Passing
STRANGE

For my good friends

Steve Bissette,

Jim DeFilippi, and

Chris DeFilippi.

If I were more prolific, you

each would have your own book.

Passing STRANGE

*True Tales of New England
Hauntings and Horrors*

Joseph A. Citro

Illustrations by David Diaz

HOUGHTON MIFFLIN COMPANY
222 BERKELEY STREET
BOSTON, MASSACHUSETTS 02116

For information about permission to reproduce selections from this book,
write to Permissions, Houghton Mifflin Company, 215 Park Avenue South,
New York, New York 10003.

Library of Congress Cataloging-in-Publication Data
Citro, Joseph A.
    Passing strange : true tales of New England hauntings and
horrors / Joseph A. Citro ; illustrations by David Diaz.
    p.   cm.
Includes bibliographical references and index.
ISBN 1-57630-018-8 (hardcover) ISBN 1-57630-059-5 (softcover)
1. Ghosts—New England. 2. Haunted places—New England.
3. Curiosities and wonders—New England. I. Title.
GR106.C57   1996
398.2'0974'05—dc20   96-32202

Printed and bound in the United States of America
QUM   10   9   8   7   6   5   4   3   2   1

Designed by Susan McClellan

Cover illustration by David Diaz

Contents

Introduction:
A Book of Wonders

> **"***There is something truer and more real than what we can see with the eyes and touch with the finger.***"**

—NATHANIEL HAWTHORNE
Rappaccini's Daughter

THE ETERNAL MOURNER

WHEN I WAS A KID, LIVING IN SOUTHERN VERMONT, my father would sometimes take the whole family for a day in the Big City. This involved a 40-mile drive from my hometown of Chester to the city of Rutland: population, some 17,000 folks at the time.

To this fidgety youngster, the journey seemed endless. I tuned out as we passed through little settlements like Gassetts, Ludlow, and Mount Holly. Then I yawned as we skirted brooks and crossed bridges. And all the while I battled nausea as our Plymouth swayed around the twists and turns of Route 103.

But there was one thing I looked forward to: the Bowman Mansion in the village of Cuttingsville.

It was a spooky old place, deserted, faded, scary as a haunted house in a horror comic. But what gave me the biggest shudder was directly across the road. It was something in the cemetery . . .

I remember preparing myself the moment we drove into town. I'd lean forward from the backseat, my head bobbing up front, right between my father's and mother's. I held my breath as the road curved gently to the right and the graveyard panorama opened up.

Then it appeared!

There, directly across from the house, was a somber granite mausoleum—a tomb. And as always—right on its steps—I saw the ghostly figure of a man, completely white and absolutely motionless. He looked exactly like a ghost, kneeling there on the granite stairs of the crypt.

I could imagine a car full of uninitiated travelers cruising into Cuttingsville for the first time. I could picture their vehicle swerving dangerously as its astonished driver gawked too long at the spectral supplicant.

It wasn't a ghost, of course. It was a marble statue. And it's still there, just exactly as it was when I was a boy. The marble mourner is John P. Bowman himself.

My father had grown up in the area, so he had a lot of stories about the mausoleum, the mansion, and the man. He told me that Bowman had been a rich industrialist who'd lived there with his wife and daughter. Following a tragedy, the details of which no one seemed to remember, Mr. Bowman's wife and child had passed away, leaving the grieving millionaire alone in his spooky old house.

As Dad told it, Mr. Bowman's beliefs were a tad peculiar. Supposedly, he passed the years as a recluse, studying occult sciences and performing odd rituals. He believed he would find a way to literally come back from the dead. On the off chance that his family would return, too, he'd had the elaborate mausoleum built to preserve their bodies, just in case they'd be needing them again.

After a while, grief and the years took their toll on Mr. Bowman. He became ill. Following a period of suffering and decline, he too passed away. Then his body was moved to join his family in the vault across the street.

According to local lore, Mr. Bowman left a rather unusual will. It provided that the remainder of his substantial fortune would be used for upkeep on the house and the mausoleum. Caretakers were maintained on the premises. Servants were employed to clean the place and to change the bed linens each week. Every night—so the story went—they'd set the table for an evening meal.

In fact, my father's rendition of the story was even more optimistic: the cook and butler would actually prepare and serve a full, formal meal every evening.

Bowman wanted everything to be ready if he, his wife, or his daughter should arrive home unannounced. And if they were to show up hungry, supper would be waiting.

It was a great story, and for years I carried it around as if it were fact. I even picked up enticing additions along the way. Like the tale—told by people who'd supposedly visited the place—of the faint, sad sobbing of an infant who could never be located among the maze of the mansion's empty rooms.

Later, when I was in high school, some of us would make the occasional pilgrimage from Chester to Cuttingsville, usually around Halloween. We'd tell the story again and again, customizing the details to fit the situation. If the moon was right, we'd sneak up to the mausoleum. Looking through the barred door revealed a spacious interior. Magically, it seemed vastly larger than the outside—an optical illusion effected by the clever placement of mirrors.

Sometimes we'd dare each other to look directly into Bowman's marble eyes. Then we'd scamper across the road and peer through the windows of his deserted mansion. Even now, one friend swears he saw a wispy, transparent shape drifting through the haunted halls.

As an adult, in preparing this book, I decided to get the real scoop on Mr. John P. Bowman. Turns out, the stories I'd grown up with were . . . well . . . slightly inaccurate.

I'll save those for another time, but for now, here's the point. Mr. Bowman is important to me because of the questions he, his home, and his tomb provoked in my developing imagination. Those questions led directly to this book.

And even now, 40 years later, I haven't been able to answer any of them to my own satisfaction. First, there's that all-important question implicit in my father's stories about Mr. Bowman: Can the dead sometimes return?

Once I permitted myself to ask that, a parade of other questions followed.

Can ghosts be real?

What about vampires, UFOs, and sea serpents?

Are we alone on this little mud ball of ours? Or are other things—spirits, angels, and even devils—sharing our space and time?

Not new questions, to be sure. They have been asked and answered over and over in continuing cycles ever since . . . well, for the purposes of this book, ever since New England was born.

From the moment of its birth, New England has been a weird place. Maybe weirder than Old England. Since day one, Yankees have, with alarming regularity, experienced odd encounters—on land, sea, even in the air.

For example, way back in 1682, Richard Chamberlain, secretary for the colony of New Hampshire, witnessed and recorded the activities of an invisible presence at the home of George Walton of Great Island. For three months the entity wreaked havoc, hurling stones, bricks, and heavy household implements, including mauls and crowbars. It took Chamberlain sixteen years to work up the courage to tell the odd tale. In 1698, he published the details in a curious pamphlet called *Lithobolia or The Stone Throwing Devil.*

Even earlier, in March 1639, John Winthrop, governor of the Massachusetts Bay Colony, recorded a clear, detailed unemotional account of a luminous object over what is now the Back Bay section of Boston. It seemed to play zigzag games in the sky. Numerous witnesses agreed its movements resembled those of a pig trying to avoid capture by racing "hither an yon." It vanished, but only for a while.

Then in January 1695, two similar moon-sized luminous objects played aerial tag over Boston Harbor. Several witnesses heard a voice in the sky repeating "in a most dreadful manner," the words "boy . . . boy . . . come away . . . come away." Two weeks later the light returned and a new group of witnesses heard the same unearthly summons.

To this day, no one knows who was calling or where the "boy" was being summoned to.

All we know for sure is that the questions never change. And, as we will see, neither does our Yankee kingdom. It's still the place that jailed women for witchcraft, cowered at strange lights in the sky, and bestowed the title "haunted" on any house full of inexplicable disturbances.

Today we're living on the same land where Puritan zealots marched into the wilderness—and saw devils crouching behind every tree. The only difference is that now there is far less wilderness and perhaps many more devils.

TELLERS AND TALES

NEW ENGLANDERS ARE EVER EAGER to tell their stories. As folklorist Richard M. Dorson wrote, "Pioneer families crowded around the hearth ... entertained themselves with tales of mystery and marvel. . . . [L]acking books, loving horrors, bred in demonology, and surrounded by dread animals and savages, colonial Americans turned naturally into vivid spinners and eager consumers of folkyarn. Cradled and nurtured in the wonder-laden atmosphere of a new world and stimulated by a brimstone theology that clothed evil in human form, this native flair for storytelling found continuous expression and ready opportunity with the nation's growth."

Is it any wonder, then, that New England bred native sons such as Nathaniel Hawthorne, H.P. Lovecraft, Stephen King, and many others who practiced and refined the art of the marvelous tale?

In the same way that New England can be seen as the cradle of American civilization, the New England Gothicists can be credited with formulating an American sense of the supernatural. They brought New England wonders to the whole world.

This is not to say the horrors they describe are entirely fabricated. No matter what our wonder writers can imagine, equally strange—or stranger—events have actually occurred here. They're recorded in newspapers, diaries, and the folk annals of the region.

Although H.P. Lovecraft seems to have been the ultimate rationalist, Nathaniel Hawthorne saw a ghost.

And so did Stephen King.

Hawthorne's paranormal meeting occurred in the 1830s, while he was employed at the Boston Customs House. Every day he'd go to the Athenaeum to do research. And every day he would see the elderly Dr. Harris, a retired clergyman, seated by the fire, reading the *Boston Post*.

We can only guess at Hawthorne's astonishment when someone informed him that Dr. Harris had died some time ago. Nonetheless, for weeks after that Hawthorne continued to see Dr. Harris. Seated by the fire. Reading his newspaper.

We might well ask, why didn't Hawthorne confront the old man, either snatch the paper out of his hand or at the very least say something to him?

Well, he was never able to explain that entirely.

"Perhaps," he wrote, "I was loth to destroy the illusion, and to rob myself of so good a ghost story, which might have been explained in some very commonplace way."

Also, there was an element of self-consciousness at work: ". . . what an absurd figure I would have made, solemnly . . . addressing what must have appeared in the eyes of all the rest of the company as an empty chair."

Then too, Hawthorne was trapped in the era's conventions of social protocol. He wrote, "In the reading room of the Athenaeum, conversation is strictly forbidden. . . . "Besides," concluded this mannered New Englander, "I had never been introduced to Dr. Harris."

Stephen King met his specter at a political fund-raiser held in an old Maine house during the winter. All the guests had left their heavy coats on a bed in an upstairs room. When it was time to leave, Mr. King climbed the stairs to get his and his wife's coats.

King, quoted in the *Boston Sunday Herald*, describes the event this way: "I was upstairs rummaging around through the coats trying to find ours. And over the top of my glasses, where things get kind of fuzzy and vague, I saw an old man in a blue suit with a bald head, sitting in a chair in the corner looking at me."

King's immediate reaction was to feel guilty, fearing the man might suspect he was pawing through the coats looking for something to steal. In a moment, he extricated his wife's coat from the pile and looked up to find " . . . there was nobody there in the corner at all."

Though convinced the old man's apparition was really present, Mr. King says he is reluctant to tell the story because of the kinds of books he writes. To illustrate, he said, "[I]f Stephen King reported a UFO to the air force they would laugh themselves into a hernia."

It is unlikely Hawthorne and King were both seeing the venerable Dr. Harris, but their sightings are not dissimilar. In the final analysis, neither is especially interesting. They are not good stories; they are not dramatic.

In this book, I have tried to identify stories that are not only dramatic but allegedly true.

If I had been an editor preparing an anthology to be titled something like *New England's Greatest Ghost Stories*, I would have pored over the fiction of Hawthorne, Lovecraft, King, Warton, Jackson, Hautala, Daniels, D'Ammassa, and many other spirited New Englanders who've tried to catalog all imaginable ghoulies and ghosties and long-leggedie beasties native to our region. I'd have been hoping to find stories not frequently anthologized, but that possessed the power to lower a reader's blood temperature a few degrees.

However, this is not that kind of anthology.

Professional writers of horror fiction are not the only people who perpetuate stories about the bizarre side of New England life.

Real things happen to real people. Sometimes the braver among them choose to tell the tales. Some stories find their way into print. Others—like my father's account of John P. Bowman—get passed along by word-of-mouth.

Perhaps, like the metaphorical ball of snow, the stories get bigger and pick up a little alien matter as they roll along. But eventually, they become part of our environment and ultimately part of ourselves.

And that's what this book is about—stories.

It is not a scholarly attempt to trace the narratives to their sources. It is not an effort to separate the fact from the fiction. And it most certainly is not a thesis that aims to prove or disprove the presence of the supernatural in our daily lives.

It is a book of real stories told by real people.

I have not enhanced them at all. I have only drawn upon written records and oral testimony to present other people's stories in my own way. Essentially, I am an editor, an anthologizer.

Frankly, I have never been able to decide how to integrate the supernatural into my personal belief system. When I'm at the keyboard writing a novel, a short story, or the tales that comprise this book, I believe. Otherwise, I'm a skeptic. I know that skepticism is healthy and good; it doubts, while at the same time it emphatically permits the possibility that the events chronicled here may in fact have happened.

Even if you militantly disbelieve in ghosts and their kin, that need not inhibit your enjoyment of these tales. But if I might make a small suggestion: try to suspend that disbelief while you read these pages. If you can do that, you'll have a lot more fun.

It's the kind of fun I had every time we drove through Cuttingsville. It's the kind of fun our Yankee forefathers and mothers enjoyed while seated around the hearth.

And above all, it's the kind of fun that lets the tradition continue . . .

THRICE-TOLD TALES

I HOPE YOU WILL NOT FIND ANY TALES here that suffer from overexposure. I won't tell you about Vermont's Lake Champlain Monster or New Hampshire's classic UFO abduction case involving Barney and Betty Hill. I won't be writing about the Salem witch trials or speculating about whether Lizzie Borden did in fact give her father forty whacks. Plenty of other authors have addressed these issues.

As editor of this anthology, I have tried to discover lesser-known tales, but they all had to meet a certain subjective, self-imposed, impossible-to-articulate "strangeness level."

This standard is best expressed in an idiom sometimes used by my adopted aunt, who passed away in 1975 at age 100. There is much I remember about this independent old New Englander, including some of her colorful language: she called a bicycle a wheel and a porch a piazza, and she could name every wildflower and bird.

But there is a certain phrase she used that has lodged itself forever in my writer's memory. If something was strange, she would say so: "That's strange."

But if an event surpassed even that, if something was exceptionally uncanny, she'd say, "That's passing strange."

I hope you'll find the stories in this book to be passing strange.

If not, I think I might do well to avoid wherever it is you come from.

PART I

SPIRITED COMMUNICATION

❝Beyond a doubt you are selected as the material of some new experiment. Perhaps the result is to be death; perhaps a fate more awful still.❞

—NATHANIEL HAWTHORNE
Rappaccini's Daughter

The Nightmare *on* Elm Street

STRATFORD, CONNECTICUT, SETTLED IN 1639, HAS LONG BEEN A CENTER FOR shipbuilding and oystering. Today it's home to the renowned Shakespeare Theater. It has always been considered a peaceful and comfortable small New England town.

And perhaps it was the notion of tranquillity that inspired Rev. Eliakim Phelps to move there with his family. On February 22, 1848, they bought a grand, sprawling Greek Revival-style mansion on Elm Street.

It was a three-story affair, built in 1826 for George R. Dowell, a sea captain about to retire. There were some eccentricities in its construction. For example, the main hallway was 70 feet long by 12 feet wide. At each end twin staircases met at a second-floor landing. This odd design was intended to replicate the layout of a clipper ship.

Dr. Phelps, like Captain Dowell before him, anticipated retirement years that would be comfortable and serene.

But the preacher's tranquillity was to be short-lived, for specters more terrifying than anything imagined by Stratford's bard were about to descend on the aging clergyman and his family.

The trouble began on Sunday morning, March 10, 1850. Dr. Phelps, his wife, and their four children were returning from church services. Because their maid was away, Dr. Phelps had been especially careful about securing the house. He had locked not only the outside doors, but the inside doors and windows as well. The only keys were in his pocket.

You can imagine his consternation when he stepped into the yard and saw the front door wide open. Interior doors were open too. At first, Phelps believed there had been a burglary.

He entered the house with great caution to find everything in chaos: Someone had knocked over the tables and chairs. China lay smashed on the carpet, books and clothing littered the floors. Even the fireplace tools were scattered helter-skelter.

Yet, mysteriously, Dr. Phelps noticed his gold watch and the family silver were in plain sight and undisturbed. Though the place was a mess, nothing was missing.

An unlocked window suggested the family's arrival home had interrupted the vandals, perhaps scaring them away before they had an opportunity to steal any valuables.

Dr. Phelps led his puzzled family up the stairs to inspect the bedrooms. They listened, nerves taut, fearing the villains might still be on the premises, wondering what sort of maniac might be waiting on the second floor.

What they found in a bedroom chilled each of them more than a blast of March wind off nearby Long Island Sound. Someone had spread a sheet atop one of the beds and on that sheet someone had placed one of Mrs. Phelps's cotton nightgowns. Stockings had been positioned at its bottom to suggest protruding feet. Its arms were folded over its chest exactly like the arms of a corpse prepared for burial.

What could the family have imagined upon seeing the fantastic flattened effigy? What unfathomable message was the mysterious intruder trying to convey?

When the family returned to church for the afternoon session, Dr. Phelps remained at home. Armed with a pistol, he hid, standing guard, waiting for the intruders to return. Though he watched and listened with heightened awareness, he failed to detect any sound or motion. But when he left his hiding place to patrol the house, Dr. Phelps made more strange discoveries.

Upon opening a downstairs door, he was surprised to see a crowd of women in his previously empty dining room. They had entered noiselessly and stood silent and unmoving, frozen in postures of religious devotion. Some bowed so low their foreheads almost touched the floor. Several had Bibles open beside them. All seemed focused on a tiny, demonic figure suspended from a cord in the center of the room.

The eleven female figures were so incredibly lifelike that it took Dr. Phelps several seconds to realize they were dummies. Closer examination revealed they were fashioned from the family's old clothing, stuffed with rags, muffs, and other materials gathered from all over the house.

This terrifying tableau had been completely constructed during the comparatively brief period the family was in church. Somehow, it had been set up while Dr. Phelps was standing guard. It seemed impossible. Artistry capable of fooling the eye should have taken much longer to create—but there it was: eleven female figures worshipping a grotesque dwarf in the home of a retired Presbyterian minister.

Why? Who might have done such a thing? What could it mean?

An account of the event published in the *New Haven Journal* said, "From this time on the rooms were closely watched, and the figures appeared every few days when no human being could have entered the room. They were constructed and arranged, I am convinced, by no visible power. The clothing from which the figures were made was somehow gathered from all parts of the house, in spite of a strict watch. In all about 30 figures were constructed during the haunt."

Whatever their significance, on that Sunday morning the Phelpses had no way of knowing this was only the beginning. The arrival of those strange, silent, and sinister effigies marked the beginning of a madness that would seize the family and hold them hostage for almost a year.

The likes of these flamboyant and frightening events had never been seen before. And to this day, have never been equaled.

RAPPING WITH SPIRITS

BEFORE WE TAKE A COMPLETE LOOK at this nightmare on Elm Street, we have to leave New England for an overview of what was going on in America at the time—a phenomenon called "Spiritualism."

It is difficult to pinpoint the moment modern Spiritualism began. Most authorities say the seminal event occurred in Hydesville, New York, a century and a half ago. But clearly, what culminated there blossomed from diverse roots.

By mid-nineteenth century, for example, the mystical writing of Emanuel Swedenborg had reached, and influenced, the popular culture. The entrancing techniques of Anton Mesmer were practiced widely and successfully in parlors and dining rooms all over the United States. And within eighteen reclusive colonies, rapturous American Shakers carried on dialogues with departed friends and relatives.

These mystical events, paradoxically combined with a new faith in science, altered the American consciousness. Suddenly, many of us truly believed that scientific method would eventually explain all things—physical and spiritual. So in retrospect, what happened at Hydesville—just 30 miles east of Rochester, New York—should have come as no surprise.

It was 1848. Hydesville was nothing more than a scattering of isolated farmhouses containing a total population of about forty souls.

One of the smallest, most humble residences was that of John D. Fox, his wife Margaret, and their two young daughters, Margaretta, 15, and Catherine, 12.

They were simple, unpretentious people of modest means and limited aspirations. But somehow, the Fox sisters changed the world. And luckily, in the whole history of spiritualism and psychic study, few incidents have been as carefully, fully, and immediately documented.

In 1848, within the claustrophobic confines of that rude dwelling, something began. The Foxes' cramped cottage was suddenly disturbed by a series of otherworldly occurrences. Partitions shook, furniture trembled, footsteps sounded in empty rooms. Loud, persistent knocking echoed from walls and doors. When Mr. and Mrs. Fox could find no explanation for these disturbances, they concluded that their house was haunted.

Then, on that fatal Friday night, March 31, 1848—less than a week after Dr. Phelps and his family moved into their Connecticut mansion—the two Fox girls became so frightened by the commotion that they fled to their parents' room, hoping to get some sleep.

The racket continued.

Mrs. Fox picks up the story, excerpted here from her sworn statement four days later:

"The children heard rapping and tried to make similar sounds by snapping their fingers. My youngest child, Cathie, said, 'Mr. Splitfoot, do as I do!', clapping her hands. The sound instantly followed with the same number of raps. When she stopped the sound ceased for a short time. Then Margaretta said, in sport, 'No, do just as I do. Count one, two, three, four,' striking one hand against the other at the same time; and the raps came as before."

Through trial and error, an elaborate system of communication was established between the family and the unknown rapper. Questions were answered by the spirit's knocking once for "yes," twice for "no." Words were spelled out by tapping the alphabet.

In time, the entity identified himself as a 31-year-old peddler who'd been murdered by a former occupant of the Foxes' home. Some reports tell us that human bones were later found in the basement; others say we have only the spirit's word about his worldly identity. But in either case, direct communication seemed to be established with the spirit world. For many nineteenth-century Americans, this was, quite literally, the greatest single event in human history.

Why? Because it finally put an end to thousands of years of speculation; it proved once and for all that we can communicate with the dead. In the minds of millions, it was conclusively established that physical death was not the end of life, but merely a short step in spiritual ascendancy.

Further, it showed that brief biological life was only part of the spiritual process. This seemed to confirm Christian thinking about the afterlife: Yes, we retained our individual identities in the hereafter.

Consequently, many Christians embraced spiritualism, first incorporating it into their own religious beliefs, then making it into a new religion—Spiritualism, with a capital "S." The concept took off, grew, and spread rapidly to the masses, here and abroad.

This new revelation, Spiritualism, swiftly became part of the consciousness of all Americans in the mid-1800s.

Which brings us back to New England and one of the strangest hauntings of all.

OF TABLES AND TABLEAUX

BY THE TIME DR. PHELPS moved to Stratford he had become, by virtue of his position as a religious leader, aware of most nineteenth-century developments in mysticism. He openly expressed interest in clairvoyance and for years he had been fascinated by mesmerism, especially its potential to heal. He'd even experimented with inducing the trance state in some of his family members. At that time, it must be remembered, these dabblings would hardly have been considered eccentricities. In fact, there is no reason to believe Dr. Phelps was ever anything but a model Presbyterian clergyman.

Eliakim Phelps, D.D., was born in Belchertown, Massachusetts, to an old, respected, and prosperous New England family. He was a graduate of Union and Andover Seminaries and had ministered to congregations in Geneva and Huntington, New York. He was well known in religious circles for having served many years as secretary of the American Educational Society in New York and the American Society of Philadelphia. Widowed in his early fifties, all his children were independent adults.

A NEW FAMILY

AT 59 YEARS OF AGE, Dr. Phelps experienced more changes in his life. Not only did he relocate from Philadelphia to Stratford, but he also became a newlywed. He'd married a widow several years his junior. And the new Mrs. Phelps had three children: Anna, 16; Henry, 11; and another girl, 6. Together Dr. and Mrs. Phelps produced a son, who was 3 years old when the strangeness began.

Some accounts suggest that the family was not entirely happy. Apparently, Mrs. Phelps was not well and she grew to dislike her new town and her neighbors. Anna, her daughter, had a nervous disposition. But it was 11-year-old Henry who seemed to suffer the most. He missed his dead father and quite possibly resented the "old man" his mother had married.

It was at this point that something—call it a spirit—took up residence in the home of Dr. Eliakim Phelps and his new family.

And quite possibly this "thing" was there by invitation.

TAPPING ON DEATH'S DOOR

O N MARCH 4, 1850, about two years after they'd moved in, an old friend of Dr. Phelps's arrived for a visit. It is easy to imagine the two graying gentlemen, puffing tobacco, sipping brandy, talking of spiritual matters. No doubt this new phenomenon of Spiritualism came up. The Fox sisters' "spirit rappings" were probably discussed. One thing led to another and eventually the two men decided to try their hands at contacting the spirits.

This was Phelps's first attempt at a seance . . . and it worked!

The men heard intermittent, disorganized rappings, but neither considered theirs to be an extraordinary contact. All in all, it was a benign experiment; who could have predicted the supernatural backlash it provoked?

By March 10, the episode was probably forgotten when the family returned from church to discover the crowd of motionless, unbidden guests already described.

The next day, Monday, the haunting's pace picked up. An assortment of objects began to move about the house. An umbrella leapt from its place in the hall and soared 25 feet through the air. Smaller objects—forks, spoons, knives, nails, and keys—sailed from locations where no visible person could have propelled them. The force, whatever it was, must have become exhausted, for by evening the activity had ceased.

But next morning, it was up and at it again, launching a smorgasbord of objects through the rooms.

Understandably frightened, Mrs. Phelps pleaded with her husband to summon help. He called Rev. John Mitchell, a friend and fellow retired clergyman. Mitchell, a no-nonsense cleric with a reputation for sound judgment, listened to the story and theorized the obvious: the maid or the older children were playing little tricks. As an experiment, he locked the suspects away, but the disturbance continued.

The puzzled Rev. Mitchell—perhaps the first to systematically investigate the phenomena—later wrote that he actually witnessed moving objects. That, and similar evidence, convinced him the events did not occur through trickery; they were explicable.

On the 14th, the presence made a contribution to the morning meal. A large potato dropped out of nowhere and onto the breakfast table. Escalating chaos and commotion continued for the rest of the day, culminating when Dr. and Mrs. Phelps sat with Rev. Mitchell behind the closed doors of the parlor. They witnessed forty-six objects—mostly clothing from upstairs closets—appear and drop out of the air.

In the weeks to come, many observers saw things fly through the air. Most said these projectiles were traveling at abnormally slow speeds. Sometimes they would touch down very lightly, as if carefully placed on furniture or the floor. Dr. Phelps reported that he and many others had seen objects change direction in flight.

Like Rev. Mitchell, the modern reader is likely to suspect trickery. However, we must consider that Dr. Phelps was very hospitable to curiosity seekers, reporters, and investigators. He permitted them to come in and observe as long as they wanted—and dozens of people did just that. Many witnessed bizarre disturbances firsthand.

Consequently, Phelps assured readers of the *Boston Transcript*: "I can produce scores of persons whose character for intelligence, piety and competence to judge this matter no one who knows them will question, who will make solemn oath that they have witnessed the same things. As for the reliability of the facts they can be proved by testimony a hundred-fold greater than is ordinarily required in our court of justice in cases of life and death."

Even Austin Phelps, Dr. Phelps's adult son from his first marriage, arrived in Stratford to get to the bottom of things.

Austin, a professor from the nearby Andover Theological Seminary, was accompanied by his uncle Abner Phelps, a well-known Boston physician and Massachusetts legislator. Neither man enjoyed the family's growing notoriety, nor did they entirely approve of Dr. Phelps's marriage to "that younger woman."

Upon arrival, they were convinced they would quickly discover the trickster among the family members. When they left, they were convinced the manifestations were genuine.

During the first night, they heard loud pounding which seemed to be coming from the knocker on the front door. They took turns flinging the door open, only to find nothing visible on the porch.

Finally, they positioned themselves on both sides of the door, Austin outside on the steps, Uncle Abner inside in the hall. The loud rapping continued between them, yet neither man could ascertain its source.

During the night, the two guests were repeatedly disturbed by loud pounding. On the second night, they figured they had finally found the culprit; they determined the noise was coming from Anna's bedroom door.

Again they took their positions on both sides of Anna's door. The pounding continued. It came, Austin wrote, ". . . on the door between us. Said I, 'Doctor, the knocking is outside of the door.' 'No,' he said, 'it is on the inside.'

"The young lady was in bed, covered up and out of reach of the door. We examined the panel and found dents where it had been struck."

It is difficult to fully understand, much less communicate in writing, the complexity and relentless nature of the disturbances. Often it was nonstop pandemonium, as if the spirit world were waging psychological warfare against the family. They heard screams, indistinct voices, rappings, poundings. Noises synchronously resounded from various parts of the house. Sometimes they were deafening.

Objects sailed through occupied and unoccupied rooms. Glass broke. Pottery smashed. Spoons levitated and bent in midair. Seventy-one windows shattered. Marble-topped tables reared up on two legs like startled stallions.

And some of the inexplicable antics were so far beyond bizarre they seemed part of some animator's alternate reality. For example, H.B. Taylor reported in the *Bridgeport Standard* that in the presence of several people, a brass candlestick jumped off the mantel and pounded itself against the floor until it eventually broke.

Fireplace tools danced around the floor like cartoon characters. Turnips appeared with astonishing regularity. Sometimes they moved through the air; sometimes weird symbols were carved upon them.

Once the entire family witnessed what they described as a "vegetable growth" that suddenly appeared on the sitting-room carpet. It was as if the flowery patterns in the carpet came to life and grew. Then—astonishing as it seems—cabalistic symbols formed on the leaves before the whole vision vanished entirely.

And, perhaps weirdest of all, the tableau of stuffed figures continued to reappear. Dr. Webster reported in the *New Haven Journal*, "In a short space of time so many figures were constructed that it would not have been possible for half a dozen women, working steadily for several hours, to have completed their design, and arrange the picturesque tableau. Yet these things happened in a short space of time, with the whole house on the watch. In all, about 30 figures were constructed during this period."

One effigy, formed from Mrs. Phelps's dress, was so realistic the youngest child, upon entering the room with his sister, whispered, "Be still, Ma is saying prayers."

A TURN FOR THE WORST

IN SPITE OF ITS OCCASIONAL ARTISTRY, there was no reason to believe the presence was in any way benevolent.

From the start, Dr. Phelps suspected his visiting spirits might be demonic. And perhaps that was the case, because their pranks quickly turned menacing.

They plagued Anna with more than sleep deprivation. In the *New York Sun* of April 29, 1850, a visiting reporter named Beach wrote that he, Mrs. Phelps, and Anna were alone in the room, where he was able to observe their every move. At one point he saw Anna's right arm jerk and stiffen as she cried, "I am pinched!"

Beach quickly rolled back her sleeve, exposing severe fresh pinch marks on her arm. Sometimes she was slapped. Those around her saw only the jerk of her head, yet they reported hearing loud smacks. Then they watched red welts appear on her face. According to H.B. Taylor of the *Bridgeport Standard*, an attempt was made on Anna's life. Once, while sleeping, something pressed a pillow over her head and tied tape around her neck, almost strangling her.

But young Henry seemed to be singled out for the most abuse. He was assaulted, abducted, and occasionally rendered insensible.

Once, while driving with his stepfather, he was bombarded with stones. They counted twenty on the floor of their carriage. H.B. Taylor actually saw Henry carried across the room by invisible hands and deposited on the floor. Once the boy vanished and was found outside, tied up and suspended from a tree. He had no idea how he got there. Another time, in the presence of witnesses, he was snatched up into the air, his head nearly hitting the ceiling.

In time, the attacks became more vicious. Beach's report in the *New York Sun* described how he and several others in Henry's bedroom saw a matchbox fall to the floor from the mantelpiece. Then, apparently under its own power, the box began to slide toward the bed, ultimately moving beneath it. At that moment, Henry cried that he was being burned. Mr. Beach reached under the bed and found a piece of flaming paper.

Henry regularly experienced other indignities: He was thrown by invisible hands into a cistern of water. His trouser legs were torn open in front of a visiting clergyman. And then, in a letter published in Charles W. Elliott's *Mysteries: or Glimpses of the Supernatural*, Horace Day said, "On the occasion of my visit, Mrs. Phelps hurriedly entered the room, reporting her son missing. . . . Later, [she] led the group to the back yard, where the boy was found in the hay mound, in a seemingly comatose state, from which he recovered in about an hour." Another time, he vanished, later to be discovered stuffed onto the shelf in a closet with a rope tied around his neck.

CAN WE TALK?

So what was going on? Here we apparently have an invisible entity capable of creative thought, but willing to indulge in everything from sophomoric pranks to arson, vandalism, assault, and kidnapping.

What was the Phelps family dealing with? A ghost? A poltergeist? A demon? Or some form of unconscious, perhaps involuntary, telekinesis? There are probably a million explanations from overt trickery to occult terrorism.

Immediately following his earliest attempts at communicating with the entity, Dr. Eliakim Phelps cut off all efforts at dialogue. The coded rappings had been so blasphemous Phelps forbade further discussion, concluding the invisible communicator was undoubtedly Satan or his evil minions. Unfortunately, verbatim transcripts of these abominations have been lost.

Unlike the good cleric, however, the entity wasn't eager to suspend communications. Throughout the ordeal, it apparently made numerous overtures, first by rapping, then through arcane symbols scrawled on walls and clothing, and finally, with actual handwriting.

This is an especially fascinating part of the haunting. Assuming the original tableau itself was not some sort of theatrical communication attempt (though dummies praying to a demonic dwarf could be interpreted to communicate quite a bit), the nearby Bibles were pointedly opened to seemingly relevant passages. One, from the prophet Joel, seemed to prophesy all that was to come: "They shall run to and fro in the city; they shall run upon the wall; they shall climb up upon the houses; they shall enter in at all the windows like a thief."

KNOCK, KNOCK. WHO'S THERE?

A FREQUENT GUEST IN THE HOUSE, Rev. John Mitchell again tried to engage the entity via a system of raps patterned on those employed in Hydesville. The foul replies he received seemed to corroborate Dr. Phelps's suspicion that the thing was demonic.

Despite pleas from the clerics, the entity remained persistent. In his *Modern Spiritualism*, Frank Podmore writes, "Again, on one occasion, Dr. Phelps, writing at his table, and alone in the room, turned away for a moment, and upon turning back to his table found that a sheet of paper, previously blank, was now covered with strange-looking writing, the ink being still wet."

But still the thing had not identified itself.

Similarly, various family members would occasionally discover papers with messages written on them. At other times, comparable missives would magically appear from nowhere, perhaps drifting down over the dinner table. They might be signed by Sam Slick, Beelzebub, or H.P. Devil. One that fluttered into existence at Mrs. Phelps's tea party said, "Sir Sambo's compliments and begs the laddyes to accept as a token of esteem."

Another merely commented on Dr. Phelps's choice of stationery. "Very nice paper and nice ink for the Devil." Some messages were more literate, but none were more revealing. Finally, perhaps convinced he had to know his enemy if he were to banish it, Dr. Phelps agreed to another seance.

A SOUL IN HELL

THIS TIME, THE ENTITY seemed to come forth with verifiable information, including its earthly identity. It claimed it was a soul in hell, enduring never-ending torment for the sins it had committed while alive. Dr. Phelps, hoping to assuage its misery (and his own), asked what he could do to help.

The best thing, the spirit communicated through rapping, was to bring him a piece of pumpkin pie. Thinking he'd been misunderstood, Dr. Phelps asked again. Now the spirit had changed its mind, this time requesting a glass of fresh gin.

When Dr. Phelps asked why he was making such a disturbance in the house, the shade replied simply, "For fun."

At length, the spirit explained that in life it had been a law clerk who had done some financial work for Mrs. Phelps. The spirit confessed he had committed fraud for which he was assigned residence in hell (though how it got from there to the Phelps residence was never explained).

So, at last, they had some tangible evidence, or at least a clue. Dr. Phelps made a journey to the Philadelphia law office where he examined the papers in question. Yes, he discovered, there had been fraud, but the amount of money involved was not "sufficiently large to warrant prosecution." Apparently, justice in the next world is far more severe than in our own.

Nothing in this second communication attempt caused Dr. Phelps to change his original position. "I am satisfied that the communications are wholly worthless, in that they are frequently false, contradictory, and nonsensical. . . . I place no value in any of the messages, and if they are from spirits," he concluded, "they are evil spirits."

Deceit, chaos, aggression. It was like warfare. But was the house the battlefield, or the prize?

Surprisingly, Dr. Phelps later agreed to one final dialogue with his invisible guests. After months of persecution, he and the family had finally had enough. Whatever they were fighting—spirits, ghosts, or demons—the time had come to retreat. They would move away, or at least spend the winter back in Philadelphia.

Following that decision, a "spirit message" landed on the desk where Dr. Phelps was at work. It asked how soon the family would be departing and requested an immediate reply—in writing!

On a nearby scrap of paper, Dr. Phelps answered at once, writing "October I."

And so they did.

If the spirits were indeed trying to drive the family from the house, they had succeeded. On October I, 1850, Eliakim Phelps sent his wife and four children ahead to Philadelphia. He remained briefly in residence at Stratford to put things in order. The phantom pranksters did not accompany the family, nor did they remain with Dr. Phelps.

AND WHAT OF TODAY?

THE JURY IS STILL OUT on whether the house remained haunted after the Phelps family left.

Before leaving for Philadelphia, Dr. Phelps sold the place to Moses Beach, founder of the *New York Sun* newspaper. Later, Beach's son Alfred converted it into a school. After the turn of the century, it was acquired by James Albert Wales, who did extensive renovations.

In the 1940s, Wales passed it on to Maude Thompson, who converted it into a home for the elderly.

As far as I can tell, there were no new reports of hauntings until 1947, when the Phelps place was purchased by Carl Caserta and his wife, both registered nurses. For twenty years they ran it as the Restmore Convalescent Center.

Again, people started reporting odd noises, indistinct whispers, and a cellar door that just wouldn't stay closed.

However, the Casertas say the ghosts were perfectly polite, even helpful. Twice they credit a ghost for saving the lives of their elderly residents, not to mention their infant son, Gary: first, when his crib caught fire; and again years later, when he almost fell from the second floor while sleepwalking. On both occasions the Casertas were alerted by the buzzer system, but no one admitted to sounding the alarm.

The Casertas sold the house to a company that runs a chain of convalescent homes. But they boarded it up instead of renovating it.

During the years it sat empty, the old place became sort of a metaphysical Mecca, falling victim to ghost-defying vandals and a stream of disrespectful psychics, pseudo-psychics, and psychos. So much damage was done that ultimately the owners decided renovation would be far too costly.

A Stratford policeman tells of the time he was dispatched to the house on a vandalism call. He and another cop entered the building. Immediately they both felt the interior was strangely cold and unusually dark.

They heard loud, distinct noises on the third floor. Thinking that whoever was up there would have no way of escape, the policemen ran up the stairs and saw a dark-caped figure that looked vaguely like a nun. The figure ran down the hallway and dashed into a bedroom. Believing the perpetrator was trapped, the two policemen entered the room just in time to see the figure vanish into a closet. When they opened the closet door, no one was there.

The Phelps house is gone now. It burned in the early seventies. The knockings, however, remain unexplained. Local lore has it that the initial upheaval was the work of the ghost of Goody Bassett, who was hanged near there for witchcraft in 1651. A victim of misguided religious fervor, Goody may have been down on clergymen. If so, that might explain why Reverend Phelps got the worst treatment of all.

But ghost, witch, or demon, whatever it was seems to have vanished. Presumably, it went back to where it had come from, leaving everyone to speculate just where that place might be.

The Machiasport Madonna

IN THE PREVIOUS CHAPTER, I TOUCHED ON AMERICAN SPIRITUALISM AND HOW IT supposedly originated with the Fox family in Hydesville, New York. Of course, what happened at the Fox home was not unique. Prior to the so-called "Rochester Rappings," people all over the world had been interacting with spirits for thousands of years.

Although we continue to say Modern Spiritualism began with the Fox family, it's just another way of saying that in 1848, circumstances were just exactly right for an age-old phenomenon to take on new life and spread.

If American history had unfolded differently, books about Spiritualism would probably proclaim that it began not in New York, but in New England, in the little seacoast village of Machiasport, Maine. And it could be argued that it began there as early as 1799, a good half-century before the New York events.

To me, the story of Capt. Abner Blaisdel and his family is far stranger than that of the Fox sisters, and in many ways it's more thought-provoking.

Today, we have no idea what reality propelled the Machiasport phenomena, but we have plenty of documentation to prove that something powerfully strange really happened there.

In fact, I've heard Machiasport's specter referred to as "America's First Ghost." Of course, that too is inaccurate. Ghostly visions were seen on this continent long before the European intrusion. And in truth, we have no way of knowing what folks saw in Machiasport was really a ghost at all.

But take a look at the facts and decide for yourself.

HEADING DOWN EAST

MACHIASPORT LIES OFF ROUTE I, on Machias Bay, way up above L.L. Bean, Belfast, and Ellsworth. It's so far north that it's almost in Canada.

The area is rich in legend, thanks in part to Sam Bellamy, the "Robin Hood of the High Seas." There, in the early 1700s, Bellamy planned to establish his utopia, an independent kingdom populated by pirates. After forcing captured seamen into slave labor to build his fortress, Bellamy drowned in a nautical altercation, his ship sank, and his retirement plans dissolved.

For the most part, Machiasport is noted historically because that's where the first naval battle of the American Revolution was fought, on June 12, 1775. The hardy citizens were sick and tired of paying British taxes and giving up their lumber without profit. Col. Jeremiah O'Brien used a local merchant ship staffed with pitch-fork-packing locals to attack and capture the British vessel *Margaretta*, five days before Bunker Hill. Fort O'Brien and the sturdy souls who manned it became part of the new nation's national defense system.

And in the realm of the paranormal, Machiasport is remembered because it was there, on August 9, 1799, that Capt. Abner Blaisdel and his family began to notice odd noises in their house.

Though irritating and distracting, the sounds didn't interfere with the family's day-to-day lives. Still, they were persistent, continuing intermittently for the rest of the year. Then, with the beginning of the new year, things escalated.

On January 2, 1800, Abner and his daughter Lydia began to hear a new and unfamiliar sound in their home. Strangely, it was as if someone were talking, though the words were unintelligible.

Upon investigation, they discovered that the voice seemed to be coming from the cellar. And it sounded like a woman. Although they could see no one, they were able to carry on a conversation with the disembodied stranger.

The entity said that she was the deceased wife of Capt. George Butler, a local man known slightly to the Blaisdel family. Further, the presence said her name was Nelly and that her father was David Hooper, who lived about six miles from the Blaisdel home.

At Nelly's request, Captain Blaisdel sent for her father and her earthbound husband. George Butler was not available just then, and Hooper was slow to respond. No doubt he felt somewhat inconvenienced to be summoned on a cold, stormy day for what would certainly prove to be a fool's errand. But Abner Blaisdel was a respected member of the community; he'd not annoy a man for the sport of it.

So, with the arctic breath of the Atlantic chilling him to the bone, David Hooper traveled the six snowy miles to find out what all the fuss was about.

Blaisdel met him at the front door, then cautiously explained how Hooper's daughter's ghost had been hanging around the cellar for the last six months.

Blaisdel had no idea why she'd picked his house. It would have been easier for all concerned if she'd appeared directly to her father, or her husband, or someone at least related to her. Blaisdel himself felt out of the loop.

By all accounts, David Hooper was a crusty old coot, not one to be easily convinced of his daughter's postmortem shenanigans. But then again, Blaisdel didn't have a reputation for jokes or fantastic stories either.

Determined to get to the bottom of things, the two men descended into the cellar.

And again the voice began speaking.

Hooper was able to pose a series of questions no one but his daughter could answer. And the voice always responded correctly. The shaken old man quickly became a believer. Later he wrote, "I believe it was her voice. She gave such clear and irresistible tokens of her being the spirit of my daughter as gave me no less satisfaction than admiration and delight."

But the ghost did not go so far as to appear to her father.

A MERE MASS OF LIGHT

W HEN SHE FINALLY CHOSE TO SHOW HERSELF, she was again drawn to Blaisdel's family rather than her own. While crossing a nearby field, Abner's son Paul saw something that so terrified him he ran home in a panic. He choked out that he had seen the figure of a woman as it "floated over the fields."

The next night, Paul was to regret his reaction to the specter. Nelly's voice, speaking from the cellar, was furious at the boy for his rudeness. She demanded to know why Paul hadn't greeted her properly when he saw her outside.

Between January and February of 1800, just about everyone in the area had heard about Nelly Butler's alleged return from the dead.

Apparently, Nelly was not a timid, retiring specter. In fact, she was abnormally aggressive and outspoken. Not only did she blast young Blaisdel for his bad manners, she also got into the habit of herding people into the cellar of Captain Blaisdel's house to lecture them about their moral behavior. Somehow, she seemed to know far more than she should about the private lives of the population. She passed among the spectators, talking incessantly, haranguing on religious themes.

This proselytizing procedure had started in May of 1800 when Nelly materialized, wearing "a shining white garment," to twenty people in Blaisdel's cellar. One witness said, "At first the apparition was a mere mass of light, then it grew into a personal form, about as tall as myself . . . the glow of the apparition had a constant tremulous motion. At last the personal form became shapeless, expanded every way and then vanished in a moment."

At another time, Nelly assembled a group of 200 people, enough to rival the congregation of any clergyman in the area. Once gathered, the persnickety prophetess would admonish them with religious sermons and predictions—many of which apparently came true. Nelly foretold the death of Blaisdel's wife and father. She even foresaw the marriage of her widowed husband, George, to Lydia Blaisdel.

Her voice was described as "shrill but mild and pleasant."

At one point, Captain Blaisdel asked Nelly why she chose to speak to people in the cellar? Why not in the house proper, where folks could be more comfortable?

"I do not wish to frighten the children," she told him.

A DANGEROUS VISION?

A LOCAL MINISTER, REV. ABRAHAM CUMMINGS, was concerned that his parishioners—along with other locals—were becoming too preoccupied with Nelly. Cummings did not believe in ghosts, but when he learned that whatever it was presumed to speak on religious matters, he became alarmed.

Determined to investigate, he interviewed several of the eyewitnesses. He found that many people reported exactly the same thing: that Nelly had said, "Although my body is consumed and turned to dust, my soul is as much alive as before I left my body."

The apparition's message was decidedly Christian, but Rev. Cummings was not at all convinced it was coming from a supernatural being. He was certain the whole thing was a hoax. Further, he figured Captain Blaisdel was the culprit behind it.

But on his way to confront Blaisdel, Rev. Cummings had an experience that would change his view of this world and the next. He had a personal audience with the spirit that called itself Nelly Butler. In his book *Unbidden Guests*, William Oliver Stevens describes that meeting:

"About twelve rods ahead of [Rev. Cummings] there was a slight knoll . . . [where] he could see a group of white rocks . . . showing dimly against the dark turf. . . . Two or three minutes later . . . one of those . . . white rocks had risen off the ground, and had now taken the shape of a globe of light with a rosy tinge. As he went toward it he kept his eye on it for fear it might disappear, but he had not gone more than five paces when the glowing mass flashed right to where he was [and] resolved itself into the shape and dress of a woman, but small, the size of a child of seven. He thought: 'You are not tall enough for the woman who has been appearing among us.' Immediately the figure expanded to normal size . . . and now she appeared glorious, with rays of light shining from her head all about, and reaching to the ground."

Most accounts say this was the last time Nelly Butler was seen. Apparently, her mission was done because she had accomplished one important thing: she'd converted Rev. Cummings. He spent the rest of his life traveling and preaching, telling of the wonderful things he had seen and of the heavenly life that was to come. He even recorded the whole incident in a small book called *Immortality Proved by the Testimony of Science* published in 1859, and now considered quite rare.

One would think that because of the clarity of the apparition, the number of witnesses, its spiritual message and prophecies, the clergyman apostle, and the evocation of the word "science," this episode on the northern coast of Maine would have been the incident to propel Modern Spiritualism into the public consciousness. Instead, its influence remained rather provincial. Today, the events at Machiasport are all but forgotten.

Still, the modern reader has to speculate a little about what really happened there. This was one of the most witnessed ghosts in history. That and the conversion of a skeptical cleric seem to argue that something real but supernatural did occur in rural Maine. One is struck by the description of the vision: a glowing lady in white with light radiating from her head. If it hadn't identified itself as Nelly, it would sound very much like the visions seen in Lourdes, Fátima, and Guadeloupe.

Angelic? Spiritual? Demonic? Or maybe extraterrestrial? Who can say? Whatever such visitations are intended to communicate, more often than not all they do is confuse. Many of them are so baffling it is far easier to say, simply, that they never happened at all.

Spear; *Or,* *The* Modern Prometheus

IN 1818, A FRAIL YOUNG WOMAN NAMED MARY GAVE BIRTH TO A TERRIFYING, undying monster. At just 20 years of age, Mary Wollstonecraft Shelley created *Frankenstein.* Her gothic masterpiece speculated that science could restore the spark of life to a collage of old body parts.

It was fiction, of course, but here in America it would pose questions about our two newest faiths—one in science, the other in spirits.

In 1850s Massachusetts, Spiritualism and science would collide head-on in bizarre experiments conducted by a kindly Universalist minister named John Murray Spear.

Motivated by spirits, Rev. Spear embarked on an alchemic journey that would blend science and religion in a manner never dreamed about in the gothic imagination. For under the direction of a "high society of angels," Rev. John Murray Spear was directed to create . . . dare I say it? . . . life!

And the weird thing is, some of his followers say he did just exactly that.

MAN WITH A PLAN

BORN IN BOSTON on September 16, 1804, and named after the founder of Universalism, John Murray Spear was brought up in a family that reinforced compassion and humanitarian values. His father died when John was a child, leaving him and his brother, Charles, to provide for their mother and grandparents.

When other boys were in school, John and Charles went to work in a cotton factory in Dorchester. There, thanks to a Sunday school teacher who was also a factory clerk, John learned to read and write. Education facilitated gaining an apprenticeship with a shoemaker in Abington, Massachusetts, an occupation that promised John a modest future.

But all the while, John had a dream he had yet to begin fulfilling: like his namesake John Murray, he wanted to be a preacher. According to a biographical sketch by Mrs. H.F.M. Brown of Cleveland, Ohio, Spear was precisely suited for the ministry. She describes his gentleness of spirit, generosity, and love for all living things, especially pets, children, and the aged.

With his amiable but determined temperament, newfound academic skills, and strong sense of destiny, young John began to study for the ministry. Though he was self-taught, he preached his first sermon right after Christmas of 1828 in Brewster. It was well-received and shortly afterwards, in 1830, he was ordained a Universalist minister.

The next year, he married, and the couple eventually produced five children.

According to all reports, John Murray Spear was a fine young man, full of purpose and passion. He did God's work by helping individual blacks to establish freedom and by aiding the poor, the homeless, and the incarcerated. In 1845, the family moved to Boston where, according to Mrs. Brown, "Summer and winter, early and late, through storm and sunshine, he might be seen in the byways and dens and hovels of New England's metropolis, relieving the suffering, or moving noiselessly among the victims of the law at the courthouse, whispering hopes to the hopeless, gently and lovingly rebuking and encouraging the fallen."

In time, Spear established himself as an influential religious leader. In his book *The Heyday of Spiritualism*, Slater Brown describes Spear as "honest, self-sacrificing, dedicated to good works [and] highly respected by all who knew him."

He was considered intelligent, and courageous enough to publicly champion many social issues that even today are sometimes considered unpopular: women's rights, pacifism, prison reform, and the abolition of the death penalty.

SPEAR AND SPIRITS

ONCE, WHILE SPEAKING OUT AGAINST SLAVERY in Portland, Maine, Spear was attacked by a raging mob and pummeled into unconsciousness. During the winter of 1844 and '45, his good friend Oliver Dennett nursed him back to health.

Ironically, shortly after Spear recovered, Dennett died.

Like most Americans at that time, John expressed some curiosity about Spiritualism, but he wasn't convinced of it until March 31, 1852, when, while wide awake, he noticed that his hand had—seemingly of its own accord—picked up a pen and started to write. The note, in an unfamiliar script, directed him to go to Abington to lend aid to a man he didn't even know, someone called David Vining.

More curious still, this note, generated through "automatic writing," was signed *Oliver.*

Through this mysterious process, Spear was reunited with his deceased friend Oliver Dennett. In life, Oliver had nursed John back to health. In death, Oliver became John's "spirit guide," passing along assignments from more ascended entities.

These entities often instructed John to provide medical aid to afflicted individuals. He complied willingly, though admittedly Spear knew nothing about medicine.

Spear would never know where the spirits would send him or who he'd encounter when he arrived. The mysterious powers dispatched him on healing missions to places like Salem, Georgetown, and Boston. Always eager to help, he'd willingly travel on foot, by night, in the worst of weather. His only reward was that he was permitted to alleviate the suffering of others.

When he arrived at his assigned destination, he was routinely pleased to discover that—just as the spirits had promised—he could actually help his ailing clients.

As time passed, the spirits' influence over him seemed to grow more powerful. Occasionally, he would fall into a trance and give public lectures, often speaking intelligently on subjects he knew little or nothing about. After Spear delivered twelve lectures on geology at Hamilton College, a learned faculty member complimented him, saying he had "taken up the subject just where the books left off."

But all this was minor. The spirits had far greater plans for Rev. Spear.

If these miraculous tasks were supernaturally designed tests of Spear's commitment to the spirits, he apparently passed with flying colors. The unseen authorities rewarded him by sending him to Rochester, New York, not far from Hydesville, Spiritualism's birthplace. There, during a seance, he was informed that a select group of entities was working on "the ultimate establishment of a divine social state on earth."

And Spear, who was divinely inspired and eternally cooperative, was to be the midwife who'd deliver "Heaven's last and best gift to Man."

Imagine Spear's satisfaction. He, a humble cleric from Boston, Massachusetts, was about to change the world! If this sounds like the prediction of a "Second Coming," I suspect that was the intent.

After that revelation, John Murray Spear willingly gave up his consciousness so a group of seven bodiless engineers could seize his limbs and vocal cords. Calling themselves the "Association of Electrizers," the spirits used their volunteer puppet to direct the construction of a living machine, a new life-form.

In October of 1853, Spear began construction of what he called his "New Motor," an animate mechanical contrivance that would draw its power from "nature's warehouse of infinite magnetic force."

Creating and controlling life has, for centuries, been the mortal's dream of divinity. Spear, however, seems to have been exempt from such hubris. His goals were never selfish. Having witnessed humanity's suffering at its worst, he truly believed he'd been given the opportunity to improve everything for everybody. Spear did not hesitate to risk all he had, including his reputation, under the guidance of his "Electrizers."

First, he chose a perfect location for his experiments. In Lynn, Massachusetts, there is an elevated piece of land believed to have special spiritual properties. Today, we might call it a "power center."

In the so-called High Rock section, 170 feet above the city proper, several noted Spiritualists had enjoyed religious ecstasy in a stone cottage and tower built by another Spiritualist, Jesse Hutchinson. Because several noted Spiritualists had seen angels there, Spear was certain the area would be most conducive to his divine creation.

THE CONTRAPTION'S CONCEPTION

INCORPOREAL DESIGNERS JOINED FORCES with corporal builders to construct the "Electrical Infant." Since, as journalist S. Crosly Hewitt wrote, Rev. Spear was "quite destitute of either inventive genius, scientific knowledge in either of the departments involved, physics and biology, or even ordinary chemical abilities," all the entranced cleric could do was pass along angelic instructions.

He ordered each part of the creation to be carefully machined according to specifications. Magnets, wheels, and pulleys were incorporated. Metal bars, wires, insulators, and unknown chemical compounds all had their place. Parts were added willy-nilly according to afterthought and inspiration. Zinc and copper were important materials for reasons that were never disclosed. And specific sections of the contraption apparently corresponded to the brains, hearts, and lungs of more conventional humans.

Contemporary descriptions say it was assembled on a dining room table at High Rock. Two metal supports at the center held a revolving steel shaft. This in turn supported a horizontal steel appendage from which hung two steel balls, each enclosing a magnet. Under these was an oval platform fashioned from metal and magnets. Above this hovered several zinc and copper plates—the brain of the machine. Small steel bars containing magnets surrounded the structure. Positive and negative connections rooted the thing in the earth.

The occult principles involved, according to Spear, were as follows: "All things in nature, whether animal, vegetable or mineral, are either male or female. Minerals were classified; the female distinguished from the male, so the female metals could be located on one side of the mechanism, and the male on the other. Then certain wires were carefully arranged and critically located; absorbers of the elements were nicely adjusted, with powerful condensers of the electrical fluids. Projections were made from the edifice wherein the mechanism was located, and points were raised; these caught the fluids invisible to the human eye; they were condensed; and, by this peculiar arrangement, the fluids passed to the points desired; pulsatory motion appeared . . . the results were of a highly satisfactory character—such as were never before attained on this earth; [electric] fluids were caught and permanent motion secured."

It is disappointing that no photographs or drawings of this hybrid of *homunculus* and *perpetuum mobile* seem to have survived. From the vague descriptions that remain, one is tempted to visualize a monstrous fusion of aluminum Christmas tree and television antenna that cost Rev. Spear and his followers the monumental sum of $2,000!

Nine months later—and I suspect this time frame was not a coincidence—in June 1854, the machine was complete. Although the gestation period was of a conventional duration, we note the reverse of normal conception and birth. Among mundane humanity, the spark of life is given, and the body grows. With the electrical infant, the body is constructed, then the life spark bestowed.

But not yet! According to the Electrizers, a series of "ministrations" were still needed to bestow life and motion.

Initially, small clusters of believers, each group representing a different socioeconomic division, paraded past the machine, touching it, transferring into it something of their own essence. But the "father" was, of course, Spear himself.

That entitlement came, perhaps, from divine right, but it may also have been because Spear was the only one trusting enough to undergo the mysterious "operation" the spirit engineers required. In part, this called for Spear to be wrapped in a cage made of metal plates, strips, bands, jewels, and precious metals. When properly positioned, he fell into a trance from which he woke an hour later, totally exhausted. During that time, according to a clairvoyant witness, a sort of umbilical cord of light fed the machine from the vital forces of Spear's body and soul.

The seed had been planted.

And now all was ready for the Mary of the new dispensation.

THE ELECTRICAL INFANT'S MOTHER

T HE REVEREND WAS ASSISTED by two newspaper editors, S. Crosby Hewitt and Alonzo Newton, who chronicled the whole experience. Although the various contemporary accounts attempt to protect the identity of the mother, we can be quite certain she was Mrs. S.J. Newton, wife of Alonzo.

She had been chosen to play a very special role in what was to come. After passing into "the superior state," Spear expressed the spirits' high regard for their chosen vessel. "There is before this woman," the spirits said, "a new and beautiful labor," which they promised to detail the next day at precisely ten in the morning.

One can appreciate the lady's position. A Spiritualist herself, she must have been immensely honored to find herself singled out by the exalted entities who spoke directly to her through the mouth of so famous and respected a spiritual leader.

Without hesitation she presented herself to the gathering at High Rock the next morning. And here begins the sexual, and perhaps most scandalous, part of the process.

Again in the "superior state," and on bended knee, Spear took the lady's hand and said, "Receive now this blessed power!" He closed her fingers and breathed upon her fist, saying, "This hand shall be unfolded to dispense blessings." Then, with great finality, he said, "It is done!"

But it wasn't done; it was only beginning . . .

Already a mother by more traditional means, Mrs. Newton no doubt recognized the familiar indications right away. She began experiencing the symptoms of actual gestation accompanied with "some very singular characteristics," which, perhaps happily, history fails to record.

None of the sources from this genteel era describe the specifics of her suffering, but apparently the "agonizing sensations of parturition" continued for a good two hours. During this painful ordeal, it was Mrs. Newton's personal perception that "the most interior and refined elements of her spiritual being were imparted to, and absorbed by, the appropriate portions of the mechanism. . . ."

But what the observers saw was even more astonishing.

As Boston's *New Era* headline reported, "THE THING MOVES!"

Pulsations, tiny indications of life, were evident to all beholders. Cries of triumph rose from the spectators and, on a hilltop in Lynn, Massachusetts, a new age was born.

The *New Era* continued, "Hence we most confidently assert that the advent of the science of sciences, the philosophy of all philosophies, and not long hence he [meaning the machine, a male, of course] will go alone. Then he will dispute with the doctors in the temples of science."

Together, Spear and his followers, under the guidance of benevolent supra-mundane forces, had witnessed this Last, Best Gift to Man.

How Mrs. Newton's lowly human husband—the St. Joseph in this drama—must have felt can never be known. But if he were in fact Alonzo Newton, he wrote that life equal to that of his new stepson "doubtless never before existed, either on earth, or in the waters under the earth, but whether in the heavens above, no opinion will be ventured."

ARRESTED DEVELOPMENT

ALTHOUGH MRS. NEWTON'S MATERNAL INSTINCTS would not permit her to desert her mechanical offspring—indeed she continued to nurse the motor for weeks—she cannot have been too happy with its development. Even visitors skeptical of the entire endeavor admitted the thing had moved a little. But most attributed it to magnetic forces, oxidation, and wind.

One disappointed Spiritualist wrote that the New Motive Power would not be capable of turning a coffee mill.

And what of the Electrizer spirits themselves? When an embarrassed Rev. Spear inquired as to why they had forsaken him, they reminded him to be patient. "It needs maternal care," they said, "like other newborn babes. It hungers for that nourishment on which it can feed and by which it can expand and grow."

In a last effort to give it that vital nourishment it craved, Spear had the thing shipped to Randolph, New York, an area known among Spiritualists for its "lofty electrical position." Yet, in spite of all efforts, the thing refused to budge. "The new motor would not move to any purpose," one skeptical commentator observed. "This was the only drawback in its great benefits to mankind."

At that point the end was near.

In a description worthy of a gothic novelist, psychologist Dr. Nandor Fordor explained in his book *Between Two Worlds*: "As the news of the living machine spread, disquieting rumors arose. It was whispered that strange practices had taken place and that [the medium] was indeed the mother of the strange machine. . . . The public mind was aroused against the machine which exposed motherhood to ridicule. Resentment grew to such a pitch that . . . the populace marched on the machine. . . ."

And in a scene reminiscent of an earlier attempt at life-giving, *Frankenstein*, the angry mob tore Spear's creation to pieces and trampled it under their feet.

Heartbroken, Rev. John Murray Spear never sired another mechanical offspring.

The whole fascinating episode is wonderfully odd on many levels.

Considering that the main player in this bizarre drama was a holy man, what we seem to be witnessing here is a grotesque parody of the birth, life, and death of Jesus, complete with an immaculate conception of sorts, a Mary by proxy, and a mechanical Messiah. Most conspicuous, however, is the absence of a Resurrection.

Odd, too, that the living machine's birthplace, its Bethlehem, should be Lynn, Massachusetts, a city where its nonsentient brothers and sisters—turbines, generators, jet engines, and electrical lamps—would soon proliferate.

That a worthy cleric like Spear should fall victim to such a ruse is testament to the misleading nature of the whole Spiritualist movement. As Andrew Jackson Davis pointed out, Spear and his supporters had labored nine months constructing the motor when they might have devoted their time and energies to something of real benefit to humanity.

While today it is easy to dismiss all the players as naive and in some cases moronic, I don't really think that is the case. In fact, Spear himself admitted questioning his own sanity at the very beginning of the New Motive Power communications.

Or, in our twenty-first century smugness, we may be tempted to believe we are dealing with hoax after hoax. Maybe. But I think we should be cautious when we point our finger at the hoaxer.

The evidence for unexplained phenomena associated with Spiritualism seems overwhelming. Raps came from nowhere. Tables levitated apparently under their own power. Messages appeared. Forms materialized. Mediums went into trances, giving answers to questions before they were asked and demonstrating knowledge of things they'd never learned.

I'll go out on a limb here and state that preternatural forces did seem to be at work in Lynn, Massachusetts. If Rev. Spear wasn't deceiving himself and his followers, then something was deceiving him. Something that frustrated his altruism, mocked his belief system, then deserted him entirely, leaving him red-faced and wondering what in the world had happened.

The Chittenden Investigation

IN THE PRECEDING CHAPTERS, WE HAVE LOOKED AT SOME COMPELLING, IF NOT completely convincing, paranormal events that occurred in New England during the rise of American Spiritualism.

Needless to say, hundreds of individuals flocked to Stratford, Hydesville, Machiasport, and Lynn, hoping to observe the fantastic phenomena firsthand. At the very least, we can see the Spiritualistic movement was good for tourism, one of New England's oldest industries. In spite of all the publicity these bizarre events received, there was never much of any systematic, ongoing, disinterested, scientific investigation.

However, another spectral spectacular was intensely investigated. This ten-week probe was to be the first formal case of ghostbusting in the history of Vermont.

WORKING IN THE GHOST SHOP

THE YEAR WAS 1874. The Spiritualist press was buzzing with reports of highly peculiar goings-on in a remote Vermont farmhouse in the tiny mountain town of Chittenden. Allegedly, all manner of strange phenomena were taking place in the home of William and Horatio Eddy, two middle-aged, nearly illiterate brothers, and their sister, Mary.

Their isolated and unkempt two-and-a-half-story building seemed to be infested with supernatural creatures, ghosts, and spectral phenomena of such magnitude as to be unrivaled before or since. The events at the Eddy farm were so powerful and strange that people came from all over the world to witness them. In some circles, Chittenden, Vermont, became known as "The Spirit Capital of the Universe."

But to residents of Chittenden, the Eddy house was a shunned place. Some called it "the ghost shop"; others swore it was "the abode of the Devil."

SUMMER 1874

IN NEW YORK CITY, a successful 42-year-old lawyer stopped in a newsstand and bought a paper. His name was Henry Steel Olcott, and by his own admission he "had paid no attention to the Spiritualist movement." But for some reason, during this break from the case he was working on for the city, the new religious movement crossed his mind. In his memoirs he writes, "I do not know what association of ideas made my mind pass from the mechanical constructions of water metres to modern spiritualism, but in any event I . . . bought a copy of the *Banner of Light*."

In it, he read an incredible story that was to change his life. It was an article about the Eddy brothers and their mediumistic wonders. "I saw at once," Olcott wrote, "that, if it were true that visitors [to the Eddy farm] could see, even touch and converse with deceased relatives who had found means to reconstruct their bodies and clothing so as to be temporarily solid, visible, and tangible, this was the most important fact in modern physical science."

He was determined to go and see for himself.

He convinced an influential newspaper, the *New York Daily Graphic*, to send him to Vermont to do some investigative reporting.

One might be tempted to ask, just what qualifications did this man-off-the-street have to determine whether William and Horatio were villains or visionaries?

Well, let's take a look at his resume. Olcott was born in Orange, New Jersey, in 1832 of solid Presbyterian stock. He attended college in New York City, then went on to study scientific agriculture. While still in his early twenties, Olcott received international recognition for his work on a model farm and for founding an agricultural school. Along the way he published three scientific works. In recognition of the young man's extraordinary achievements, the U.S. government offered him the

Chief Commissionership of Agriculture, the country's highest position in the field.

Other countries tried to tempt him away with similar offers, but instead, he accepted the position of agriculture editor for Horace Greeley's newspaper, the *New York Tribune*.

When the Civil War broke out, Olcott enlisted. His intellect and cunning won him an appointment as a special investigator to root out corruption in military arsenals and naval shipyards. He proved especially clever at detecting fraud. For this, he was promoted to colonel and received the personal congratulations of Secretary of War Stanton. In fact, Colonel Olcott proved so adept at sleuthing that he was appointed to a three-member panel to investigate the assassination of President Lincoln. After the war, Olcott studied law and became a wealthy and successful member of the New York bar.

In short, Olcott was a high achiever, well-trained in scientific and investigative techniques. He'd earned international recognition as a scientist before becoming a journalist, an investigator, and a lawyer.

With all this in mind, we might be more tempted to ask, could there have been a better person for the job?

So Colonel Olcott traveled to Vermont, accompanied by an artist named Alfred Kappes. Together they'd investigate the weird goings-on at the Eddy farmstead. Their report for the *Daily Graphic* would expose, once and for all, whether William and Horatio Eddy were humbugs or heroes. If they were gifted clairvoyants, Olcott would tell the world there really was some validity to this "spiritualism" business. If they were ingenious charlatans, he'd expose them and let public contempt do its worst.

In either event, Olcott was determined to be fair. As Sir Arthur Conan Doyle says in his comprehensive book, *The History of Spiritualism*, "Olcott . . . was a man of clear brain and outstanding ability, with a high sense of honor . . . loyal to a fault, unselfish, and with that rare moral courage which will follow truth and accept results even when they oppose one's expectations and desires. He was no mystical dreamer but a very practical man of affairs. . . ."

UPON ARRIVAL

I IMAGINE OLCOTT'S JOURNEY to the Eddy farm as a scene straight out of H.P. Lovecraft. Picture him arriving at the train station in Rutland during the height of summer's heat. Imagine the bumpy, dusty, sweaty, seven-mile journey by stagecoach into a "grassy valley shut in by the slopes of the Green Mountains."

Then Chittenden itself, a town of roughly 800 people. Olcott describes it as "plain, dull, and uninteresting." From there he headed south, where eventually he arrived at "the home of the Devil."

And imagine meeting the Eddys for the first time. Somber, sinister, and silent, they must have been an unnerving pair. Olcott wrote, "There is nothing about [them] to inspire confidence on first acquaintance. The brothers . . . are . . . distant, and curt to strangers . . . [they] look more like hard-working rough farmers than prophets or priests [with their] dark complexions, black hair and eyes, stiff joints, [and] clumsy carriage. . . ." And being true Yankees, they also spoke with a thick Vermont dialect that made them difficult to understand.

But in the ten weeks Colonel Olcott spent with the brothers, it wasn't eldritch Lovecraftian horrors that he witnessed. Instead, it proved to be an unrelenting phantasmagoria, a mind-numbing array of spiritual phenomena that left the writer and artist at a complete loss for words.

Like any competent investigator or journalist, Olcott set about getting background on his subjects. He learned that the brothers were descended from a long line of psychics. Mary Bradley, their maternal grandmother, four times removed, had been convicted of witchcraft during the madness in Salem, Massachusetts, in 1692. She escaped with the help of friends.

Their grandmother possessed "second sight"; the boys remembered her going into trances and speaking with entities no one else could see.

Their mother, Julia, frightened her neighbors with predictions and visions. Zephaniah, her husband—an abusive, narrow-minded bigot—discouraged all displays of her powers, maintaining they were the handiwork of the Devil.

Mrs. Eddy quickly learned to hide her gifts.

But the powers couldn't be concealed or controlled when the couple began having children. Inexplicable pounding shook the barren walls of the ramshackle farmhouse. Disembodied voices whispered near the children. Occasionally, the defenseless infants were transported from their cribs by unseen hands. They were likely to be discovered anywhere in the house, and sometimes outside.

As William and Horatio matured, the occult forces strengthened. Soon spirits became visible. On several occasions, Zephaniah watched his sons playing with unfamiliar children, children that would vanish when he approached.

The Eddy brothers couldn't go to school; their intangible companions made it impossible. A deafening concussion disrupted the one-room schoolhouse. Invisible hands snatched books from terrified children. Desks levitated. Objects—inkwells, chalk, and rulers—soared around the room.

Zephaniah tried to put a stop to things in the only way he knew how. He beat his sons repeatedly, but the strange antics continued. When he realized he couldn't control what was happening, Zephaniah became furious. Every time the boys fell spontaneously into a trance, he'd taunt them by calling them lazy or accusing them of being minions of the Evil One. When they didn't respond, he'd try to rouse them by punching or pinching them until their skin was black and blue. But the boys didn't waken.

Once, on the advice of a sympathetic Christian friend named Anson Ladd, Zephaniah doused the boys with boiling water. When his sons didn't even grimace, he permitted Ladd to drop a red-hot coal into William's hand to exorcise the Devil. The boy didn't stir, but he bore a scar on his palm until his dying day.

On occasion, the spirits apparently rose up to defend the boys. They'd materialize in front of Zephaniah and drive him from the house.

Simply put, it was more than the man could tolerate.

Realizing the potential for profit in his sons' frustrating abilities, Zephaniah rented them to a traveling showman who, for fourteen years, dragged them around the United States, Canada, and Europe. As part of the performance, the showman would challenge audience members to wake the boys from their trances.

Zephaniah and Anson Ladd looked gentle compared to audiences full of skeptics and self-proclaimed "psychic investigators." Unmercifully punched, poked, prodded, and pinched, the boys were left indelibly scarred and permanently misshapen—but their psychic gifts were never discredited. The Eddys were mobbed in Lynn, Massachusetts, stoned in Danvers, even shot at. William Eddy was irreparably disfigured by bullet wounds.

Only after the parents died were the boys able to return safely home. Along with their sister, Mary, they kept the farm and opened their home as a modest bed and breakfast, calling it The Green Tavern.

It is difficult to imagine a more horrible childhood. No wonder they grew into cold, suspicious, unfriendly men, who, Olcott reported, ". . . make newcomers feel ill at ease and unwelcome."

Clearly, William and Horatio were not glib and affable con men.

They were something else. But what?

During Olcott's first day at Chittenden, he witnessed an outdoor seance.

In the bright moonlight of a warm summer evening, a group of ten participants carefully made their way along a well-trodden path. After entering a deep ravine near a mountain brook, they assembled in front of a cave. It had been formed ages ago when two gigantic flat stones had toppled together, creating a kind of arch. Olcott learned that it was known as "Honto's Cave," named after the good-natured Native American spirit who often appeared there.

Upon inspection, Olcott saw the giant stone slabs were so tightly pressed together that nothing but a tiny animal could go in or out from the back.

The medium, Horatio Eddy, sat on a camp stool under the arched stones. Spectators, seated on crude wooden planks laid across boulders, watched as Horatio was concealed within a makeshift "spirit cabinet," fashioned from shawls draped across saplings.

As Horatio spoke quietly, a gigantic Native American walked from within the darkness of the cave. While the medium addressed the specter, someone cried, "Look! Look up there!"

On the top of the cave, where even a mountain goat could not have climbed, the figure of another gigantic Indian stood silhouetted against the moonlit sky.

To the right a spectral female, probably Honto, had appeared on a ledge. In all, ten such figures materialized over the course of the evening. They vanished all at once.

"Within a few minutes," Olcott wrote, "the spirit of a man named Alas Sprague emerged . . . and walked far from the cabinet in the brilliant rays of the moon. Then appeared the brother of one of the spectators and was duly and truly identified. All dematerialized while in plain view of ten observers."

After the seance, Olcott and his companion made a careful search of the grounds looking for footprints in the soft earth. They found no such evidence.

THE INSIDE SCOOP

A S CONVINCING AS OLCOTT found this incredible display, he knew it would be far easier to detect fraud in the more controlled confines of the house. He and Mr. Kappes carefully examined the 17-by-35½-foot "circle room" above the kitchen of the Eddys' mysterious farmhouse. Using carpenters and engineers as consultants, Olcott convinced himself the walls and floor were every bit as solid as they appeared. So, what he witnessed night after night in that room became all the more puzzling.

Judging from his writings, the seances progressed something like this: Every night of the week except Sunday, guests and visitors assembled on wooden benches before a platform lighted only by a kerosene lamp recessed in a barrel.

William Eddy, the primary medium, would mount the platform and enter his "spirit cabinet," which was nothing more than a tiny closet. For a suspenseful moment, all would be silent. Then soft voices would speak or sing in the distance, often accompanied by music. Tambourines came to life and soared around the stage; ectoplasmic hands appeared, grappling, waving, touching the spectators.

Tension mounted.

Shortly, from behind the curtained door of William Eddy's "spirit cabinet," ethereal forms began to emerge. One at a time or in groups. Twenty, even thirty in the course of an evening.

Some were completely visible and seemingly solid. Others were partially materialized. Still others remained transparent as they moved before the awed spectators.

These apparitions varied in size from that of an infant to well over six feet (Will Eddy himself was only 5 feet 9 inches). Most of the ghostly visitors were elderly

Vermonters or American Indians, but in time, a vast array of representative nation-alities appeared in costume: black Africans, Russians, Kurds, Orientals, and more.

Where did they come from?

Olcott had fully familiarized himself with the methods of stage magicians and fraudulent mediums. His detailed examinations of the spirit cabinet disclosed only plaster and lathe. No trapdoors, no hidden compartments, no room for anyone but the medium himself.

Then, in sort of a carnival of souls, the apparitions performed, singing, danc-ing, chatting with the spectators; they'd produce weapons, scarves, and musical in-struments. All told, the events at the Eddy farmhouse included every manifestation known to psychic science at the time: rappings, moving objects, spirit paintings and drawings, prophesying, speaking in strange tongues, healing, disembodied voices, ghostly writing, musical instruments playing, human levitation, uncanny hands appearing, clairvoyance, remote vision, teleportation, and more.

But most amazing were the full-body materializations. Some 400 in all during the ten weeks Olcott spent there. He concluded that such a show, night after night, would require a whole company of actors and several trunks full of costumes.

Yet his thorough inspection of the premises revealed no place to hide people or props. Further, if the phantoms were in fact actors, how could they be so convinc-ing night after night? Spectators repeatedly recognized deceased friends and rela-tives among the apparitions. One woman spoke at length, in Russian, to the specter of her dead husband. Others conversed with their loved ones in their native di-alects. The semi-literate Eddys hadn't really mastered their own tongue; how could they hold fluent conversations in no fewer than six foreign languages?

Additionally, such an elaborate show would be expensive to put on every night. They'd have to pay the actors, not to mention purchase expensive costumes and the sophisticated equipment required to produce "magical illusions."

The brothers were poor. They, along with sister Mary, did all the housework themselves. Half the visitors didn't pay, the rest gave only $8 a week for room and board. No charge was ever made for the seances.

Olcott's ten-week stay was an admirable feat of endurance, considering the plain food, hard living, and unfriendly hosts. He came away disliking the gloomy brothers, yet absolutely confident they could bring back the dead.

Not only did he chronicle his adventure for the *New York Daily Graphic*, but he also wrote a book called *People From the Other World*. This study, some 500 pages long, is full of precise drawings of the apparitions, the grounds, and the house—including details of its construction. Reading it today, one might find it difficult to imagine any precaution this fair-minded researcher didn't take.

In all, Colonel Olcott recorded the appearance of well over 400 different supernatural entities. He collected hundreds of eyewitness testimonies and dozens of sworn affidavits from laborers, lawyers, farmers, physicians, merchants, musicians, bankers, bakers, housewives, and historians. All had personally observed the manifestation of men, women, children, and even babies, most of whom emerged from the spirit cabinet, then roamed freely around the "circle room."

For example, this is part of the sworn testimony of eyewitness Franklin Bolles of Hartford, Connecticut: "My wife's mother . . . appeared to us . . . looking so natural that we recognized her instantly. . . . But suddenly, as if she had exhausted all her power of materialization . . . her form melted down to the floor, and disappeared. . . . The figure did not dissolve into a mist and disperse laterally, but sank down and disappeared, as if every particle comprising her frame had suddenly lost its cohesion with every other, and the whole fell into a heap together."

A Doctor Hodges of Stoneham, Massachusetts, along with four other witnesses, signed a document saying: "We certify . . . that Santum was out on the platform when another Indian of almost as great a stature came out, and the two passed each other as they walked up and down. At the same time a conversation was being carried on between [spirits known as] George Dix, Mayflower, old Mrs. Morse, and Mrs. Eaton inside the cabinet. We recognized the familiar voice of each."

Along with such eyewitness testimony, Olcott reproduced dozens of statements from respectable carpenters and tradespeople who had examined everything for trickery. At the conclusion of every seance, the spirit cabinet and William were thoroughly searched. Both showed the same result: a chair with a man tied to it—and nothing else. No Indian buckskins, no costumes or clothing, no musical instruments, spears, daggers, or pistols—just a man in a deep trance . . .

LOOKING BACKWARD

Eventually, the Eddy brothers and sister Mary went their separate ways. As Agnes Gould, a 96-year-old Chittenden resident recalled in 1980, the family began to feud among themselves. "They'd get jealous of each other's power," she said, "each other's success."

Horatio moved out, taking a house across the street, where he devoted himself to light gardening, occasional seances, and doing magic tricks for children brave enough to approach him. Mary relocated to the nearby village of East Pittsford, where she became a full-time, professional medium, giving seances in her home and traveling to various Spiritualist gatherings. And William dropped out of public life entirely, becoming something of a hermit in the old family place.

On September 8, 1922, Horatio became the first brother to cross over into the land of the spirits. His house was so cluttered that funeral services were conducted on the porch.

William lived for another ten years. He was a familiar figure around town, sporting a full black beard and dark hair, even in old age. He never married and refused to participate in the sort of "theatrical spiritualism" practiced by his brother and sister.

Coincidentally—or perhaps by design?—William Eddy's life paralleled the entire birth, rise, and eventual decline of American Spiritualism. When he died on October 25, 1932, at age 99, a magnificent and magical era died as well.

If William Eddy had any real secrets about this life or the next, he took them with him to the grave. Ever since then, as far as we know, he's held his silence.

WHAT HAPPENED?

What are we to make of this odd tale? One is tempted simply to dismiss the events, to say that in a simpler, less-sophisticated era, investigators were, well, simpler and less sophisticated.

No modern examiner, we aver, would be so easily duped.

And that sums it up: In the final analysis, it all comes down to Olcott. Was he a dependable witness? Should we trust his perceptions and conclusions?

His documentation—corroborated by several other investigators—suggests we're not dealing with a hoax. Though skeptical and analytical throughout, Olcott came away completely convinced the Eddys brought back the spirits of the dead.

But, we may ask, if the dead don't return, then what were those incredible creatures? Could they have been ectoplasmic extensions of the sullen, sleeping William? Did he, through some biological process yet unknown, produce the visions from the power of his mind or the matter of his body? Or could the creatures have been something else, something stranger, like elemental pranksters posing as departed loved ones, their deceptions motivated by forces, drives, and desires we cannot even guess at?

The theatrical quality of the demonstrations suggests someone—or something—was putting on a show.

Madam Helena Blavatsky, whom Olcott met at Chittenden, had a chilling explanation that hints at sinister purpose. Though she didn't believe the dead return to earth, she believed nonhuman spirits exist, spirits who can, on occasion, interact with human beings.

She postulated that the Eddys, unwittingly, had given such spirits a passageway into our world. Attempting to contact the departed, she explained, "only opens the door to a swarm of 'spooks' . . . to which the medium becomes a slave for life." She warned that these and similar experiments could interfere with the evolution of human souls, for some spirits "are most dangerous."

Could Chittenden's wonder show have been staged by cunning malevolent spirits? Was it their intent to divert people's attention from more worthwhile spiritual development? Maybe. This whole country—indeed the entire western world—was "distracted" by Spiritualism for more than half a century.

Our only conclusion can be that wherever the truth lies, something grand and mysterious happened in Chittenden, Vermont, in the nineteenth century. The Eddy visions so influenced Colonel Olcott that he came away a changed man, a believer.

In 1875, Olcott and Madam Blavatsky co-founded the Theosophical Society, whose membership included some of the greatest minds of the day. The society's noble motto, then as now, is "There is no religion higher than the Truth."

PART II

BARNYARD TALES and TERRORS

*"Our entire farm was overrun by freaks,
flouting with impunity their huge vestigial claws
and limbs, bunches and distentions, superfluous
organs and double sets of teeth."*

— HOWARD FRANK MOSHER

Disappearances

Funny Farms

THE TERM "NEW ENGLAND" CONJURES MORE THAN SPIRITS OF THE DEAD. It conjures images—different ones for different people.

For some, New England is picturesque seacoast towns, rocky shores, and wind-blasted Cape Cod cottages. Others picture snow-dusted mountain villages, après-ski cocktails, and inflated gas prices. Those more nostalgically inclined might recall bandstands on vast village greens, 4-H clubs, and firemen's carnivals, while the more romantic see white picket fences, with church steeples and colonial houses to match.

Regardless of your preferred stereotype, one staple of New England imagery is, and always has been, the farm. It's obvious: farming has been essential to New England culture and economy since Pilgrims began evolving into Yankees.

Those from "away" routinely associate New England farms with hard work and solid values. And the purposeful Yankees populating the farms, of course, are too busy to be anything but taciturn and too honest to be anything but direct.

Generally, we don't associate the New England farm with mystery, madness, and death. But as the following stories show, New England, like its Old World counterpart, has enough bizarre and baffling occurrences to confound even a Harvard-educated Sherlock Holmes.

The Mystery of the Perforated Pond

ROCKY RIDGE FARM IS ABOUT ONE HUNDRED ACRES OF SCENIC LAND, REMOTELY situated near the Maine-New Hampshire border. From the high position of his house, owner William McCarthy can enjoy a satisfying vista that includes his "horse pond," near the bottom of a hill.

Sometime during the morning of January 10, 1977, farmer McCarthy looked out and saw a panorama that was perfectly normal . . . except for one thing: he saw a hole in the ice of that pond.

A month earlier, when the ice was new and fragile, he would have thought nothing of it. But by mid-January, Wakefield, New Hampshire, was solidly bound in winter's cold embrace, and the ice on his "horse pond" was a good 18 inches thick. It was, as McCarthy himself attested, strong enough to drive a tank over.

When he inspected the mysterious hole close up, he found it was perfectly round and about 3 feet in diameter. Its position was close enough to the center of the pond to suggest that whatever caused it had been aimed.

Now that *was* strange. What—other than an ice fisherman with a 3-foot auger—could make such a hole? It would certainly require great force. If caused by a falling object—some kind of space junk, maybe—it must have fallen from a considerable height.

Understandably curious, Mr. McCarthy found a long stick and began poking around with it. He says he definitely struck *something* submerged in 3 feet of pond water. As Mr. McCarthy peered into the hole, he saw at first nothing but impenetrably dark water. But then, he said, "I . . . saw what appeared to be a square black object."

A square black object?

He continued to poke around "without hitting anything else that I could tell." Soon he called his wife, Dorothy, to get her take on this mysterious business. She gave the scene a good inspection but was equally baffled. Not knowing what else to do, the puzzled farmer went inside and phoned the town police.

That was a mistake, for this one innocent phone call touched off a national furor.

First, police showed up with a bunch of civil defense workers in tow. As CD workers checked the hole, their Geiger counters began clicking up a storm. Something was giving off an abnormally high amount of radiation. In fact, the count was so high the officials ordered everyone to stay away from the pond.

Then they instructed Mr. McCarthy and his family not to tell anyone about what happened.

Although he'd just made the one phone call, word somehow got out. Suddenly Bill McCarthy found himself surrounded not only by civil defense workers and police, but also by National Guardsmen and a whole army of press people, photographers, and television news crews. By the end of the afternoon, the New Hampshire Attorney General's office, the state police, and even the Pentagon were in on the act.

Things happened incredibly fast; the McCarthy farm had never been so busy.

Over the next few hours, the family saw parades of determined officials and civilians arrive mildly curious and depart totally bewildered. The state police tried to rope off the area, but undaunted throngs of curiosity seekers just ducked under the ropes.

A team of workers were brought in to make the hole in the pond larger, but that proved unsafe and revealed nothing. Every airfield within a 100-mile radius was checked. No military or civilian craft had dropped or lost anything over New Hampshire. No meteors had been reported, and experts ruled out natural thawing, hot springs, satellite debris, and oversized ice fishermen.

By nightfall, after a lot of dashing around, scribbling, affirmative head-nodding, and secretive buzzing, someone gave the order to pump out the pond. But this too proved impossible, so everyone but the appointed guards gave up for the night.

The next morning, the underwater mystery suddenly plunged a few fathoms deeper. For some reason, someone thought to check the radiation count again. New readings showed the radioactivity in and around the pond had vanished. It was as if whatever was in the water at sundown on Monday was gone on Tuesday. Vanished.

And so, apparently, had the black box McCarthy said he had seen. Perhaps, as the officials said, it had never been there at all. But certain eyewitnesses maintained that National Guardsmen had removed *something* from the pond, and hauled it away in the back of a truck.

State officials countered by admitting they had instructed a chemist to take samples of water and soil, which he'd carried away in a black box.

Radiation control people said the same thing. But no one admitted to taking anything from the pond that shouldn't have been there in the first place.

In short, the *official* statement to the press is that nothing was discovered. The implication was that nothing had ever been there.

However, in the days to come, as the confusion began deescalating, Mr. McCarthy noticed another strange thing: the hole never seemed to refreeze. Even after a windy subzero New Hampshire night, only a slush would form in the opening.

So there you have it. After all is said and done, we can be certain of only one fact: *something* made that hole.

Are we then to assume that whatever punctured the ice on William McCarthy's pond originated beneath the water? Did it project upward and, like an underwater cruise missile, then vanish into the sky?

Or should we believe that whatever crashed down through the ice then made a subsurface U-turn and flew back out via the same hole?

Not very likely.

It is sad to think that today, twenty years after the fact, we don't know any more than we did in January of 1977. All we can say for sure is that whatever deep-sixed in McCarthy's pond made a big splash, but only in the papers.

Which brings me around to another circular subject.

Back in October of 1971, a different kind of circle was discovered on another New Hampshire farm. It was a distinct, round pattern formed by swirled, flattened grass in a field.

Today, we would call it a "crop-circle." In those days, such things were less frequently encountered, and less publicized. They were referred to as "flying saucer nests" —that is, if they were discussed at all.

Anyway, several field investigators from the Aerial Phenomena Research Organization of Tucson, Arizona, came all the way to New England to check things out. They showed up with their clipboards, their cameras, and their Geiger counters, but soon left in frustration. It seems that the farmer and the good people of Walpole, New Hampshire, were either too sensible or too publicity-shy to report their information.

It is a case where, perhaps, taciturnity is the appropriate response. I can't help wondering if farmer McCarthy would agree.

The Incident *at* Orwell

WHEN IT COMES TO WEIRD THINGS HAPPENING ON NEW ENGLAND FARMS, Mr. McCarthy's punctured pond is just the tip of the iceberg. And as mystifying as it is, at least no one was hurt, nor was any serious damage done to property or livestock.

The same cannot be said of this next mysterious incident, when a remote farmyard in Orwell, Vermont, was the scene of some grisly goings-on during a four-day period in late October 1991.

On Sunday, farmer Kenneth Pope found one of his heifers with scratches and deep puncture wounds on its face. He figured the animal had somehow gotten loose and hurt itself—maybe on a barbed-wire fence or protruding nail.

Then things got worse. Two days later, on Tuesday, he discovered four more cattle with their faces sliced to ribbons. Mr. Pope wasn't sure what had done it—dogs, maybe—but as an added precaution, he closed and carefully locked the barn door that night.

In spite of his security efforts, something got in. Its only means of entry was a window positioned so that a dog could not possibly get through.

Whatever the wily intruder was, it seemed extraordinarily purposeful. And canny. It bypassed calves in a calf house outside the barn, and it ignored the full-grown, free-roaming cattle. Instead, it went directly to the place where the 4-to-9-month-old cows were tied and helpless in stalls. A week and a half earlier, these heifers had been dehorned. Maybe the interloper had been attracted by the smell of the dehorning wounds. In any event, whatever it was mutilated the remaining cattle, leaving them suffering but not dead.

Mr. Pope called veterinarian Kent Anderson to examine the maimed animals.

The doctor paid special attention to the deep parallel lacerations on their faces and noses. In some cases, most of the flesh had been torn away. Facial bones had been crushed into the sinuses. Whatever had done this had to be strong and weigh well over 100 pounds. The damage was so extensive that Dr. Anderson recommended the suffering animals be killed, resulting in more than a $10,000 loss for Kenneth Pope. And a major mystery for the veterinarian, the farmer, and the community.

"I wouldn't rule out dogs," Dr. Anderson said. But he knew dogs were not likely suspects. The wounded animals had no bite marks anywhere but on the fronts of their heads.

But if not dogs, what manner of beast could be responsible for such a savage mutilation of fourteen heifers and one cow? What sort of creature would mangle its prey, then leave it alive?

Whatever it was hadn't killed for food. It was almost as if it had simply been playing with its victims.

When Pope and Anderson considered all the evidence, their best guess was that a large cat was responsible, a cat far bigger than a house cat, bobcat, or lynx. After all, members of the cat family will toy with their victims, often attacking without killing.

Trouble is, cats big enough to do that kind of damage do not live in Vermont.

Or at least they're not supposed to. Though that has never stopped Vermonters and other New Englanders from seeing these giant phantom felines from time to time.

But if it was *not* a cat, then just what was it?

A Shocking Tale

A SIMILAR SCENARIO BUT FAR MORE BAFFLING MYSTERY UNFOLDS IN THIS next barnyard tale. However, there is no way a cat or dog or any other known critter can be blamed for the damage.

The grisly events occurred at a deceptively tranquil New England farm, scenic enough to grace any postcard or promotional calendar.

Winter again. A wet, foggy night in February 1984.

The innocent-looking barn was part of Honeymoon Valley Farm, a successful dairy operation beautifully situated between Route 5 and the Connecticut River, in Dummerston, Vermont. Owned by Robert Ranney and his wife, Judy, the farm was a photographer's dream, hardly the sort of place to be visited by anything . . . unnatural.

Yet Mr. Ranney discovered a terrifying tragedy unlike anything he'd ever seen before. At about three in the morning, as always, he headed out after the milking cows. As he walked past the barn where the heifers were kept, something caught his eye.

"I saw one heifer that looked like she might need help," Mr. Ranney said. "And I looked in the barn . . ."

What he saw was a nightmarish tableau, a gruesome sight the memory of which would be with him the rest of his life.

Twenty-three of his twenty-nine heifers were dead. "At first," he said, "it looked like they were all dead." No blood. No wounds. No sign of a struggle. Just dead.

How could it be? Only a few hours earlier all the little animals had been perfectly all right. And now . . .

Well, according to one account, the twenty-three dead heifers were lying in a perfect circle with feed still in their mouths.

The surviving six cows were unharmed.

When he'd recovered from the shock, the first thing Mr. Ranney did was call his veterinarian. After examining the cows, the vet couldn't escape an odd conclusion: the animals had been electrocuted. But try as he might, the vet couldn't figure out how it had happened.

However, he assured Mr. Ranney that the animals apparently had died instantly; none of them had suffered. This he determined because there were no signs of a struggle nor evidence the cows had tried to escape. Whatever happened must have happened very fast—instantly—making the deaths even more of a puzzle.

Because of the value of the livestock—worth more than $1,000 a head—an insurance investigator was required to inspect the scene. He agreed that all twenty-three cows had died instantly, probably by electrocution. However, he couldn't determine any way the killings could have been achieved intentionally, by design, and with such precision. With that disclosure, foul play was ruled out, but it didn't look like an accident either. Suddenly, the events took on an added layer of mystery.

Then more investigators checked the scene, including electricians, but not one of them could discover any reason for the eerie electrical deaths.

Mr. Ranney voiced a theory of his own: "What it looked like was lightning. . . . I've seen plenty of cows hit by lightning out in the field, and that's what these cows looked like."

Although the lightning theory has merit, there were absolutely no signs of a strike: the barn door remained closed; there were no burns or scorch marks on the roof, beams, or floor; and none of the hay had ignited. More telling, perhaps, is that none of the dead cows had split hoofs. Lightning will generally leave that mark if no other.

So what happened?

The most bizarre theory was put forth several days later by another examiner, an ex-policeman from Rutland, Vermont, named William Chapleau. Chapleau inspected the scene on behalf of a private investigative organization called MUFON, an acronym for Mutual UFO Network.

While scanning the area with a Geiger counter, Chapleau found high radiation at the center of the barn and in the cornfield where the cows had been buried. Noting the proximity of the farm to the Vermont Yankee Nuclear Power Plant in Vernon,

Chapleau's first guess was that the animals had been killed by some kind of freak radioactive discharge. He soon learned, however, that the power plant had been shut down at the time.

Then—having eliminated all other possibilities to his own satisfaction—Chapleau ventured that the animals may have been killed by a UFO.

On the night the cows died, four people had contacted him about a "torpedo-shaped" UFO over the Vernon Nuclear Plant, just a few miles away. Also, a ball of light had been seen that same night in nearby Hinsdale, New Hampshire.

According to Chapleau, no other explanation for the strange deaths has ever emerged.

About a decade later, on October 21, 1994, I discussed the incident with Mrs. Ranney. Although the family had moved away from Dummerston, she remembered everything clearly.

I wanted to be sure I had the facts straight, so I asked her if I had recorded everything accurately. In general, yes, but she told me I had the dates wrong. In reality, the tragedy happened on February 14, 1984.

The eerie thought of a St. Valentine's Day Massacre gave me a little shudder; I'm sure she noticed. Finally, I asked her if the gruesome events had ever been explained?

No, she said, it is as much a mystery today as it was the night it happened. In ten years, no realistic theory—including stray voltage—has ever been offered.

Then she gave me one more chilling detail.

The burial of the twenty-three cows had been unceremonious. They simply bulldozed a big hole in the field and pushed all the bodies into it. Then they covered them with dirt and planted corn over everything.

But, she told me, as weird as it sounds, the corn has never grown on the circle defined by the dead cows' grave.

Natural or unnatural? Who can say? If there is a connection among the cows, the UFO, the nuclear plant, and a barren patch of cornfield, the evidence seems entirely circumstantial.

A hole in the ice of a pond, too round to be natural.

A circular swirl in a hillside pasture.

A semicircle of electrocuted heifers and a round grave where corn will never grow . . . Mundane or miraculous, whatever the explanation may be, these baffling events make us feel as if we're going round in circles.

The **Problem** *of* **Old Hairy**

THE PRECEDING STORIES ARE FRUSTRATING, AS TRUE MYSTERIES ARE LIKELY TO BE. The problem is, nothing is found. We don't know what broke farmer McCarthy's ice, we're not sure what maimed Mr. Pope's livestock, and we have no idea at all what zapped the Ranneys' heifers.

There were, as far as we've learned, no witnesses to any of these events. With no witnesses, and no evidence, we'll probably never know what happened.

But imagine what it might have been like to catch the phantom perpetrator before it killed the Ranneys' cows. Or picture entering Pope's barn in time to stop the slaughter of his heifers.

Could that be what happened on August 23, 1982? Could John Fuller and David Buckley have stopped something—who knows what?—before it happened?

It was a Monday night. Rainy, as is often the pattern when strange things happen. Fuller and Buckley were working at a dairy farm in Ellington, Connecticut. At around midnight, it was their routine to go to the barn to check on the cows. As they stepped inside and out of the rain, they ran into something that scared them half to death.

There they were, face to face with some variety of nightmare creature.

The thing appeared alien, yet something seemed vaguely human about it. Perhaps it was its casual, humanlike posture as it sat there on the edge of a feed bin, watching the cows. Its manner seemed nonchalant as one of its hirsute hands dangled into the bin, playing with the silage, stirring it or maybe reaching for a handful to eat.

The men described the creature as huge and hairy, 6 to 7 feet tall, probably weighing some 300 pounds. Its head was about the size of a man's; its nose more human than animal.

When it saw them, the creature stood up and made a halting move in their direction. At that point David and John screamed, ran out of the barn, and didn't stop until they reached a telephone to call the police.

Though he made an earnest effort, Sgt. Fred Bird of the Connecticut State Police could not find any evidence of a monster at the scene. Because of the wet ground, footprints were undetectable. The creature—whatever it might have been—had vanished without a trace. We have no idea about its intent, though apparently it had harmed neither property nor livestock. But who knows what might have happened if John and David hadn't walked in when they did?

Reviewing these strange events today, it is tempting to toss off the whole thing as a prank. But Fuller and Buckley were not known as jokesters. Nor were they susceptible to hallucinations. And neither man was considered especially squeamish.

The fact is, both men were badly shaken by the confrontation. Buckley's brother said, "It isn't like Dave to get that excited. . . . I certainly believe he saw something."

So if the men weren't playing a joke, could someone have been joking with them?

Sergeant Bird thought it unlikely. "You play a practical joke like that around a farm," he said, "and you're liable to wind up dead. People out in the country have guns, and they don't like to see their animals spooked."

PART III

WILD LANDS

❝*Most people simply knew that certain hilly regions were considered as highly unhealthy, unprofitable, and generally unlucky to live in, and that the farther one kept from them the better off one usually was.***❞**

— H.P. LOVECRAFT
The Whisperer in the Darkness

From the
Mountains
of Madness

GHOSTS HAUNT HOUSES.

Poltergeists haunt people.

But is it something else that haunts regions or areas of land?

For years, investigators of the strange have theorized that certain places, like certain people, are extraordinarily vulnerable to "mysterious forces."

Various labels have been used to describe these "haunted" areas. My favorite, of course, would be "Twilight Zones." But before Rod Serling, there was that eldritch New England horror writer H.P. Lovecraft, who discussed "dimensional gateways."

Among Fortean researchers, those longtime collectors of anomalous phenomena, we have the terrifying speculations of John A. Keel, who used the term "windows" to describe these interdimensional trapdoors. And zoologist Ivan Sanderson one-upped Keel when he coined the slightly more chilling "vile vortices."

Ever since Vincent Gaddis's term "Bermuda Triangle" became part of the language, writers have used "triangle" to designate some of these odd areas. Researcher Loren Coleman identified the Bay State's "Bridgewater Triangle." I even swiped the term to write about Vermont's "Bennington Triangle," described at length later in this section.

Zones. Vortices. Triangles.

Of these terms, the most useful, it seems to me, is also the most neutral: "window areas." These are places where a porthole or window seems to be open between this world and some other.

Looking out through these windows, human beings might see any assortment of anomalies, from pterodactyls and flying saucers to more earthbound enigmas like lake monsters or 8-foot shambling man-beasts. The more out of sync the apparitions are with our conventional three-dimensional reality, the more conspicuous they become.

If a man or woman were to trip and fall through one of these gateways, who can say where they would end up? Possibly back in sixteenth-century France. Or in some unrecognizable city where people speak a language completely foreign to even the polyglot's ear. But what if someone, or something, from the other side were to tumble in this direction? What would that be like?

Perhaps the people in Dover, Massachusetts, can answer that, as we'll soon see. Or maybe those brave souls stationed high atop New England's highest peak can give us some insight. We'll find out very shortly.

But for now, what are the symptoms of these mystery-charged regions? How would we know if we were standing in one?

THINGS THAT GO BOOM

CALL THEM WINDOWS, VORTICES, OTHER DIMENSIONS, or simply haunted spots, there are plenty of places in New England that enjoy sinister reputations. One of the most familiar is in Connecticut.

Since precolonial times, many strange things have happened in the vicinity of East Haddam. Best known among the various phenomena are the weird, loud noises. People have been hearing them for centuries. Native Americans called the area *Mackimoodus,* which translates as *place of noises.* One of the many explanations from folklore is that the sounds are the underground rumblings of an Indian god who became upset at the Englishman's god's arrival. Can't blame him.

In his 1729 account, the Reverend Mr. Hosmer describes the Moodus Noises as earthquakes, but with this peculiarity: "They seem to have their centre, rise and origin among us. . . ." That they are so localized and so persistent makes them especially puzzling.

Rev. Hosmer continues, saying, "Now whether there be any thing diabolical in these things, I know not. . . . Whether it be fire or air distressed in the subterraneous caverns of the earth, cannot be known; for there is no eruption, no explosion perceptible, but the sounds and tremors, which sometimes are very fearful and dreadful. I myself heard eight or ten sounds successively, and imitating small arms, in the space of five minutes."

The so-called Moodus Noises have never been successfully traced or explained. They remain one of New England's most vexing conundrums.

As you can see, the scientifically minded minister was no better equipped to account for them than we are today. But the eighteenth century was generally a quieter time. Though they are still heard occasionally, modern environmental noises make them less noticeable.

ON TOP OF NEW ENGLAND

WE'LL BEGIN MAPPING NEW ENGLAND window areas by moving from the depths of Connecticut to the highest spot around—over a mile in the air. From there we should get a perfect overview.

Our vehicle, New Hampshire's famous Cog Railroad, has very little in common with a rocketship. Yet since the mid-nineteenth century, it has transported people to an alien world where the topography is as unearthly as that of any faraway planet—the summit of Mt. Washington.

It is a remote and desolate place. At 6,288 feet above sea level, Mt. Washington is not only the highest point in New England, but also one of the coldest spots in America. Weather conditions are among the worst in the world. Temperatures reach minus 50 degrees Fahrenheit in winter, and in summer can routinely drop below freezing. Ice can form any time of year.

The highest wind velocity ever recorded roared across the summit—231 miles per hour. Steady 100-mph winds are frequent. Hurricanes, 75 mph and more, can occur more than 100 days a year.

As you travel up the mountain, by railroad, automobile, or on foot, the changes are remarkable. The air becomes thinner. At 4,000 feet, fir trees look stunted and scraggly. A few more steps and they're gone altogether, exposing snow and ice and rock.

When the air is clear and the weather fine, the world seems to spread out below you: you can see four states and part of Canada. With a telescope or binoculars, Whiteface Mountain in New York's Adirondacks rests on the horizon. To the south, there's Cape Ann, Massachusetts, some 130 miles away. At night, coastal lighthouse beacons separate city lights from the stars.

In winter, there's hardly a more inhospitable environment on earth. The road and railway are closed, useless. The only means of ascent is by tractor. And once on top, nighttime becomes a uniquely terrifying experience. Imagine yourself far from the safety of civilization, closer than ever before to the infinite, feeling the rage of pounding winds and snow that cuts like glass.

Here, people understand the concept of "isolation."

THE FORCE MAY BE WITH YOU

HARD TO BELIEVE, BUT A FEW HARDY SOULS live in these insufferable conditions. They're the year-round staff of WMTW-TV's Channel 8 Transmitter and of the Mt. Washington Observatory.

But nonhuman things can survive here as well: birds, bobcats, deer, even a tiny rare rodent, called the yellownosed vole. And there's vegetation, the kind usually found in the faraway arctic.

But something else makes its home on that mountaintop.

Something not vegetable, animal, or human. It was known centuries ago to Native Americans and it's known today to anyone who's spent time on the summit—especially during winter.

People swear it's a living thing, though it's not physical at all. Those who have had a run-in with it somehow know intuitively that it is not a ghost, either. Over the years, it has come to be known simply as "The Presence."

Many strange occurrences, physical and psychic, have been documented over the years, all attributed to the Presence. Mountaintop workers in the weather-station buildings describe hearing voices and footsteps in empty rooms; they've seen articles moved or suspended in midair. The invisible Presence has done everything from tossing curtains and clothing to attacking human beings.

Different people experience it in different ways, so everyone has his or her pet theory to explain it. Native Americans avoided the mountaintop, believing a great spirit dwelled there. Early colonial explorers suspected pretty much the same thing.

There it waits for whatever reason. Ever-present, illusive, unseen, brooding above the tree line.

Some people call it playful, curious, capricious, and benign. Maybe they sense something watching them, lurking secretly around a bend in the trail or following behind, close but out of sight. Others report glimpsing something fleeting in their peripheral vision. It's there, and then it's gone.

Most who've experienced the Presence say they don't feel menaced by it. "If this *thing* wasn't friendly," said William Harris after a quarter century on the mountain, "it would have gotten me good—a long time ago."

But others aren't so sure . . .

The late Lee Vincent, director of WMTW-TV's transmitter, occupied the summit outpost for years. He made a study of the Presence, wrote about it in his books, and included it in his lectures. Generally, he maintained, the Presence becomes much more active after something violent occurs on the mountain.

If that is true, the Presence has had numerous opportunities to act up, for there have been many violent episodes in the area. On average, since 1888, two people each year have lost their lives in the White Mountains.

In the 1960s, a small plane carrying two Santa Clauses and their pilot crashed. They were the so-called "Flying Santas" who parachute into shopping centers as publicity gags. Following the crash and the three deaths, there were three psychic experiences on the mountain, all directed toward the same person.

But probably the most violent episode in the mountain's history was the cog railroad accident of September 17, 1967, the only blemish on an otherwise perfect safety record.

Carrying around seventy-five people, the train got to Skyline Switch but didn't stop. In fact, it never stopped there because the switch was *always* left in the straight position. Except this time. Before the crew could react, the front cog wheel lost its grip. The engine flopped on its side, releasing the coach, which rolled back, accelerated, and plunged off the wooden Long Trestle. Many were injured in the fall. Eight were killed.

To this day, the reason for the accident remains unexplained. I suspect the cause will never be known for sure. It could have been a railroad man's negligence. Or possibly some irresponsible hiker had tampered with the switching mechanism, not realizing what he or she was doing. Whether it was deliberate and malicious or completely an accident, *something* moved the switch.

Though most authorities agree it was the fault of human error, others have offered less tangible and far more sinister explanations.

Afterwards, weird things began happening to John Davis of East Burke, Vermont, a railroad employee who worked and lived at the Tip-Top House hotel. He'd find the safe open, but nothing would be missing. Chairs somehow changed position overnight. Money rearranged itself in the cash register. No matter how closely he watched, he couldn't discover the culprit.

The company summoned the state police to investigate. Officers searched the building, went over it again with a German shepherd, then remained in the hotel overnight. Predictably, they found nothing.

Peter Zwirken of the weather observatory tells an especially perplexing tale about a blustery evening when a knock came at the door. It was surprising because the men thought everyone was together there in the room.

One brave soul walked over and opened the door on a typical snowy, stormy night. But no one was there. When the man glanced downward, he saw right there on the doorstep a large, heavy bronze plaque.

Clustering around, the men recognized it as a memorial to a climber who had died of exposure on the mountain. Normally, the plaque was securely affixed to a stone foundation a mile away at Crawford Path. Zwirken concluded, "It had been ripped off its foundation and somehow transported to our door atop Mt. Washington. No mortal could have accomplished such a feat."

SEEING THINGS

ALTHOUGH THE PRESENCE is normally thought of as invisible, occasionally people get a glimpse of something that is utterly beyond their comprehension.

Lee Vincent himself reported such a visual experience in his book *Instant Legends from the Rock Pile*. It happened on a cold, clear January night in 1964. Sixty-five-mile-an-hour winds pounded away at Vincent as he made his way between buildings. Not surprisingly, he lost his footing and fell, whacking his elbow.

Before rising, something caught his attention, freezing him in place. He saw a huge, silver-topped cloud formation slowly ascending from the black abyss of the Great Gulf. But something about it wasn't as it should be: curiously, the cloud was moving at a right angle to the wind. Clouds simply do not move against the wind in nature as we know it.

"Panic gripped me," Vincent wrote. "I rolled over, clawing my way back to the top." He raced to the safety of the TV station, convinced the cloud was following him. Safely inside, he bolted the door before daring to look back toward the hotel. There he saw the mysterious vapor being absorbed into the wooden shingles of the hotel walls.

INVESTIGATORS

AFTER SUCH AN UNNERVING EXPERIENCE, Vincent became fascinated with the mysterious mountain phenomena and began to collect testimony from his colleagues.

For example, Jon Lingel, who did odd jobs for the TV station, recounted two weird experiences on the mountaintop. One night, when he was all alone in the Yankee Network Building, he was awakened in the middle of the night by the sound of footsteps coming down the hall toward his bedroom. Wondering who could be visiting at that hour, he got up and checked.

But the hall was empty.

Moments later, he heard the footsteps again, this time accompanied by heavy breathing. He'd had enough. Jon grabbed his flashlight and leapt out into the hall to confront the intruder.

But no one was there.

Puzzled, and more than a little tense, Jon returned to bed, but his fear escalated rapidly. He got up and locked his bedroom door. Moments later, he experienced something reminiscent of a scene from Stephen King's *The Shining*.

Jon heard more sounds. For all the world it sounded as if a party was in progress on the floor below him. He distinctly heard laughter, voices, even the sharp musical tones of glasses clinking. Summoning his courage a third time, he left his room to investigate. Again, he found he was completely alone in the building.

But not for long.

Jon Lingel left the Yankee Network Building that night, vowing never to sleep there again.

Writer Austin Stevens tried to get to the bottom—or should I say the top—of things for *Yankee* magazine. Though the article is presented with an admirably balanced skepticism, *Yankee* editor Judson Hale writes in his book *Inside New England*, "Stevens went up there to investigate, and returned convinced that almost all the men stationed on Mt. Washington during the winter have, at times, experienced 'a force—a curious, watchful, malevolent force.' "

Malevolent?

Photographer Mike Micucci tells of an incident that happened shortly after he started work at the observatory. While standing on a precipitation platform, "I was pushed by something," he swears. "I was pushed and there was nobody there to push me."

Peter Zwirken concluded, "It seems to pick on people it doesn't like and then forces them off the mountain."

Marty Engstrom, longtime Channel 8 weatherman, sums it up, "All I'll say about the whole thing is—it tells you right in the Bible that there are such things and it tells you not to mess around with them."

THE WILD PLACES

THE PECULIAR PHENOMENA ATOP MT. WASHINGTON are not unique. For years, climbers of particular mountains all over the world have been reporting attacks of paralyzing, unreasoning terror. There is an impressive record of mountaineers who have run for their lives, though for no particular reason.

J. Norman Collie was seized by terror while climbing Scotland's Ben MacDhui in 1888. Suddenly, he admitted, he found himself running down the mountain in absolute horror. In 1945, P.A. Densham, an experienced mountaineer in charge of aircraft rescue, was on the same summit when he sensed a presence. Then he heard what he thought were footsteps and went to investigate. Upon arriving at the place he believed the footsteps were coming from, a heightened sense of inexplicable fright gripped him. He bolted away with such unreasoning determination that he almost plunged to his death over Lurcher's Crag.

Hamish Corrie experienced a similar "unaccountable panic" near the summit of Sgurr Dearg on Skye. And in 1910, John Buchan, climbing with a local forester, went through the same thing in the Bavarian Alps. Both panicked at the same time and fled without speaking until they collapsed, exhausted, in a valley below.

Mt. Shasta in California has many similar legends . . . and the list goes on . . .

Perhaps this "mountain madness" phenomenon was first identified in the Greek mountains thousands of years ago. There, such episodes were attributed to psychic attacks by the goat-footed god, Pan, who, of course, causes panic.

So was Pan vacationing in New Hampshire the night Mt. Washington observatory employee Will Harris sensed he was not alone during one of his solitary evening walks? Suddenly, he had the feeling that something was behind him. He looked repeatedly, but saw nothing. Yet he *knew* something was there.

Will was luckier than a co-worker who was actually chased one night by some mysterious "force." He was in one of the pressurized chambers when he sensed something invisible was in there with him. Fear and tension turned into panic until he ran out, shaking uncontrollably.

Of course, it is unlikely that any visitor passing a bright summer's day atop Mt. Washington, safe amid a giggling gaggle of tourists, would have any sort of run-in with the Presence. But those who brave the winter have a different experience. When they arrive, they might have their doubts—but no one remains a doubter for long.

The **Bennington Triangle**

VERMONT, TOO, HAS ITS HAUNTED HEIGHTS. BUT THE HISTORY OF GLASTENBURY Mountain is far more monstrous than that of Mt. Washington.

Located in the Green Mountains near Bennington, the area has always had a "reputation." It's an inaccessible region, remote, full of dark places, jutting outcroppings, vast marshlands, and quiet pools. It's easy to see how the topography might give birth to legends, if not actual monsters.

Since precolonial times, there have been strange tales of mysterious lights, untraceable sounds, and unidentifiable odors. Specters skulked among the trees. Unknown creatures—glimpsed fleetingly within the silent swampland—burned themselves forever into memory.

In olden times, Native Americans shunned the place; they believed the area was cursed. Refusing to live there, they used the land only to bury their dead.

The few colonial families who settled the now-vanished town of Glastenbury were plagued by misfortune. Many suffered recurring bouts of disease; mothers died in childbirth; and madness claimed more than its share of victims.

It was was on those sinister slopes that, during the last century, a coach full of travelers was attacked by the baffling "Bennington Monster." And there, in 1892, Henry MacDowell went haywire and murdered Jim Crowley. Declared mad, he was sentenced to life in the Waterbury Asylum. But he escaped and vanished. Some say he returned to the wilds of Glastenbury, where he remains to this day.

But all this happened a long time ago.

Today, the mountains remain as mysterious, and dark tales are still told.

Whether monsters walk and curses claim their victims may be a matter for debate.

But there's one thing we know for sure: the Glastenbury Mountain area is where one of Vermont's most frightening mysteries took place. And not too very long ago. It was covered in newspapers all around New England.

I refer to these events as "The Bennington Triangle" because they involve a series of unexplained disappearances. Beginning late in 1945, a number of people—perhaps ten in all—stepped off the face of the earth.

The mystery remains unsolved to this day. In fact, after thousands of hours of investigation, no one has ever uncovered so much as a clue.

OLD MAN RIVERS

THE STRANGENESS STARTED WITH MIDDIE RIVERS on November 12, 1945. This 74-year-old native of the region had worked as a hunting and fishing guide. He knew the area very well. And, according to a recent physical, he was in perfect health.

The weather was unusually mild that day as Rivers led four hunters up onto the mountain. But when they started to return to camp, Rivers got a bit ahead of the others. They never caught up with him. The old man vanished completely.

Volunteers and police combed the area for hours. They didn't lose hope because Rivers was an experienced woodsman; he'd know how to survive in the wild. Expanded efforts continued for a month. But no trace—nothing—was ever found.

PAULA WELDEN

PAULA WELDEN, A BENNINGTON COLLEGE SOPHOMORE from Stamford, Connecticut, was the second to go.

On Sunday, December 1, 1946, this 18-year-old left Dewey Hall for a short afternoon hike on the Long Trail. A local man gave her a lift as far as his home in Woodford Hollow. Later, at about four o'clock p.m., Ernest Whitman, an employee of the *Bennington Banner*, gave her directions. Afterwards, other witnesses saw her on the trail itself. The 5-foot-5-inch blond was easy to spot because of her bright red parka.

Monday afternoon came and Paula hadn't returned to school. The college called the sheriff's department. Joined by 400 students, faculty, and townspeople, the sherrif's men searched diligently but found nothing.

Governor Mortimer Proctor summoned the FBI, who were assisted by New York and Connecticut State Police. Search parties combed the area for weeks. In spite of their efforts, a $5,000 reward, and the aid of a famous clairvoyant, not a single clue turned up. The official search—involving bloodhounds, airplanes, helicopters, and well over 1,000 people—ended on December 22 with no results. No sign of a body. No clothing. No evidence at all. The only thing certain is that a young woman took a walk in the Vermont hills and never came back.

THIRD AND STRANGEST

ODDLY, THE THIRD PERSON VANISHED on the third anniversary of Paula Welden's disappearance. It was three years to the day: December 1, 1949. Elderly James E. Tetford had been visiting relatives in northern Vermont. His family put him on a bus in St. Albans and James started back to the Bennington Soldiers' Home, where he lived.

He never arrived. The exact location of his disappearance is obscured by the event's strangeness. Witnesses saw him get on the bus. He was aboard at the stop before Bennington. But, impossible as it sounds, he apparently never got off! Again, there were no clues. No one saw anything. Even the bus driver had no explanation.

THE YOUNGEST

ON COLUMBUS DAY OF 1950, 8-year-old Paul Jepson vanished. His mother and father were farmers and caretakers of the town dump. That's where the tragedy occurred. Paul waited in the pickup while his mother relocated some pigs. She only left him for a moment. But when she looked up, Paul was gone. It was between three and four o'clock.

He should have been easy to spot in his red jacket, but Mrs. Jepson couldn't see him anywhere. Eventually she called for help.

Well-practiced volunteers assembled to begin another search. Hundreds of civilians joined officials to comb the dump, the road, and the mountains. This time they instituted a "double-check" system: as soon as one group finished searching an area, a second group would search the same area.

Coast Guard planes and local psychics proved useless.

Bloodhounds borrowed from the New Hampshire State Police lost Paul's scent at the junction of East and Chapel Roads, west of Glastenbury Mountain. Local legend holds that the dogs lost Paul's scent at the exact spot where Paula Welden was last seen.

At one point, Paul's father disclosed an odd bit of information: lately, Paul had voiced an unaccountable "yen" to go into the mountains.

On October 14, 1950, the *Bennington Banner* reported, "The mystery of Paul's complete disappearance, and not a single clue to work on, makes the third [fourth, counting Tetford] such case of a missing person in practically the same area during the past five years."

A pattern seemed to be emerging.

ANOTHER WOMAN

ABOUT TWO WEEKS LATER, on Saturday the 28th, Freida Langer was on a hike with her cousin Herbert Elsner. They had left from their family camp on the eastern side of Glastenbury Mountain, near Somerset Reservoir.

Freida, a short, rugged woman of 53, was an experienced gun-handler and woodsperson. She was completely familiar with the area.

At about 3:45 p.m., only about one-half mile from camp, she slipped and fell into a stream. She told her cousin that she'd run the short distance back to the camp, change clothes, and hurry back to join him.

When she didn't return, Herbert went to look for her. Not only had she not reached camp, but no one saw her come out of the woods.

Alarmed by another disappearance in the same general area, local officials quickly launched another search. It turned up nothing.

On November 1, Gen. Merritt Edson, state director of public safety, initiated a second search. He issued an emphatic command: officers must stay on the job until they find Langer, dead or alive.

This effort involved helicopters, amphibious planes, and hordes of people on foot. But Edson couldn't command his men to do the impossible. They found nothing.

The *Bennington Banner* wrote, "One of the things hard to explain is how Mrs. Langer could have become so completely lost in an hour's time before dark in an area with which she was so thoroughly familiar."

On November 5, the searchers tried again, dividing into three groups of thirty. They lined up and marched side by side. It would have been hard to miss a clue if one had been there to find.

Efforts continued until the weekend of November 11, when officials launched the biggest search ever. Sportsmen and military units joined police, firemen, and community volunteers. Over 300 people scoured the woods.

And found nothing.

On the Monday following this monumental effort, Freida's family finally gave up hope.

What did the combined forces of military and civilian searchers have to show for all their efforts? Not one single worthwhile clue.

CHRISTMAN AND JONES

THREE OF THE SOURCES I USED in preparing this chapter include at least two more disappearances in the "Bennington Triangle."

On December 3, 1950, only a few days after the search for Freida Langer ended, Frances Christman left her home to visit a friend just one-half mile away. Somewhere on that brief hike she vanished without a trace.

I was able to verify that this story was reported in the Bennington newspaper. And, yes, a woman did vanish. However, earlier researchers either didn't know Vermont geography, or they just didn't read the newspapers very well. Frances Christman disappeared in Hinesburg, Vermont, a good 120 miles north of the Glastenbury area.

Other accounts of the Glastenbury tragedy include the disappearance of teenager

Martha Jeanette Jones on November 13, 1950. The time was right, the place was right. However, if researchers had kept flipping pages, they would have discovered the December 20, 1950, issue of the *Bennington Banner*, which reported that Martha Jeanette Jones had turned up in Accotink, Virginia, near a military base, working as a waitress.

In spite of the erroneous addition of Christman and Jones, the events are no less mysterious. Five human beings vanished between 1945 and 1950.

But was it just five?

In a *Burlington* (Vermont) *Free Press* article dated October 25, 1981, reporter Sally Jacobs says that two years after the Paula Welden disappearance, "a trio of hunters from Massachusetts vanished near [the ghost town of] Glastenbury. Their disappearance, like those that preceded them, remains a mystery."

And one of the *Bennington Banner* articles I reviewed made reference to a 13-year-old Bennington boy, Melvin Hills, who was lost in the same area around October 11, 1942.

If these are true, then the number of disappearances goes from five to nine.

Where did they go? How can we possibly explain such a thing?

Could the "Bennington Monster" have carried them off into the swamps of Glastenbury Mountain? Could they have tumbled through some interdimensional trapdoor in this "window area"? Or maybe they encountered a certain enchanted stone, known to the Indians for yawning and swallowing anyone who steps on it.

One *Bennington Banner* reporter even speculated that there exists something of a Yankee Shangri-La upon Glastenbury Mountain, a lost horizon into which people inadvertently step, never to be seen again. To some, that probably seems the best explanation because it discounts other less happy endings.

Alien abduction, for example. Alleged abductees, under hypnosis, claim they've been victims of sinister medical examinations, then released with holes in their memories and implants in their brains. Some, I suppose, never come back at all.

Perhaps the answer is more prosaic, something not precisely identified in the annals of American crime circa 1945—the serial killer.

The Bennington events took place over a limited amount of time: five years.

And in roughly the same area: around the Long Trail, between its intersection with Route 9 and the summit of Glastenbury Mountain. The victims' ages spanned from 8 to 75. They were about equally divided between men and women. All occurred during the last three months of the calendar year, then stopped.

Serial killers operate that way; they do their dirty work, then drift from place to place. Maybe the perpetrator was someone who visited Vermont in October, November, and December. Maybe for hunting season, or for the holidays.

Even at the time, residents imagined a particularly cunning madman known alternately as "The Bennington Ripper" or "The Mad Murderer of the Long Trail." But the truth is, no murder was ever proven.

All these complex questions are counterbalanced by some that are deceptively simple. Like, why didn't the snow on the ground during the months of these vanishings facilitate the searches? And if some of the victims wandered off and froze to death, why didn't the spring thaw expose their remains?

In line with this, there is one especially chilling footnote to the story. On May 12, 1951, the body of Freida Langer did appear, *seven months after she'd vanished!* Impossibly, the corpse was discovered among tall grasses near the flood dam of Somerset Reservoir. It was in an open, visible area where searchers simply could not have missed it. Remember, teams had repeatedly combed the area for weeks. The search for Freida Langer was, arguably, the most thorough of all.

Unfortunately, Langer's fate couldn't be determined by examining the remains; as the *Banner* said, they were in "gruesome condition."

And what of the others? No human remains were ever found. No thread of clothing. No blood. No hair. No clues at all.

MASS. HYSTERIA?

WHILE NOT ESPECIALLY MOUNTAINOUS, MASSACHUSETTS still has its share of window areas. Look around, you'll see plenty of places renowned for frequent recurrences of UFO sightings, creature manifestations, mysterious disappearances, along with high incidence of disease, crime, madness, and other colorful peculiarities. In *Curious Encounters*, researcher Loren Coleman writes of window areas: "It is almost as if Gaia's paranormal zones, her pimples, if you will, are someway being labeled and revisited by the phenomena, again and again. . . ."

For example, the land around the glassy waters of the Quabbin Reservoir near Amherst may be the frame around a window to another world. This vast mysterious area of mid-Massachusetts wilderness continues to produce strange tales of impressive variety. There are almost 80,000 wild acres around the water; how many stories could be hidden there?

Among the easiest to believe is that the Quabbin is still the home of the *Felis concolor* cougar, aka North American mountain lion, panther, puma, mountain screamer, catamount, or whatever you want to call it. This giant cat—which can be 6 feet long from nose to tail and weigh some 200 pounds—has been officially extinct in the Bay State since the last one was killed in Amherst in 1858. Since then, there have been more than 300 sightings, half of which were reported in the Quabbin area.

Among the mystery animals found in the vicinity, nothing could be more out of place than the crocodiles that are occasionally sighted around Dismal Swamp near Ware. In 1922, several crocodilian critters between 6 and 8 feet long were spotted. More recently, crocs up to 3 feet long have actually been captured there!

But other stories may be a little harder to swallow. For example, back in August 13, 1919, an explosion and brilliant flash of white light occurred above the Quabbin area between eight and nine in the evening. Then a glowing "something" descended slowly and landed on Erastus Dewey's property, some 20 feet from his front door. Rufus Graves, an Amherst professor, examined the object. It was bowl shaped, 8 inches across and 1 inch thick. This "whatsis" had a soft, fuzzy, clothlike surface that was yellowish pink in color. It contained a foul-smelling pulp that liquefied and turned blood red when exposed to the air. Afterwards, several similar objects were discovered here and there in the area.

But other UFOs, those that never seem to touch down, are more familiar sights in the skies above the Quabbin. Long before "flying saucers" became big news in the 1940s, weird celestial objects were business as usual in this haunted zone. But they weren't always in the sky; sometimes they were in the barn.

In the winter of 1906, for example, Mr. Isaac Spinney of Petersham noticed a peculiar luminescence in his barn on Nichewaug Road. Though he was on his way to bed, he paused to watch as the light seemed to die away, then flare up again full force. Spinney stood transfixed as the light went through its bright-dim cycle several times. Something about its odd nature told him it was not a fire. But what was it?

Bagging the idea of bed, Spinney raced off to tell his neighbor Seymour Williams. Together the men rushed back to the barn where the light continued to pulse. Then, as the two men watched in wonder, a glowing ball floated out of the barn and leisurely drifted off in the direction of W.B. Spooner's farm.

Spinney and Williams separated to outflank the light, but as soon as they made a gesture to trap it, the light vanished just as if someone had puffed out a candle.

When neighbors heard about the odd event, they locked their doors and armed themselves, not knowing if they were dealing with a "phantom or pyromaniac, haunt or hobo." But this particular phantom intruder seemed to have gone away for good.

Bridgewater

THE "BRIDGEWATER TRIANGLE" IS ANOTHER SO-CALLED WINDOW AREA IN THE Bay State. Because of the slightly more sinister nature of the occurrences there, it is a window perhaps best kept closed.

The region is a triangular area of some 200 square miles. Its corners are defined by the towns of Abington, Freetown, and Rehobeth. Within the triangle are the towns of Brockton, Taunton, Bridgewater, Raynham, Mansfield, Norton, and Easton, each of which could easily inspire a strange-but-true book of its own.

In the heart of the region is the largest swampland in Massachusetts, and maybe in all New England. The murky, quicksand-infested, 6,000-acre Hockomock Swamp is just 40 minutes from Boston. Sliced by busy commuter routes and power lines, scarred by roads, trails, and abandoned railroad tracks, it is vast, primitive, primeval, and essentially the same as it was 500 or more years ago.

In the language of the indigenous Native Americans, Hockomock translates as something like "Place of Spirits." For thousands of years—perhaps dating back to the last glacier—native dwellers have been sensitive to the area's strangeness. To them, it is both sacred and evil.

Loren Coleman reports that archaeologists located an 8,000-year-old burial ground on Grassy Island in Hockomock Swamp. When they excavated the graves, red ochre within began to bubble and dissolve for unknown reasons. All attempts to document the event, including the misbehaving ochre, were frustrated. For some reason, every photograph taken there failed to come out.

On a riverbank directly across from the Grassy Island Burial Ground is another major enigma of the Bridgewater Triangle, the so-called Dighton Rock. This 40-ton sandstone boulder is covered with organized markings, pictograms and hieroglyphiclike etchings that must mean . . . something.

Many of the Massachusetts ethnic groups can find some evidence on the rock to "prove" they were the first to settle the area. But in reality, nothing has ever been settled. Today, the rock is protected by Delebare State Park and questions regarding the origin of its puzzling markings are exhibited on the nearby walls. Pick a people: Vikings, Phoenicians, Egyptians, or Portuguese—it's all a guess, and the meaning of Dighton Rock remains a mystery.

The colonial era added to the region's mystery with records of a "Yellow Day," when the normally blue skies glowed with a mysterious yellow light. You can imagine what its sulfurous hue suggested to the colonists. More defined lights are also frequently reported in the area. Every January, as if on schedule, evasive balls of incandescence known as "spook lights" zip along the railroad tracks in Raynham, near the dog-racing stadium.

Baseball-sized ghost lights are almost a common sight in Bridgewater's Elm Street area. They pulsate red, blue, and orange as they bounce through the air—then they vanish.

Larger UFOs are identified there from time to time. Joseph's Restaurant in Rehobeth was apparently visited by one in 1973 during a short power failure. When the lights came back on, patrons found two perfect circles in the dirt out back.

Coleman tells that another impressive sighting, "one of the most spectacular," occurred on March 23, 1979. The witness was Jerry Lopez, a news reporter for WHDW radio in Boston. Shaped like home plate on a baseball field, the UFO was bright red on top with rows of white and red lights around the sides. Also, in front, there was a bright white headlight at the point of the diamond. This conspicuous "whatsis" was at the intersection of Routes 24 and 106, right at the center of the Bridgewater Triangle.

BIRDS AND BEASTS

BUT PERHAPS STRANGEST OF ALL is another apparition occasionally spotted in the skies above the triangle. It's another UFO, but this one seems most definitely alive.

I'm talking about a bird, a giant bird.

In 1988, two Bridgewater boys reported following man-sized, three-toed tracks, until they ran into the bird that was making them. As it flew off into the trees, they had time to see its black, wrinkled face, dark feathers, and long brown legs that dangled behind it. Its wingspan, they thought, was greater than 6 feet.

Another impressive sighting occurred at about two o'clock one summer morning in 1971. Coleman describes it this way: "Norton police sergeant Thomas Downy was driving . . . along Winter Street in Mansfield toward his home in Easton. As he approached a place known as 'Bird Hill' in Easton at the edge of the swamp, he was suddenly confronted by a tremendous winged creature over six feet tall with a wing span of between eight and twelve feet. . . . The bird flew straight up and, flapping its massive wings, disappeared over the dark trees into the swamp."

When the rattled policeman reported the sighting, his colleagues helped him search for evidence. Alas, the strange bird had flown the coop, seemingly unwilling to put in another appearance.

To me, there is a certain poetry in the notion that a man named "Downy" saw a feathered phantom on "Bird Hill."

OLD HAIRY AGAIN

MORE LAND BOUND BUT NO LESS MYSTERIOUS is another denizen of this and many other "Twilight Zones." Residents of the triangle and tourists have witnessed the infrequent appearances of giant, shambling, hair-covered man-beasts.

Reputedly, they are responsible for the unearthly screeching that occasionally issues from the bowels of Hockomock Swamp. According to the indigenous Native Americans, these eerie cries—like a banshee's wail—foretell the death of a warrior or chief.

Though these creatures are usually described as docile and retiring, something large and hairy waged war on farm animals in the early 1970s. Whatever it was allegedly killed and mutilated the pigs and sheep of several local farmers. Town and state police, accompanied by attack dogs, searched the swamp for two days and nights, but never found the culprit.

And there are still more strange members of the Triangle's Mysterious Menagerie. In 1939, CCC workers near the swamp saw a huge snake as thick and black as a stovepipe. More recently, a motorist reported running over an 8-foot-long boa constrictor that had no business being there. Another man even reported seeing a giant snapping turtle near Middleboro.

Giant cats, too, are frequently reported. Tawny colored or sometimes black, they inspire occasional lion hunts when slashed livestock are discovered.

On the other hand, sometimes people see giant black dogs as well. One of these hell-hounds, reminiscent of the Baskerville beast, was reported in Abingdon after it ripped out the throats of two ponies. The animal terrorized the community for several weeks, but evaded every attempt to capture it.

It was last seen by officer Frank Curran near some railroad tracks. He shot at it but missed. The dog—apparently unalarmed—turned away slowly and ambled off down the tracks.

None of these critters is ever seen for long. Although numerous attempts have been made to trap them, or shoot them, all such efforts have been unsuccessful. To rid the Hockomock Swamp of its unearthly wildlife, perhaps authorities could try a simple plan: let the mysterious black dogs chase the phantom cats back into oblivion.

A **Winsted Window?**

EXTRAORDINARY PHENOMENA HAVE FREQUENTLY DISRUPTED THE TOWN OF Winsted, Connecticut. The procession of oddities has gone on so long that certain researchers believe Winsted is yet another of New England's infamous window areas.

A local man, Ted Thoben, has investigated enough lights in the sky to conclude there is something definitely weird about Winsted. "Windows," he says, "are a magnetic deviation in the terrain, where these things slip through."

Things? What things?

Well, back in February of 1967, a businessman and two companions saw some sort of object suspended in the sky. They watched it for a good 15 minutes before it flashed red and green, then vanished.

In September of the same year, two 14-year-old girls were home alone on a Friday night. At about nine o'clock, one of them glanced out a second-story bedroom window and saw a bright light that just shouldn't have been there. Telling their story to the *Hartford Courant*, one said, "It looked as big as a Volkswagen." It went through a red-white-red color-changing sequence as it seemed to dance up and down in the sky.

Thoroughly absorbed by the dancing light, their attention was snapped away by an odd noise coming from the barn 50 feet away. The girls agreed it sounded like a lawnmower engine trying to start.

But who would be mowing a lawn at that time of night?

When they peeked out, it wasn't a lawnmower that they saw. Instead, next to the mailbox in the yard, they saw two indistinct figures, maybe 4 to 5 feet tall, moving in the darkness.

What the figures were about to do by the mailbox may never be known, for just then a car came around a curve. As its lights swept the area, the two figures, joined by a third, ran off into the thick brush behind the barn. At the same time, the light on the hill went out.

About 20 minutes later, the girls and their neighbor saw a faint glow return to the hilltop. But, very sensibly, no one went out to investigate.

That same year, cone-shaped objects were spotted in the Winsted skies. Red and green lights hovering soundlessly over treetops became a familiar part of the landscape.

In 1976, thirteen girl campers and their leader were hiking up Blueberry Mountain outside town. All at once, they were bothered by a high-pitched whine. Looking up, they clearly saw a silver, flat-bottomed, disk-shaped something, about 25 feet wide. It had a red dome on top and seemed to be engulfed in a purplish mist. Shortly, it vanished.

In 1977, three people, accompanied by a policeman, saw another red-topped object in the sky. It was hovering near the sewage treatment plant and seemed to be examining the ground with two beams of light. People also reported seeing similar objects diving into the local reservoir, then splashing out again.

Of course, the first explanation of any peculiar light in the sky is flying saucers. "But," Ted Thoben says, "I don't believe they come from another planet. I think they exist at a different vibratory frequency rate so that we cannot see them most of the time. They inhabit the same space as we do, and places like Winsted are the exchange point between different dimensions."

In other words, windows.

We will return to Winsted again in another chapter, for we have nowhere near exhausted the supply of local strangeness. But for now, let's move on to the granddaddy of all Connecticut window areas.

Beyond *the* Dark Entry

SOME PLACES, THOUGH WELL SITUATED AND PRIMED FOR PROSPERITY, SEEM doomed from the start. A perfect example is the defunct village of Glastenbury in southern Vermont.

Another such place is Dudleytown, Connecticut, a two-mile square plateau in the southwestern part of Cornwall. Unlike its neighbors in Litchfield County, Dudleytown died a slow and agonizing death, leaving only a barren scattering of legend-infested ruins that are carefully shunned.

Perhaps no spot in New England is more deserving of the name "ghost town," though some would judge "demon town" a more accurate description.

There are plenty of theories about what went wrong in Dudleytown, but no one has fully explained the mysterious series of tragedies. Some theorists are practical in their postmortems, saying that in spite of the sylvan beauty of the area, the land itself was poor, rocky, too far from navigable water or major highways, and way too mountainous. Others blame progress, saying the opening of the West and the growth of industry in urban centers lured the population away.

But there are those who say such rational explanations don't account for the unwholesomeness that happened there. They offer other explanations which, at least at first, seem far more fanciful. For example, did the first settlers tangle with Indian magic when they built on Mohawk land? Was preternatural retaliation the consequence of encroaching civilization?

Most believers assert it was the name "Dudley," and not the land on which they settled, that bore the malediction. If that is so, then the curse is an old one, originating long before the town was founded in 1740. For the original settlers of Dudleytown, some believe, may have brought the curse with them from England.

In any event, disasters of every type seemed to plague the men and women of Dudleytown. And there was no escaping the curse's savagery; it cut down those who stood their ground, and followed those who tried to escape, leaving in its wake a pathetic trail of broken lives and escalating madness.

I have found no record of the curse's utterance, yet there is plenty of evidence of its effect. The most common belief is that it was placed on the Dudley family by no less a divinely sanctioned power than the British monarchy.

A FAMILY CURSED?

I F SO, THEN THE FAMILY'S TROUBLE STARTED with Edmund Dudley, who, around 1509, was executed by King Henry VIII for stealing tax money from the royal treasury.

Later, Edmund's son John, Duke of Northumberland, conspired to control the English throne. His scheme was to effect a marriage between his son Guilford and Lady Jane Grey, the great-granddaughter of Henry VII. To accomplish this, Dudley and his second son, Robert, Earl of Leicester, persuaded the young and dying King Edward to pass the crown to Dudley's daughter-in-law, Lady Jane.

Though Jane was queen for a day, the Dudley machinations were discovered and all concerned were sentenced to death. John was executed in 1553. Five months later, Lady Jane and her husband Guilford Dudley were beheaded. Although Robert was pardoned, he was never free of royal suspicion.

Another Dudley assault on England occurred when Guilford's brother returned from France, bringing the plague with him. The infection he spread killed thousands of his countrymen. Some blame him for weakening the empire because of vast military losses.

Through maliciousness, malfeasance, and mistake, the Dudleys had acquired a bad reputation. No doubt many individuals cursed their name.

William Dudley, a direct descendant of Robert's, figured the New World would not only offer fresh opportunities, but also a far better chance of keeping his head.

A NEW LIFE

IN 1747, WILLIAM'S GREAT-GRANDSONS—Abiel, Barzillai, Gideon, and Abijah—settled on some undeveloped acres near Cornwall, Connecticut, bestowing on the unsullied land the accursed name of Dudley. They subsisted by hunting, raising buckwheat, and logging.

Other families followed. Jones, Carter, Tanner, Patterson, and more. Everyone pitched in and worked hard, applying their determination, strong constitutions, and versatile skills to the formation of a town.

When nearby Salisbury discovered iron, Dudleytown seized the opportunity to supply charcoal for the furnaces. Dudleytown lumbermen were quick to harvest unlimited acres of pine, oak, maple, and chestnut.

The flourishing town produced its fair share of notable citizens, too. Mary Cheney married publisher and presidential candidate Horace Greeley. Selectman Deacon Thomas Porter left town to become a Vermont supreme court judge. His son, Ebenezer, became the respected president of Andover Seminary.

It almost looked as if the town would thrive, yet all the time something was just a little wrong. Disaster seemed to follow, as if the family curse had finally discovered the new whereabouts of the Dudley clan.

MORE THAN MADNESS

INSANITY SEIZED ABIEL DUDLEY. He squandered his earnings and ended up the town pauper. Abiel's affliction was so complete he had to be cared for by a custodian. Townsmen applied for the job by submitting the lowest bid to maintain this once-respected town father. Abiel died an impoverished madman at 90 years of age.

Abiel's three brothers also died peculiar deaths. One was cut to pieces by savage attackers, allegedly Indians, but, as we shall see, there were other possibilities.

In 1759, Nathaniel Carter bought what had been Abiel's house in the center of town. Maybe that was a mistake. Though Carter's family moved to New York four years later, a series of misfortunes followed. One of his children died of illness. In

October of 1764, hostile Indians killed his wife Sarah and his youngest son. Then they burned the house and made off with the remaining three children. Carter was away and missed the slaughter, but on his way home he was attacked and hacked to pieces. At length, when his two daughters were finally recovered, they remained sickly and were "stark mad until death."

Back in Dudleytown, Nathaniel's brother Adoniram suffered a strange fate. In 1774, some horrible unidentified contagion struck down his whole family. Yet it didn't afflict anyone else, just the Carters.

For a few decades, perhaps the virus lay dormant along with the curse, for in 1813 a less focused epidemic wiped out scores of Dudleytown residents, including many members of the pioneering Jones family.

Mary Greeley hanged herself a few days before her husband, Horace, lost the presidential election in 1872. Greeley, himself, feeling great disappointment and loss, degenerated rapidly and died insane on November 29, 1872.

Gershon Hollister was murdered in William Tanner's home. Some said Tanner did it, but Tanner denied it. Apparently, the rigors of the resulting investigation proved too much for William. He too succumbed to madness, railing on about demons and ghosts and asserting that Hollister had been savaged by some awesome, unknown beast. Tanner remained in this tortured state until his death at age 104.

A freak bolt of lightning ended the life of Gen. Herman Swift's wife. Though the stable New Englander had been advisor to George Washington and a Revolutionary War hero, the resulting loss and loneliness soon drove General Swift into irreparable dementia.

It seemed as if every family suffered. Deaths came in unprecedented numbers. Madness seemed to claim far more than its fair share of the population. Where at first people only whispered about being cursed, now they spoke about it outright.

Word spread. Frightened residents moved away, often abandoning their belongings. Not surprisingly, no new families moved in.

By the late nineteenth century, there was only one citizen left in Dudleytown, a Pole whose name was long ago forgotten. This solitary immigrant had seen opportunity in the abandoned homes and neglected farmland. He moved into the old

Rogers estate and worked hard raising sheep. But loneliness touched him before he was seized by madness. When he evacuated, Dudleytown was all but dead.

AND THEN THERE WERE NONE

A STURDY IRISHMAN NAMED PATRICK BROPHY fancied the idea of having a whole town to himself. He publicly stated that he feared no ghosts, nor wild animals, either. So in 1892, he moved in with his wife, two sons, and a flock of sheep in tow. Rapid-fire misfortunes met him immediately. His sheep died, his sons vanished, and consumption killed his wife.

The Irishman now stood alone, just as the Pole before him. Though determined not to leave, Pat Brophy was forced out when a mysterious fire destroyed his house and everything he owned. A week later, he stumbled into Cornwall, raving maniacally about giant animals with cloven hooves and the ghastly green spirits that had chased and tried to capture him.

Many thought this would be the end, but Dudleytown had one more bit of evil to perform.

Around 1920, while touring back-country Connecticut, William C. Clark and his wife discovered Dudleytown. It was love at first sight. The couple made the mistake of thinking this isolated, romantic spot was just the sort of place they'd always dreamed about. Greatly satisfied with the prospect of country living, they bought several hundred acres.

Clark, a busy New York physician and professor of medicine, would appreciate this bucolic respite from city life. Visualizing their rural residence-to-be as a vacation home, Dr. and Mrs. Clark planned to make good use of the great outdoors. They both enjoyed hunting, fishing, and swimming.

Being a pioneering sort, Dr. Clark cleared a perfect piece of land and built their rustic home from the felled hemlock. The able-bodied physician laid pipe to a spring and he even fashioned a swimming pool in a brook not far from the house.

Meanwhile, residents of the surrounding towns whispered among themselves, speculating that this was just the sort of vital young couple that would put an end to this "curse" business once and for all. At the same time, summer after summer, they paid close attention to see if misfortune would show any signs of reasserting itself.

During the summer of 1924, while vacationing at "the cottage," Dr. Clark was called back to the city on an emergency. For some reason, Mrs. Clark was especially reluctant to let him go. She was strangely quiet as they waited at the train station. Repeatedly, she made him promise that he would return as quickly as possible.

She attributed it to the fact that she had never spent a night alone at the cabin. In spite of her nervousness, she laughed at herself a little bit for being so squeamish.

After the train pulled out, Mrs. Clark remained alone on the platform for a long time, staring off down the empty tracks.

No one knows what happened while Dr. Clark was away. But when he returned within 36 hours, he knew immediately that something was wrong.

No one was at the train station to meet him.

He hired a ride part of the way, then ran through the shadowy woods, hurrying back to the cabin. There was no sign of life anywhere around. Things seemed unnaturally still. Even the owls were quiet.

When he rushed to the door, he found it not only unlocked but slightly open. Holding his breath, Dr. Clark stepped into the dark interior.

Then he heard something that would sear a scar into his memory for all time. It was a sound he'd heard before, but always in the confines of a hospital ward. Coming from beyond their bedroom door was the shrill, near hysterical laughter of one hopelessly insane.

In the brief time that Dr. Clark was away, his wife had gone irreversibly mad. And for the rest of her life she carried on about ghosts, and weird animal-like creatures that were pursuing her.

RESTING IN PEACE

D R. CLARK'S DEPARTURE extinguished all mortal life in Dudleytown. The last of the original houses fell into its cellar hole by 1925, and since then, the wilderness has slowly reclaimed everything it once possessed.

And we are left to ask what happened.

There must be some reason Dudleytown disappeared almost a century ago while neighboring communities continue to prosper.

Did the Dudley brothers merely pick a bad spot for their settlement? Or was there some dark magic in this usurped Mohawk hunting ground? Could some shaman's words echo from beyond the grave, destroying all they touch?

Then again, maybe there really was a Dudley curse, imported by eighteenth century immigrants who thus damned themselves and everyone who crossed their paths.

Or it could be the land itself. Maybe the Dudleys chose a "window area," one of Ivan Sanderson's "vile vortexes," where supernatural forces encroach at will on our three-dimensional reality.

There is no way to tell. But if you wish to travel to Dudleytown in search of an answer, it is unlikely you'll find the vanished community on any map. Just follow Route 7 to Cornwall, and try to locate the ominous sounding, though aptly named, "Dark Entry Road." From there, what's left of the road winds up a mountain, precariously near a deep, narrow gorge, leading up to Dudleytown.

If you get that far, you can probably find artifacts of the extinct village. Cellar holes, graves, pieces of timber, maybe even an old smelting furnace with scatterings of slag. But be careful, for something may still lurk among the wilds and ruins.

Contemporary visitors invariably find the place "forbidding" and come away vaguely frightened, often not knowing why. They say they sense that something is watching them, or they feel unaccountably cold even on sunny summer days. One man, long curious to explore the place, told me, "I wanted to leave from the first moment I got there."

Some people have had more tangible experiences. There's the story of an ill-fated television documentary about Dudleytown that was plagued with equipment failure, personal illness, and ruined film.

Other explorers report visions of looming dark shapes in the daytime or lights that flicker helter-skelter through the trees at night.

And many visitors hear screeching sounds. Owls perhaps. But it's as likely a chorus of woodland demons, or the souls of Dudleytown inhabitants who cannot escape the site of their earthly demise.

Suggestion? Superstition? Or some atavistic human response to something ancient, unsettling, and apparently dangerous?

All we know for sure is that Dudleytown is no more. And to this day, no one has tried to rebuild it.

The Town *that* Won't Die

As we have seen, even in a state as populated as modern Connecticut, it is possible, even today, to find remote and mysterious areas that continue to exist only because of the stories attached to them. In addition to demonic Dudleytown, the Nutmeg State has another ghost town that is equally enigmatic, but in a very different way.

Although it is not as menacing as Dudleytown, it poses some fascinating questions about the nature of hauntings. While Dudleytown seemed eager to get rid of its residents, Bara-Hack seems reluctant to let them go. And today, while the town is long gone, the population . . . ? Well, maybe they never got around to leaving.

If you decide to go and see for yourself, don't start by looking for it on any map, for Bara-Hack is a lost village, buried deep in the northeastern Connecticut woods. It's almost directly across the state from Dudleytown, close to Abington Four Corners in the township of Pomfret. You'll find its remains at the end of a disused path that follows Mashomoquet Brook.

There's something pastoral, almost friendly about Bara-Hack's address. Even its name reinforces a quiet sense of intimacy and hospitality: Bara-Hack is a Welsh term that translates as "breaking bread."

But over the years people have begun to refer to Bara-Hack by another name. They call it "The Village of Voices."

This isolated settlement was pioneered around 1780 by two Welsh families who carried their dream far into the colonial wilderness.

Stories about these first settlers vary somewhat. One founder was Jonathan Randall, who moved to Bara-Hack from Cranston, Rhode Island. Local lore has it that

Randall owned slaves; and it was the slaves who first noticed something was amiss in Bara-Hack.

After the first of the new population started to die, some of the slaves claimed to see the departed as phantoms, resting leisurely in the branches of a certain tree near the village cemetery.

Another original settler, Obadiah Higginbotham, had deserted from the British army. Presumably he would have welcomed the protective isolation of the Connecticut wilds.

Higginbotham went into business manufacturing looms and spinning wheels. His factory did well, surviving at least until the Civil War. Some pinpoint the factory's post-war failure as the event that initiated the chain of abandonment and relocation that eventually led to the death of the town.

A GHOST TOWN

IN ALL, THE COMMUNITY LASTED ONLY ABOUT A CENTURY. By 1890—the date etched into the most recent gravestone—all the villagers had died or moved away. Almost immediately afterwards, visitors and passersby started to perceive strange things there. It is not so much what anyone saw or felt—it's what they *heard*. It was as if the vanished population were carrying on business as usual just beyond the curtain of slowly encroaching trees.

And that is exactly the impression countless visitors have had. As they approach—night or day—they discover the ruins of this empty village are alive with noise. Though nothing is visible, they might distinctly hear the untrained voices of children in song; wagon wheels grinding heavily on gravel paths, chickens squawking, cows mooing; men and women in conversation. Incredible as it seems, all the sounds of life still echo in Bara-Hack, though the last occupant left more than a century ago.

Fewer than thirty years after Bara-Hack's demise, its reputation was thoroughly ensconced and documented. In 1927, naturalist Odell Shepard described the isolated ruins this way: "Although there is no human habitation for a long distance round about and no one goes there except the very few who go to listen, yet there is always a hum and stir of human life . . . the voices of mothers who have long been dust calling their children into homes that are now mere holes in the earth. . . . It is as though sounds were able in this place to get round that incomprehensible corner, to pierce that mysterious soundproof wall that we call Time."

This strange "hole in time" phenomenon is so well attested to that for years people have called Bara-Hack haunted. But if it is a haunting, it is a very unusual one. It is as if the town itself were the ghost, and what may sound like individuals are merely parts of its complex personality.

A SOUND ANALYSIS

OVER THE YEARS, A FAIR NUMBER OF PEOPLE have visited the site, yet Bara-Hack is not well-known in New England ghost lore. Only a few have written about it and fewer still have rigorously investigated. I have been able to find only one record of a systematic and somewhat scientific examination of the strange phenomena at the "Village of Sounds."

In 1971 and 1972, an investigator from Rhode Island named Paul F. Eno conducted a series of visits to Bara-Hack. With him, acting as guide, was Harry Chase, who had lived for years in the area and who had a long-term interest in the history of the region and the mysteries of the vanished community. Chase had documented his own explorations of Bara-Hack with a series of photographs, dating back to 1948. Many show white, ghostly images that are too indistinct to be acceptable as hard evidence of spirit activity.

But they do show something . . .

Eno's group claims to have recorded many puzzling phenomena. They reported hearing dogs bark, the sounds of cattle, and indistinct human voices. They also heard one other frequently reported sound: the ghostly ring of children's laughter. Unfortunately, all efforts to get these eerie sounds on tape failed.

Perhaps the most vexing of their experiences involved something they saw near the small graveyard. Eno claims that for more than seven minutes his team witnessed a ghostly bearded face hovering over the western wall of the cemetery. And more unsettling still is what they saw in the branches of a nearby elm tree—"a babylike figure reclining on a branch."

Finally, just as Eno's group departed, they claim to have heard the clamor of a man shouting commands as he drove an invisible team and wagon. The ghostly teamster clattered off through the dark, impassable woodland, heading into the mysterious dimension where the secret of Bara-Hack, the town that won't give up its dead, has been kept for centuries.

*Here had been their houses, represented
today by a few gaping cellar holes out
of which tall trees were growing; but
here is the Village of Voices. For the
place is peopled still. . . .*

—ODELL SHEPARD
The Harvest of a Quiet Eye

PART IV

COSMIC RELIEF

"Oho," quoth he,
"the old Earth is frolicsome to-night!"

— NATHANIEL HAWTHORNE
My Kinsman, Major Molineux

The Cosmic Comedian

THE UNIVERSE IS NOT WITHOUT A SENSE OF HUMOR.

While dashing about, trying to avoid all the outrageous slings and arrows Fate hurls at us, we'll occasionally slip on an empyrean banana peel and land on our metaphysical behinds. The resulting laughter may be distant, soft, and decidedly sinister, but it is laughter nonetheless.

With that in mind, perhaps this is a good point to take a little detour through the "lighter" side of weird New England. The following exhibits from the Cosmic Comedian's bag of tricks should be very amusing. It's safe to laugh, until similar things start happening to you . . .

The Horrible Harlequins

It is easy to presume the entire history of New England weirdness began at Salem, Massachusetts, in 1692. The witches' story has been told many times.

However, a far stranger and apparently unrelated occurrence was going on just 15 miles up the coast, in nearby Cape Ann. This puzzling episode, when considered in conjunction with the Salem madness, could lead one to believe another Revolution preceded the American War of Independence by almost a century.

But the question is, just who was doing the rebelling? The colonists were definitely battling something, but what?

Today, almost totally eclipsed by the Salem insanity, Cape Ann's caper is all but forgotten. Yet the whole thing was carefully recorded by Cotton Mather in his *Magnalia Christi Americana*, based on extensive testimony from Rev. John Emerson of Gloucester. Unfortunately, no record of the events gives us any real clues to solve the mystery.

Briefly, what happened is this: A band of oddly dressed outsiders kept a cluster of colonial towns in terrified confusion for two solid weeks. As Samuel Adams Drake says, "The witnesses are all persons of character and credibility. Moreover, their testimony remains unshaken by any subsequent revelations to this day."

The most coherent chronicle of these events focuses on one Ebenezer Babson, yeoman farmer from Cape Ann. Night after night during the summer of 1692, Babson and his family heard noises outside their home. The commotion sounded as if a group of people were stomping around, and in some cases running. The unnerving clamor proved most vexing, for every time Babson looked out a window or door, there was no one to be seen.

Fearing an attack of some kind, he cautioned his wife and children to be careful.

Though the sounds continued every night, the attack never came.

Then one midsummer evening as he was returning home alone, Mr. Babson saw the door of his house open and close. Two strangers were leaving. Before he could call to them, they spotted him and ran off, disappearing into a nearby cornfield.

Understandably alarmed, Babson ran home to check on the welfare of his loved ones. But when he questioned his family about the strange men, they seemed puzzled. They said no one had visited during his absence.

Though taken considerably aback, Babson was not indecisive. Trusting the testimony of his own senses, he seized his rifle and took off after the intruders.

He couldn't find any tracks to follow, but he entered the cornfield as they had done. He fought his way through the tall stalks, heading across the field. When he emerged on the other side, he stood very still, looking and listening. The droning of odd voices disturbed the still evening air. "The man of the house is now come," reported an unfamiliar speaker, "else we might have taken the house."

At that point, two forms appeared from behind a log. They saw Babson and bolted. The puzzled farmer lost sight of them as they vanished into the swamp.

Now, Mr. Babson was convinced he and his family were about to be attacked. He hurried home, unable to shake a growing sense of menace.

With great haste, the Babsons relocated to the well-manned wooden fort nearby. Upon entering the protective structure, everyone immediately heard a great turmoil outside. It sounded as if a number of individuals had followed the Babsons to the garrison.

Thoroughly provoked, the stout-hearted Babson decided to confront those who taunted him. He about-faced and stomped outside again, just in time to see what appeared to be the same two men running down the hill toward the swamp. Having seen what apparently were scouts, everyone in the fort became convinced a siege was imminent. Trouble was, no one could figure out by whom. Needless to say, Indians were the first suspects. But these strangers didn't look anything like Indians.

Babson guessed they might be French, judging by their odd attire and the way they carried their weapons. And, of course, bands of highwaymen, pirates, or marauders weren't completely out of the question either.

A suspense-filled night passed slowly within the sturdy wooden walls, but the anticipated attack never came.

Two nights later, Babson saw the two strangers again. They were waiting for him outside the garrison.

And they were armed.

As if in perfect synchronization, both started toward him "at the top of their speed." Babson turned and escaped back into the fort. As soon as he was safely inside, the tromping of many men was clearly audible beyond the walls. Within the fortification, everyone listened, waiting for an attack that never happened.

Later, Babson and his companion John Brown saw a trio of strangers. Without hesitation, the colonists raised their rifles but were unable to shoot "owing to the strangers' dodging about in so lively a manner that they could not take aim."

By now the people of Cape Ann were in a feverish state of excitement and alarm. Everyone was speculating about the identity of these "unaccountable troublers." Some thought they were French. Some thought they were British. But many were beginning to believe they were "devils in the form of men." Was this some demonic charade designed to bewilder the citizens and trick them into a series of wild-goose chases?

Then, on July 14, 1692, not only Babson and Brown, but all the men of the garrison saw a half-dozen strangers, all within gunshot range. Rather than pursue them, the colonists held back, suspecting an ambush.

After the armed colonists had readied themselves, they sallied forth as the half-dozen strangers scattered. Babson overtook two of them. With one clearly in his gun sight, he pulled the trigger. Oddly, his ever-trusty weapon misfired for the first time.

As the frolicking phantoms tried to get away, Babson called to his fellows, "Here they are!" When his comrades raced to his side, everyone saw three more of the mysterious men emerge from the swamp, walking in perfect formation, shoulder to shoulder.

Babson reflexively raised his gun and fired a single shot. This time the results were far better then he would have anticipated—the trio of strangers tumbled to the ground.

"Come! Look! I've killed three of them," he cried.

But as the colonists approached, the downed men rose to their feet and cavorted away, "apparently without hurt or wound of any kind." Before all three disappeared into the swamp, one turned and with his "silver gun" he fired a round at his would-be slayer. The shot narrowly missed Babson, burying itself in a tree. Curious, Babson dug out the bullet. He found it to be thin and pointed, completely unlike the rough lead balls the colonists were using.

Anyway, the bedeviled Babson took refuge behind the tree to reload as his comrades clustered around him. We can only imagine the nature of their conversation.

Inspired mostly by desperation, they momentarily struck on a plan. After identifying the spot where they thought the fugitives were hiding, they all charged together.

As before, the strangers scattered and ran. However, one unfortunate straggler was cornered by the colonial vigilantes. Babson stepped forward and shot the man. Everyone saw him fall.

The crowd rushed to examine their prize, only to discover the body wasn't there.

Frustrated now, and more than a little frightened, Babson and the men searched to no avail. The body had simply vanished.

Cautiously, they ventured a short way into the swamp. Soon they heard voices. Deep within the lightless marshland, the speakers were "going on . . . in some outlandish jargon [the colonials] could not understand. . . ."

Fatigued and completely demoralized, the men returned to the garrison. No sooner were they snugly within its protective wooden walls than the cry arose, "Look, they are there!"

Sure enough, the phantoms had reappeared. This time they were perceived as fleeting shapes, dashing from stone to stone. Similar dark forms crouched behind fences. Others leapt from tree to bush—always well out of gunshot range.

What could it mean?

Just exactly what was going on?

Early the next morning, Ebenezer Babson made his way to the harbor to be sure everyone was prepared—for what, he didn't know. By now, no one doubted that some kind of devastating attack was close at hand. But the colonists still had no idea who their enemy was or what the whole strange ruckus was all about.

On his way back to the fort, Babson encountered two strangers who sprang out at him, blocking his path. Guns raised, they fired repeatedly in his direction. Though the bullets struck around him—and Babson had no doubt that they were real—not one of them hit him.

Aid was not far behind. Fellow townsmen quickly arrived on the scene, opening fire on the attackers. The foray drove them off, but as usual failed to harm them. The stymied militiamen chattered tensely about what each had long suspected: the enemy was not made of mortal flesh and blood. Perhaps harming them would be impossible.

Contact with the odd visitants continued for days.

While scouting, two men from the garrison observed about a dozen of the outsiders in an apple orchard where "they seemed to be performing some strange incantations." A scout, Richard Dolliver, fired where the cluster of strangers was the thickest. As usual, they scattered but did not fall.

Now the citizens of Gloucester were convinced they were helpless in the clutches of Darkness. The infernal invaders had everyone thoroughly terrified: by day they were afraid to venture outside; at night they cowered behind fortified walls, praying for sunrise.

What manner of man, they wondered, could move through the swamps without leaving tracks and vanish without a trace? How could they fight legions of demons impervious to flintlock and sword?

Fearing the worst, the colonists continued to reinforce their warning to surrounding towns. In an effort to help, Captain Appleton arrived from Ipswich, leading sixty heavily armed men. The reinforcements, along with Appleton's good-natured bravado, gave the frightened Gloucesterites new hope.

But in response, the phantom attackers became more bold and openly contemptuous. They appeared in full daylight, popping out of bushes and peering from behind trees. It was impossible to calculate their number, though it seemed as if vast forces were amassing outside the garrison.

Volleys of musket fire proved time after time that none could be killed, nor even wounded.

At night, the phantoms threw stones, beat upon the walls of the fort with heavy clubs, and taunted the colonists with their presence and indestructibility. Eventually, displaying the sublime confidence of one who knows he cannot be harmed, they would not even run when the colonists chased them.

As if to complete some mysterious, metaphysical circle, Ebenezer Babson was one of the last to confront the invaders. Outside town one day, he observed three of them walking along the road. He concealed himself in a thicket at the roadside and readied his weapon. Suspense mounting, he held his fire until the three came within an easy stone's throw. Then he stood up and pulled the trigger.

To Babson's horror, the gun did not fire.

The three phantoms didn't even break stride. As they passed the petrified farmer, they "took no other notice of him than to give him a disdainful look as they walked by."

Moments later, Babson tried his weapon again and it worked perfectly.

After more than a fortnight enduring this inexplicable terrorism, the colonists knew the war was lost. Though there was not so much as a casualty on either side, they knew they were helpless. As poet John Greenleaf Whittier has his disheartened captain instruct:

> *Lay aside your useless weapons;*
> *skill and prowess naught avail;*
> *They who do the Devil's service*
> *wear their master's coat of mail.*

In other words, the colonists gave up.

And when that was done, the invaders seemed to give up, too. They disappeared and—as far as we know—they have never come back.

But what a puzzle they have bequeathed us!

Who were they? What were they? Why did they taunt the colonists yet never do them any real harm?

The modern mind is conditioned to put everything into categories, but where shall we file Cape Ann's "spectre leaguers"?

Were they demons? Ghosts? Extraterrestrials? Frenchmen? Maybe even a group of mischievous college students time-traveling from the future?

Or were they other-dimensional beings, harmless elemental spirits who, according to many occultists, inhabit the world right along with us? If so, perhaps they were making a stand, trying to repel the self-same occupying colonists who, in another hundred years, would successfully repel the forces of an oppressive British King?

Where's Roger?

TODAY WE REMEMBER ROGER WILLIAMS AS A RELIGIOUS NONCONFORMIST. His strong convictions repeatedly got him into trouble, from the time he arrived in New England until he founded the state of Rhode Island.

By championing unreasonable causes—like religious freedom, complete separation of church and state, and compensation to Native Americans for their land—Williams got thrown out of Massachusetts in 1635.

The next year, he headed into the wilds around Narragansett Bay, where he set about practicing what he preached: he purchased lands from the Narragansett tribe and established a community based on religious freedom and democratic ideals. He called this settlement "Providence," in gratitude "for God's merciful providence unto me in my distress."

While all that may be true, it has nothing whatsoever to do with Roger Williams's postmortem adventures. At least I don't think it does . . .

Anyway, after Williams passed away in 1683, he was buried beside his wife on their farm, in the shade of one of their apple trees. Though Williams was universally respected and much-loved by fellow colonists, he was given but a modest headstone.

Many years after his death, a concerned group of citizens decided the founder of Rhode Island should be entitled to a far more elaborate headstone, not to mention a nobler site for his final resting place.

In preparing this memorial upgrade, a commission was authorized to disinter Mr. and Mrs. Williams and move them to their new digs, so to speak. But when the crew opened the graves, they received the surprise of their lives. The corpses were missing.

This event has been described as the most remarkable grave-robbing ever. And it was a real mystery. Where were the bodies? Who took them? And *why?*

The solution was not immediately obvious. Then, after much talk and a little more

digging, they rooted out the villain. In fact, the cheeky perpetrator had been standing there all the while, right in plain sight.

Not far from the empty graves there stood a healthy apple tree, known for its exceptional fruit. But when it was examined, the Rhode Islanders clustered around it
quickly lost their taste for fruit.

It seems the roots of that robust tree had somehow found their way to the coffins
of Mr. and Mrs. Williams. They burrowed through the rotting wood, and kept
moving.

One large root now filled the spot formerly occupied by Roger Williams's head.
It then penetrated the chest cavity, following the course of the spine to the feet, where
it angled upward. A similar process had displaced Mrs. Williams's remains.

The roots had completely absorbed the couple. Stranger still, the bloated tubers
bore a striking resemblance to recumbent human forms. The thick main shafts,
with their weave-work of veiny branches looked for all the world like the exposed cir-
culatory systems of two human bodies.

Though the graves were empty, there was no doubt about what had become of the
venerated couple. Nature had bestowed its own honor, preserving them in her own
strange way before humankind got around to it.

Still, I wonder if there is some sort of message here? As a cleric, Roger Williams
would have known full well what happened the last time a founding father yielded
to temptation by consuming an apple. What can be the portent, one wonders, when
just the opposite happens?

The *Wicked* Water Sprite

WHENEVER I'M INVITED TO SPEAK ABOUT MY EXPLORATIONS INTO THE ODDER side of New England, someone invariably asks me to identify the strangest thing I've come across. People like to think in superlatives, I guess. So I try to respond that way. However, for the following story, I'm not really sure which superlative to use. It isn't horrifying or even scary in any conventional sense. But when I discovered it a few years back, I was convinced then, as I am now, that it is one of the oddest, most offbeat, and puzzling things I've ever run across. Perhaps the superlative that best fits is "most off the wall."

And this is no legend or myth. I've spoken to witnesses. I've interviewed one of the family members. I'm completely satisfied that it is absolutely true.

Most anomalies fall readily into classifiable types: ghosts, monsters, UFOs, haunted houses, psychic experiences, and so on. Occasionally, however, something so monumentally strange comes along that it's completely unclassifiable.

Such an event occurred in a Windsor, Vermont, home back in 1955.

A physician, his wife, and their two daughters had lived for nine years in their comfortable two-story home on Cherry Street. There was nothing odd about the house itself. In fact, it could not have been more normal, with its brown shingled exterior, white trim, and attached garage.

But starting on Monday, September 20, 1955, normalcy became a thing of the past as the family plunged headlong into Vermont's own version of *The Twilight Zone*.

On that day, one of the daughters noticed a quantity of water had collected in the concave seat of a wooden chair in her bedroom. As she was about to clean it up, she noticed a second puddle on the floor. Where had it come from? Nothing had spilled. Nothing was leaking. It wasn't raining outside and no water pipes ran through her room.

Almost immediately, other family members began noticing pools of water here and there on the first and second floors of the house.

What started as a trickle quickly became a downpour. Over the first two days, the family collected thirteen pails of water. But no one could determine where it was coming from—it just seemed to appear.

This water from nowhere saturated the contents of their bureau drawers and soaked the clothing in their closets. Dishes, cups, and glasses filled with water. Continual mopping and sponging did no good; it was like trying to bail out a sinking ship.

Mattresses, pillows, and living room furniture got so wet they had to be removed from the house.

The puzzled M.D. called in friends and neighbors, hoping someone could make sense of this unique water problem. The puzzled Windsorites looked around, scratched their heads, shrugged, and observed that the air didn't seem to be unusually damp. Or warm. Or cold. They didn't notice any mist or haze. And—try as they might—they could discern no possible source for the accumulating water. The neighbors were also quick to point out that nothing remotely similar was going on in any of their houses nearby.

Yet water continued to appear. In drawers. Bowls. Dishes. On chairs and all over the floor. The *Claremont* (New Hampshire) *Daily Eagle* reported that on occasion it actually rained inside the house.

The doctor described one instance when he was carrying a bowl of grapes from the kitchen. By the time he got to the living room, the bowl had filled with water almost in front of his eyes.

The family called in various experts, hoping to get to the bottom of things: plumbers, electricians, insulation installers, furnace specialists—even a dowser— but no one could offer a realistic explanation. However, the baffled experts were able to make a few interesting observations: there were no broken waterlines or sweating pipes; there was no problem with groundwater or seepage from a well or spring. Perhaps odder still, the walls and ceilings were not afflicted. They, and the insulation *inside* the walls, remained perfectly dry. And—perhaps most remarkable for a Vermont house—there was no water in the basement.

Sometimes things would appear to be drying out, then the family would leave, only to return to a house that seemed to have been flooded.

So where was the water coming from? How could it just appear before their eyes? And why now, after living in the house for nine years with no similar problems?

The doctor said, "To . . . stand in the middle of a room, feeling no dampness, and to watch the water mount on the boards about you, is an experience almost terrifying!"

Things climaxed during the first weekend in October. Water cascaded from the kitchen cupboards, streamed from under the electric stove, and dripped from the living room piano. The family had finally had enough. They had already moved what furniture they wanted to save into the garage; now they too moved out, driven from their home by the fantastic flood.

All four moved into a trailer in their front yard. Where—it may be important to note—the phenomenon did not follow.

When the Associated Press picked up the story, newspapers from all around the world began phoning to get more information. Letters with questions, explanations, and prayers arrived almost every day. Endless lines of curiosity seekers paraded by the house on foot and in cars. Numerous eccentrics imposed themselves into the situation, with scenarios involving divine or demonic intervention.

Then, about a month after the phenomenon started, it stopped. The end, like the beginning, came without explanation. In hopes of cutting off the flow of curiosity seekers, the doctor issued a press release saying the problem had been solved. But it hadn't been solved—it just stopped.

Over the weekend of October 22 and 23, the family began moving back into their house. Life returned to something resembling normal. And, little by little, the high strangeness in Windsor slipped from memory.

Today, whenever I reflect on this strange tale, I can almost believe there really is some sort of cosmic joker who enjoys involving unsuspecting souls in outlandish antics such as these. And if the unsettling events at Windsor were a cosmic joke, I should close by telling you the punch line.

You may have noticed that I never mentioned the name of the unfortunate family. Believe it or not, their name was Waterman.

Water, Water Everywhere

FOR A LONG TIME, I THOUGHT DR. WATERMAN'S SITUATION WAS UNIQUE. THEN I discovered that after concluding its wet work with the Waterman family, Windsor's Water Sprite apparently picked up and moved south. About a decade later, it—or one of its pesky kinfolk—reappeared, taking up residence with the Francis Martin family of Methuen, Massachusetts.

Commencing on Tuesday, October 25, 1963, Mr. and Mrs. Martin and their 11-year-old daughter confronted their uninvited guest in the TV room. They were watching some evening programs when someone noticed a peculiar wet spot on the wall. Before anyone could react, they heard a loud popping sound, like a firecracker. Or perhaps "champagne cork" would be a better analogy because right after the *pop*, a stream of water squirted from the wet patch on the wall, arcing directly into the room, and splattering on the floor.

It was as if a water pipe had burst, but, oddly, there were no pipes at all behind that particular wall. This fantastic fountain ran for a good two hours while similar waterspouts began erupting here and there all over the house. It was as if someone were turning on invisible faucets hooked up to nonexistent waterlines. Each spout would last about 20 seconds, then recur at approximately 15-minute intervals.

More curiously, after a waterspout erupted, no hole in the wall or wall covering was detectable.

When mops and dehumidifying equipment proved useless, the mystified Martins called for help. Neighbors and local officials trooped through. A crew of city firemen, the leaders of which possessed extensive architectural knowledge, examined the building for leaks. They determined the roof was flawless. After several hours of investigation, no one was able to find so much as a single suspicious imperfection.

Since no one could find the water's source, no one could shut it off. By Friday, persistent wetness, unexpected geysers, and a general feeling of distorted reality had thoroughly dampened their spirits. Events forced the Martin family to leave, abandoning their home to the spurts and the experts.

Luckily, they had relatives close by who offered to take them in.

Nonetheless, every day they'd trudge dutifully back to clean up and continue their search for the water's source. Surrounded by the usual cavalcade of skeptics—plumbers, building inspectors, and police—everyone scratched their hair thin trying to come up with a slightly cogent explanation.

One witness testified that he saw water cascading down the staircase like a waterfall. Another measured a 1-inch accumulation on the floor. Sometimes a quart or so would splash out of nowhere all at once. By November 1, water was bubbling and shooting from the walls and furniture in five rooms at the same time.

A national roofing company from Boston dispatched an engineer to test the home. Right away he noted the accumulation of more than a quart of water on the sofa. Naturally suspecting a leak, he tore down a section of plasterboard nearby only to find it, and the insulation behind it, "dry as a bone."

He and six other examiners concluded formally that there was nothing whatsoever wrong with the building structurally.

Still, the baffled family members and confused consultants tried everything they could think of. They shut off the water supply to the house and drained all the pipes. They made sure the heat was turned off and they opened all the windows to encourage ventilation. They even raised the shades to admit the maximum amount of sunlight. All to no avail.

Nothing helped.

Pops sounded and water spouted.

Now living with Mrs. Martin's parents, the family hoped for succor. Their sanctuary was the middle floor of a three-story apartment house in nearby Lawrence. Bizarre as it seems, when the Martins moved in, the water sprite tagged along with them. The whole popping and splashing scenario began all over again at the new location.

Again, experts examined the roof and the plumbing. They investigated every nook, cranny, and crawl space. Water kept pouring in. Even as they watched, no one could determine its source.

It may be important to note that the walls squirted only in the apartment where the Martins were staying. No unusual moisture bedeviled the families above or below.

Needless to say, suspicion fell on the daughter. The experts could find no natural law to explain the problem. So instead, local police were willing to believe that dozens of people had all been completely bamboozled by an 11-year-old girl.

Was she a scapegoat? Well, here's what happened: Twelve adults were milling around in the in-laws' five-room Lawrence apartment. Water was splashing in every room. Amid all this commotion, one of the cops caught the girl at the kitchen sink having a glass of water—and that was evidence enough. The police called the problem "solved" and went back to the station house to report everything had been the work of the mischievous youngster. On the other hand, a deputy fire chief was a bit more analytical. He had seen the girl helping to mop up the floor while water was exploding in four or five places at once.

Word leaked out, of course, and local newspapers had their Halloween story for 1963. Soon parades of gawkers found their way to the Methuen home, making life miserable for all concerned. The more aggressive curiosity seekers actually wanted to touch afflicted family members, thinking that somehow they would benefit spiritually from the contact.

Ultimately, perhaps following the example of Windsor's Waterman family, the Martins did the only thing they could do. They announced that the problem had been solved. They reported that a hole had finally been discovered in the roof of their Methuen home, which, they said, accounted for the whole thing.

Of course, that failed to explain the equally weird goings-on at the in-laws' place in Lawrence. Or where the water came from on sunny days.

Also similar to the Windsor episode, the Methuen and Lawrence phenomena were short-lived. Though differences do exist, all three cases are identical in at least one way: they were never solved. The phenomena just stopped. Ended. Ran their course and dried up.

Unlike the Windsor story, investigators did identify what may have been a couple of clues. First, just before the pop and splash, there would be a sudden and un-explainable rise in the humidity in the room.

Then, after the jet of water ceased, the source spot on the wall would feel warm, sometimes hot, to the touch. These are the sorts of maddening clues that seem to deepen rather than explain the mystery. Why should either condition result in jets of water arching from unpunctured wallpaper and plasterboard?

Natural or supernatural? Your guess is as good as mine.

If the water was obeying natural laws, as the skeptics insist it must, why didn't gravity make it trickle to the floor and form a pool? How could it possibly spew horizontally, as if under pressure, from unperforated plasterboard? And how could it flow at several locations all over the house, even when it wasn't raining outside?

In any event, the public was satisfied with the Martins' explanation, and soon the whole strange business was forgotten.

When all is said and done, the only thing I can state with confidence is that, so far, no one has offered a single explanation that holds water.

And somewhere, way off in the distance, I seem to hear a faint sardonic burst of laughter.

PART V

WHAT ROUGH BEAST?

"Each subsiding century reveals some new mystery; we build where monsters used to hide themselves."

— HENRY WADSWORTH LONGFELLOW
Kavanagh

Dover's Frail Phantom

No census of New England can ever be complete.

As much as we may enjoy the cultural variety of this 200-year-old American melting pot, there are undetected visitors among us, aliens in the most unconventional sense. We know this because we see them from time to time. They seem to just . . . well . . . materialize. Then—as if by magic—they vanish back to wherever they came from, leaving puzzled Yankees scratching their heads and wondering if they've suddenly been transported to the seventh New England state, the one called "Insanity."

Imagine this happening to you. For the next few pages, pretend you're in a car, riding around on the back roads of rural Massachusetts. You're in the backseat of Bill Bartlett's VW, sitting next to Andy Brodie. In the front seat, Mike Mazzacca is riding shotgun. Bartlett's at the wheel.

The date: April 21, 1977. About 10:30 p.m. The sky is dark but clear. The air's chilly but not cold. Bill's driving along Farm Street on the outskirts of Dover, the wealthiest community in Massachusetts. The road is a narrow, winding path between woodlands and pastures. Hard to believe things can be so rural just 15 miles from Boston.

No one in the car is mindful of Farm Street's history. It's the second-oldest road in town, originally built on Indian trails. And no one knows that in the 1600s a local man claimed he'd met the Devil face-to-face on this very stretch of road.

So of course there's no reason for anyone to guess that within minutes Bill Bartlett and his passengers will confront an oddity that Walter Webb, assistant director of the Hayden Planetarium at Boston's Science Museum, would call " . . . one of the most baffling creature episodes ever reported."

A creature soon to be dubbed "The Dover Demon."

The headlights of Bill Bartlett's VW sweep along the tumbled stone wall at the roadside. Then, in the white glare of the headlights, you see something on the wall. Something alive. It's trying to climb over the piles of rocks. At first, you think it might be a cat. Or a dog. Maybe even a raccoon. But . . . funny . . . it doesn't move exactly like an animal. It seems to be *clutching* at the rocks with its fingers and toes. And its arms look way too long; its head too big . . .

"Did you see that!" Bartlett blurts, a tremor distorting his voice.

"See what?" asks Andy.

Whatever it was, Mike and Andy had missed it; they'd been talking together, not watching the road. But *you* saw it. And Bill saw it, too; you can tell by the undisguised look of fear on his face.

As he speeds away, shaking and chattering in terror, you try to collect your thoughts. Just exactly what was that odd creature you saw climbing over the stone wall?

The most conspicuous feature was its head. It was huge, bulbous, big as a watermelon, way out of proportion to its body. The eyes were big too. Orange colored, seeming to glow as the thing stared into the headlights, looking right at you.

Although you got a good, unobstructed view of it, you couldn't make out any nose, mouth, or ears. Those features were either very small, or nonexistent. And all the proportions were wrong; the creature's thin neck didn't appear to be strong enough to support its oddly oversized head.

The body was absurdly tiny, actually smaller than the head. Its limbs were out of proportion, way too long and strangely fragile. Its fingers and toes were disproportionately long, too. You recall the way they seemed to grip at the stones, flexing, bending, molding to the contours of the rocks.

Was it an animal? Did it have teeth? A tail? If it did, you hadn't seen them.

All in all, there was something vaguely human about the little thing. But if it were human, why wasn't it wearing any clothes on this chilly April night? No, it was naked. Hairless. Its strange peach-colored skin appeared rough in the lights of the passing vehicle. From head to foot, it couldn't have been more than 4 feet tall.

What was it?

Later, you and Bill Bartlett compare notes. Bill's description matches yours perfectly. But after hours of speculation, neither of you has any idea what you might have seen.

WITNESSES

MORE THAN TEN YEARS LATER, Bill Bartlett recalled the bizarre creature. "I must confess," he admitted to writer Robert Cahill, "at seeing it, I panicked, screamed, and sped off down the road."

But his passengers, Andy and Mike, weren't ready to leave the scene. They were curious. They wanted to see it, too.

Bartlett had hesitated, fear reverberating within him. But his companions insisted and somehow Bill knew he'd be needing corroborating witnesses.

"They finally got me to go back . . ."

He turned his car around and once again drove along Farm Street. All the while, Mike and Andy called out to the creature, "Come on! Come out! We want to see you!"

When they arrived at the spot, the creature was nowhere to be seen.

But it wasn't gone . . .

Later that same night another Dover boy, 15-year-old John Baxter, would have a hair-raising midnight encounter.

John was on his way home from visiting his girlfriend Cathy Cronin. It was just a short walk from her house on Miller's Hill to Farm Street, where he planned to hitch a ride.

Considering the lateness of the hour, he was surprised to see someone coming toward him. Clearly, it wasn't an animal; it was walking upright.

Thinking it might be a friend of his, he called out.

There was no response. But the tiny figure kept moving toward him. Baxter wondered who it was and where he was going.

Now more uncertain, John Baxter called again. No response.

John stopped moving. The other figure stopped too. Whoever . . . whatever it was stood perfectly still, just 20 feet away. John became aware of the two enormous orange eyes staring at him.

The teenager started shaking in his boots as he tried to make sense of the alien vision. Was it an animal walking on its hind legs? No, more likely a child, a horribly deformed child.

Could this weird little kid be lost? Was he up to some sort of mischief?

But those unearthly eyes . . .

No, this wasn't any kid. It looked more like some kind of monkey, a shaved monkey, with a big peanutlike head.

When its long fingers began clutching at rocks by the roadside, John feared the thing might attack him. But maybe it wasn't going to use the stones for weapons, maybe it was using them to steady itself . . .

John experienced another jolt of surprise when the figure bolted off the road, heading into the nearby woods. He could hear its footfalls in the dry leaves.

And now it was John Baxter who was running. Trying to outdistance the terror that seized him.

Bill Bartlett didn't learn of John Baxter's confrontation with the pink-colored gnome until five days later. During that time, working independently, both boys sketched what they had seen. When they met, their drawings matched.

They also learned they were not the only ones who'd seen the creature.

April 22, the evening after the Bartlett-Baxter sightings, there were more reports of a spindly, peanut-headed creature.

William Taintor, 18, and Abby Brabham, 15, were driving on Springdale Avenue near downtown Dover when Abby saw the puzzling little phantom on top of a culvert over Trout Brook. It crouched on all fours, facing their oncoming car. Although Abby had heard nothing about the imp, her description tallied with Bartlett and Baxter's as to size, large oblong head, hairless body, absence of nose, ears, mouth, and tail.

But there was one remarkable conflict: she definitely perceived the eyes as green, not red or orange.

Jolted by the sight, Abby cried out for Taintor to get them out of there, fast.

Taintor got only a glimpse of the thing. As his car sped away, passing within 8 feet of the creature, he saw enough to realize that whatever stood at the roadside was like nothing he had ever seen before.

The unsettling experience left both teenagers trembling with an unfamiliar kind of fear.

INVESTIGATORS

AFTER THAT, THE REPORTS CEASED and the creature was not seen again. This extraordinary episode might have been forgotten entirely if a man named Loren Coleman, from nearby Needham, hadn't chanced to stop at the Dover Country Store on April 28.

It is a strange coincidence that Coleman was, and is, an accomplished and credible investigator of unusual phenomena. His fascinating books on the unexplained reveal an earnest but above all unbiased will to separate fact from fantasy. It was Coleman who named the creature the "Dover Demon," and it was Coleman who coordinated the efforts of at least three other determined and experienced investigators. One of them, Walter Webb, thoroughly documented the events of April 21 and 22, 1977.

Working together, the four were able to question an extraordinary number of local people, not only the witnesses themselves, but their parents, teachers, friends, even the high school principal and local police chief. Everyone agreed the young people were honest and forthright, not known for pranks, hoaxes, and other mischief.

All concerned—parents, police, and investigators—were as convinced as nonwitnesses can be that something strange was out there.

Of course, newspaper, radio, and TV reporters flocked to the area. But because there were no additional sightings, local and national media quickly lost interest. Apparently, neither the "demon" nor the witnesses had any interest in keeping the story alive.

Today, the whole incident is mostly forgotten. But those who remember, and those who rediscover it in books such as this, will always speculate about what manner of creature it was. And why did it come to Dover, Massachusetts? And why was its stay so very brief?

THEORIES

THERE ARE NOT A LOT OF THEORIES TO CHOOSE AMONG. First, of course, we must consider whether the young people were playing a prank. They all knew each other, true—so they were connected in that sense. But "connection" doesn't mean "conspiracy." Dover is a small town, just 5,000 people at the time. The odds of knowing each other were great. And of course, as the character references repeatedly stated, these were fine young people, not known as liars or conspirators.

Could someone have been playing a trick on them? Not impossible but unlikely. How could anyone short of a Hollywood special-effects animator produce anything as convincing as the creature described?

Mass hysteria—whatever that is—can be ruled out simply because the witnesses were not together when the episodes occurred. Indeed, there were three separate sightings by witnesses who had not communicated. And although each of the young people was described as terribly frightened, no one was ever called hysterical.

The descriptions of the creature bring to mind what has become a popular conception of the typical UFO occupant. We cannot rule this possibility out of course, but we must note that no UFOs were reported in the vicinity on the nights in question.

By the same token, the descriptions also call to mind Mr. Peanut and Bart Simpson. But neither of those gentlemen has ever been considered a serious suspect.

Could it have been a real demon? I don't think Coleman was earnest when he bestowed the title. He was either joking or looking for that type of catchy alliterative epithet that is always so fancied by jocular journalists.

Besides, there was nothing especially "demonic" about the little creature. It wasn't aggressive or menacing in any way. Descriptions suggest it was frail, weak, unsteady on its feet. Hardly the description of a demon.

AND FARTHER OUT . . .

OTHER THEORIES, while they cannot be eliminated out of hand, are considerably more . . . exotic. For example, little people.

Of course, we all know about Irish leprechauns and their cousins, the capricious Scandinavian elves. But we need not look abroad for the wee folk. Right here in North America people had been seeing tiny humanoid beings for centuries before the Europeans arrived.

The Cree Indians of Canada have long believed in the *Mennegishi*. These are little people whose appearance closely matches the Dover Demon. They have big, round heads, immense eyes, and no noses. Their bodies are small, with long limbs and fingers. They hang out near water and streambeds, and their purpose in life, apparently, is to play tricks on humans. The description and M.O. certainly fit.

Closer to home, the Penobscot Indians of Maine told of *Wanagemeswak*, who in many ways resemble European little folks. The Passamaquoddy share their reservations with two types of little people, the *Nagumwasuck* and the *Mekumwasuck*. Both species grow to be about 3 feet tall and both are extremely ugly. For this reason they avoid being seen. The Passamaquoddy believe that only fellow tribespeople are able to see their diminutive neighbors. So, if the Dover Demon was a wandering *Nagumwasuck* or *Mekumwasuck*, the Dover teenagers shouldn't have been able to see it.

But what, specifically, about Massachusetts where the "demon" was sighted?

Thomas Weston's 1906 *History of the Town of Middleboro, Massachusetts* (some 28 miles from Dover) discusses a race of little people called *Puk-wudjees*. Supposedly, the Native Americans believed they lived on an island from which they ventured forth, wishing neither to help nor harm the neighboring humans. They did, however, seek out murderers whom they could somehow place into an unnatural sleep, during which the spirit could leave the sleeper's body, causing if not death, then premature burial.

Other sleep-producing little folk, sometimes called "fairies," are recalled by the Scotch-Irish folk in the vicinity of Nutfield, now Derry, New Hampshire. There, a fairy queen was supposed by local Native Americans to live in Beaver Lake. Called

Tsienneto, or Neto for short, this supernatural creature occasionally did good deeds for people in distress. For example, she is said to have acted as a kind of guardian angel to Hannah Dustin of Haverhill, Massachusetts, when she was captured by unfriendly Indians in March of 1695. By putting the Indians into an unnatural sleep, the captive Mrs. Dustin was able to take their tomahawks, kill them, and head off down the Merrimac River to freedom.

Today the legendary fairy queen has been pretty thoroughly eclipsed by the legendary Hannah. You might say, Mrs. Dustin carved out a place for herself in New England horror by first killing her Indian captors, and then scalping all ten of them. To prove it, she brought the ten grisly souvenirs back home to Haverhill. Last I knew, her ax and scalping knife were on display there at the Buttonwood's Museum. I'm not sure what became of the scalps.

But the point is, no murders occurred in the vicinity of Dover, Massachusetts, on or around April 21, 1977. So apparently the puzzled teenagers were not seeing elfin royalty. Or Mrs. Dustin.

So how should we conclude? Is this chapter fact or fiction? History or romance?

In preparation for his 1989 book, Robert Cahill interviewed several of the players in this mysterious little drama. A former law officer himself, Cahill is no stranger to investigative techniques. When he talked to Carl Sheridan, the Dover police chief at the time the demon appeared, Cahill figured one former law officer would give another the straight scoop.

"Did it really happen, or was it a hoax?" Cahill asked.

"It was real," Sheridan replied. "Those boys really did see something out there."

WEE NEW ENGLANDERS

THE ABOVE LIST OF SUSPECTS for the Dover Demon's true identity by no means exhausts the New England census of little people. We Yankees have long shared New England with wee Yankees.

As already mentioned, the Passamaquoddy, the *Nagumwasuck*, and the *Mekumwasuck* all live together on two reservations in Maine.

The grotesque little people, though essentially benevolent, can be ornery if laughed at. They are believed to possess the evil eye, so if they make direct eye contact with a human being it will result in immediate death or fatal illness. Needless to say, there are many stories about eyewitnesses getting cut down by the magic stare.

In spite of the potential danger, the *Nagumwasuck* seem to be very attached to their human neighbors. If there is a death in the Passamaquoddy tribe, the *Nagumwasuck* can be heard crying in the forest. If there is a wedding or birth, the little people rejoice.

The *Mekumwasuck,* on the other hand, seem to function as guardians of the Catholic church. Ever since French Jesuit missionaries converted the Passamaquoddy in the seventeenth century, the little people have played an active role in church affairs. Like the *Nagumwasuck,* they are extremely ugly; their faces—not unlike those of the missionaries—are covered with dark hair.

An example of how the tiny protectors operate occurred in 1970 when the parish priest was away for a few days on business. During his absence, a few good ol' boys got liquored up and broke into the church to steal more wine. Their plan failed because the *Mekumwasuck* appeared and frightened the men away.

The next year at a church-sponsored dance a 16-year-old boy saw a *Mekumwasuck.* He ran to get his cousin, who also saw the grotesque little man. Word spread quickly; within minutes, everyone had run away from the dance. The message, apparently, is that the pious *Mekumwasuck* don't approve of church socials.

There's a wonderful and perhaps related story that took place in Waldoboro, Maine, sometime during January 1855. It seems J.W. McHenry was chopping wood near his home when he heard a number of loud, high-pitched screams coming from the woods on his property.

When he looked up, he saw an 18-inch-high creature covered with long black hair. As the story goes, McHenry chased the little critter and eventually caught it. Not sure what else to do with it, he brought it home and made a pet of it. Could it have been a *Mekumwasuck?* We'll be speculating more about the identity of this little fella later.

The height of ugliness may have been attained by the puzzling little creature that was spotted in Derry, New Hampshire.

On December 15, 1956, an anonymous witness was in the woods gathering Christmas trees. Suddenly, he looked up and saw something that was about 2 feet tall, and—to say the least—not especially human-looking.

Supposedly, its skin was green and wrinkled like elephant hide. Its high-domed head sported floppy ears somewhat like a bloodhound's. The nose was nothing but tiny holes. And its eyes had protective film over them like snake eyes.

Whatever it was wasn't wearing clothes. Perhaps mercifully, the witness doesn't continue his description beyond pointing out that its hands were stumps, its arms and legs were short, and its feet lacked toes.

He watched it for 20 minutes, then tried to capture it. However, its terrified screeching was so frightening that it scared the witness away!

Hard to believe this little green gargoyle could be any relation to Tsienneto, that other Derry fairy.

Moving south, F.G. Speck, in a paper about the Indians of Connecticut, talked about the *Makiawisag*, little people who lived in the woods. He recorded an event which he thought took place before 1800 in which a child named Martha Uncas was traveling with her parents in a canoe down the Yantic River. They spied some *Makiawisag* running along the shore, vaguely visible among the pine trees. Martha's mother said, "Don't look at the dwarfs. They will point their fingers at you and you cannot see them."

So what's the problem with not seeing them?

Well, supposedly, these same dwarfs occasionally arrived at people's houses, asking for something to eat. Indian legend advises that one must always give the dwarfs what they want. If someone refuses, the dwarfs will point a finger at the landowner, making it impossible for him to see them. Then they'll enter and take far more than what they had originally asked for.

In his wonderful series of columns for the *New Haven Register*, Neil Hogan tells of another—or possibly related—race of Connecticut little people. They inhabit dark hidden caves way back in the Berkshire Hills of Canaan. Called "the old men of the mountains," these reclusive fellows go around in long gray robes and, perhaps sensibly, habitually avoid contact with humankind. When we cross paths with them, however, they mess with our senses of reality and time.

For example, there's the story of a hunter who happened to spot one of the little men in the woods. Increasing his pace, the hunter tried to get a closer look at the incredible creature. As he drew nearer, however, the little man vanished, as if by magic.

Now, this hunter had heard all the stories. He knew these old men possessed vast hordes of gold and silver which they minted into triangular coins inscribed with arcane symbols.

Hoping to round up some friends and conduct a thorough search for the treasure, the hunter marked a series of trees with his knife. He clearly marked a trail from the spot where the little man had vanished, all the way back to the road.

The next day, the hunter returned with his friends, only to discover that the marks seemed to be missing. The men wandered around for hours, trying to locate just one mark—but all of them were gone, as if they'd never been there at all.

In another story, one of the more brazen little men presented himself to the wife of a local farmer and—like the *Makiawisag*—asked for something to eat. The woman—perhaps knowing better than to refuse—set out food and drink, with cheese and homemade pie for dessert. The ravenous little fellow quickly polished off every last scrap.

Assuming that the little man was now beholden to her, the woman decided to satisfy her curiosity about a couple of things. But before she could utter a single syllable, the gray-robed figure vanished from the kitchen without opening a door or window.

The puzzled woman hunted high and low for her diminutive visitor. After a while, she gave up and went back to clear the table and wash the dishes. Lo and behold, the full meal was back in place, just as if the little man had never touched it.

Then, just as she began to suspect the whole episode was nothing but a dream, she saw, there on the tabletop, seven triangular coins, inscribed with odd symbols.

It is easy to see how these stories bear a strong family resemblance to many European tales of fairy folk. Are we to conclude that multinational immigrants brought the stories with them?

Or were the stories, if not the little people themselves, here waiting on Plymouth Rock when the Europeans arrived?

New England Wailers

HISTORICALLY, THOUSANDS OF IRISH IMMIGRANTS CAME TO NEW ENGLAND TO escape the devastating potato famine of 1848.

Less historically, certain scholars maintain that another large group of Irish immigrants arrived centuries earlier. They cite evidence that indicates Irish Culdee monks colonized New England about 1,000 years before Columbus showed up. These Celtic pioneers mined for copper and built mysterious stone structures like America's Stonehenge in North Salem, New Hampshire, and the network of perplexing "beehive buildings" all over the East.

If that is true, then it's not much of a stretch to imagine they brought a few Irish oddities along with them. As we have seen, there are enough reports of little people in New England to suspect a few Leprechauns might have been stowaways on their coracles. Even *Yankee* magazine, perhaps in its unfailing spirit of whimsy, published a photograph of an alleged "little person" from Waterville, New Hampshire, in its February 1973 issue.

But another Irish import we rarely think about materializes from time to time—normally with deadly results. Luckily, sightings of this unlikely wayfarer are rare. I mean, how many Americans do you know who've had a run-in with the banshee?

According to legend, the banshee is a spirit, perhaps a guardian, that attaches itself to certain families in the same way the *Nagumwasuck* attach themselves to the Passamaquoddy. When a tribesperson dies, the *Nagumwasuck* cry, lamenting the loss.

The banshee, on the other hand, cries prior to a death. In fact, the only time it makes itself known is as a harbinger of doom.

The word banshee is derived from the Gaelic, *ban sidhe*, which means "fairy woman." She is generally imagined having long red hair and wearing a gray, flowing cloak. But it is not her appearance that one remembers. It's her horrible, bone-chilling wail. Normally, her frightful keening is heard only by family members.

Anyone who has heard the banshee's wail will not soon forget it. A composite description suggests that it starts low, almost below the level of perception; then it soars to a screeching crescendo.

The otherworldly lamentation has just enough human quality to let people know it is not a beast. Yet, somehow, it's not entirely natural, either.

Some people have described it as sounding almost like a cat. Others say it resembles the cries of a tortured bird. But all agree that no sound in nature exactly replicates it. As the cry fades, it gives the impression it's moving farther and farther away.

Fiction, you say?

Well, not everyone agrees.

A successful businessman from Boston tells of several encounters with the banshee. Although he won't release his name publicly, he has penned a full account of the experience.

He is a member of an Irish Catholic family that came to Boston in the middle of the last century, fleeing the famine. His great-great-grandfather opened a small grocery store that over the years the family has expanded into a New England-wide supermarket chain. Today, the man runs it with his two brothers.

When he was very small, about 10 years old, he heard the banshee for the first time. He was lying in bed on a bright spring morning, still half asleep, just listening to the birds singing. Then all of a sudden a weird noise began to intrude on the birds' song. Soon, he heard nothing but the noise. He says it sounded like "a demented woman."

To be certain it wasn't a product of the wind, he looked out the window. No leaves were rustling, no bushes moving. The boy got up, ran downstairs, and witnessed an upsetting sight, something he had never seen before: his father crying. But when his mother explained, he understood: his grandfather had just died.

At first, he saw no relationship between the death and the mysterious sound. His parents had never told him anything about the banshee. In fact, it wasn't until much later that he heard the legend for the first time. And that brought to mind the story of his grandfather.

Then, in 1946, the banshee cried again.

He was an officer in the air force, stationed in the Far East. As before, it occurred in the early morning. About six o'clock. But this time he was asleep when the low howling began. It woke him up.

Instantly, he knew what it was. With recognition came dread. Then terror. He wrote, "I sat bolt upright in bed, and the hair on the back of my neck prickled. The noise got louder, rising and falling like an air raid siren."

As the strange sound died away, a feeling of great sadness settled over him. Somehow he knew that his father had passed away.

And, of course, that turned out to be the case.

This Boston businessman was to hear the mournful wail one more time. About two decades later, he was on a business trip to Toronto, Canada. Exactly like the two previous times, he was in bed. And again it was morning. But this time he was fully awake, reading the morning newspaper.

Suddenly, the dreadful but all-too-familiar screech began. It quickly filled the room. Seized by a kind of panic, his first thoughts were of his wife and young son. Then his brothers. But hurried phone calls assured him the problem was not with them.

Although he had seen no clue in the morning paper, in retrospect its date might be a dead giveaway: November 22, 1963.

By early that afternoon, the businessman learned that the banshee had been crying for one of his good friends, another Irishman from Boston—President John F. Kennedy.

DOG DAYS

THERE ARE VARIATIONS TO THE BANSHEE STORY. The one we just looked at shows that the traditional Celtic banshee is alive and well and wailing in New England. In this next tale, however, we'll meet the same ominous spirit in another of its many guises.

Again, we visit the banshee-haunted state of Massachusetts and go back to June 8, 1975, when Erik and Garet Hart were playing in their grandparents' yard in South Lawrence.

For some reason, one of the boys looked up and saw that a big German shepherd was in the yard with them. Neither child had seen it arrive.

Their reflexive fear soon passed when they saw how friendly the animal seemed. It was well-groomed and healthy-looking, yet it had no collar or tags. No doubt its owner would soon whistle it back to its own yard or drive by in a car and pick it up.

Nonetheless, it seemed to feel right at home in the yard. The more the grandparents watched it, the more they realized that they'd never seen it around before. Must be just a stray passing through . . .

The family gave it food and water and everyone expected it would soon be on its way. Instead, the friendly dog seemed to want to stay around and play more games with the boys. No one objected, for the companionable beast didn't appear a bit dangerous.

All afternoon the dog and boys played in the yard. Obviously, the dog was gentle and well-trained. It would leap enthusiastically to fetch sticks, and it readily rolled over, shook hands, and sat on command.

Around five o'clock, Mrs. Hart called her sons, saying it was time to go home. The boys, however, didn't want to leave their newfound friend. They begged their mother to let them take the dog home.

Mrs. Hart was in no market for a pet, and the grandparents didn't want the trouble of keeping a dog. But Mrs. Hart understood how the boys felt and soon relented. In spite of herself, she had grown fond of the animal, too.

Delighted, Garet and Erik kissed their grandparents good-bye and raced down the driveway to the car. One of them opened the back door to welcome their new pet.

The dog eagerly followed them until it came to the edge of the property. There it stopped. It wouldn't budge from the spot. Though it had been completely obedient all afternoon, now it would not proceed beyond a certain point in the driveway. Pushing and pulling did no good; it would not even permit itself to be carried. No matter how they coaxed the animal, it would not proceed.

In her account of the incident, Mrs. Hart said it was "almost as if a wall prevented him from moving farther."

Finally, they gave up. By way of consolation, the grandparents, Ernest and Louise, agreed that the dog could stay with them. That way, the boys could come back the next day and play with it some more. Secretly, however, none of the adults really expected the animal would stay around.

But when Mrs. Hart and her sons returned the next day, the animal was still there. In that short time, grandfather had become quite fond of the dog. It seemed to love him, too; it never moved far from his side.

Mrs. Hart wrote, "My father chatted about the dog as if he had owned him all his life."

When the dog saw the boys, it eagerly played with them just as it had the day before—only it would never move beyond that invisible property line.

Now, everyone seemed happy with the arrangement. Grandfather truly wanted to keep the dog, so the boys knew they could come and play with it any time they wanted.

Mrs. Hart brought her sons to play with the new family pet twice more before disaster struck. Grandfather suffered a heart attack and was rushed to the hospital. Over the next few days the dog remained at the house. Grandmother seemed comforted by its presence and the boys loved to play with it and care for it.

On the fourth day, the dog began to moan and cry. Mrs. Hart checked him for injuries, but he was perfectly all right, just unaccountably distressed. "He just lay there making what quickly became an unnerving sound," Mrs. Hart remembered.

Grandmother said the dog's sadness was an omen.

But omen of what? Grandfather's progress was good. He was recovering. The doctor said he'd be home in a couple of weeks.

Then, on Father's Day, Grandfather took an unexpected turn for the worse. Another heart attack removed any hope of recovery. Before nightfall he had passed away.

Back home, the dog howled mournfully and could not be comforted. It would not eat or drink. It would hardly move from its place beside Grandfather's empty chair.

On the morning of the funeral, the boys left fresh food and water for the dog. When they returned home after the service, the food was untouched and the dog was gone.

Mrs. Hart and her sons searched the neighborhood and talked to everyone, hoping somebody might have seen the animal leave. A dog that size just couldn't vanish without being seen.

Grandmother shook her head saying, "You won't find him."

"Why not?" Mrs. Hart asked. "He's a big dog. Someone must have seen him."

"No," Grandmother said, "you don't understand. He was a banshee."

She went on to explain all about spirit visitations and supernatural warnings of impending death. She could even recall how her own grandmother claimed to have heard the banshee back in Ireland.

Of the lost dog, she said, "You heard its wail. It knew your father was passing before we did—and it's gone now. Its mission is done. No one saw it come. No one saw it leave. You won't find it."

It seemed as if Grandmother was right. Although Erik, Garet, and Mrs. Hart continued to search, they—and no one in that neighborhood—ever saw the dog again.

But soon after, I suspect, somewhere, and maybe not in New England, a big, dark, friendly-looking German shepherd appeared suddenly in somebody else's back yard . . .

MORE TAILS

THERE ARE MANY MORE STORIES ABOUT DOGS AND DEATH. The almost alien topography of the volcanic hills around Meriden, Connecticut, offers a veritable smorgasbord of odd legends and stories. It is a craggy landscape, full of deep gorges, strange outcroppings, dark forests, and clear, beautiful waters—a perfect setting for tales of the paranormal.

West Peak, the most western of the three Hanging Hills, is attractive to picnickers, campers, and geologists, but also to an array of supernatural creatures.

One of them, a tiny black dog of indeterminate pedigree, displays an unsettling balance of amiability and menace. Over the years, a number of deaths have come to be associated with this little animal; at the same time, he is said to be responsible for a certain amount of good fortune as well.

In fact, sightings of the Black Dog of West Peak have given birth to a saying which circumstance has repeatedly proven to be true: If you meet the Black Dog once, it shall be for joy; if twice, it shall be for sorrow; and the third time shall bring death.

Those who have seen it once or twice describe it as small, short-haired, sad-eyed, and looking vaguely like a spaniel. It is always described as dark colored, but most frequently it's said to be black. It is always friendly and appears delighted to greet its human visitors. In short, there is nothing obviously strange about the animal. However, regardless of when it is seen, winter or summer, it leaves no footprints. And it's silent. Silent as the grave. Even when it throws its head back and appears to howl, no sound escapes from its throat.

Around the turn of the century, W.H.C. Pynchon, a geologist from New York City, came to the Hanging Hills to study the unusual rock formations. He ended up studying the Black Dog as well, and later recorded his findings in the *Connecticut Quarterly*.

It was on a beautiful spring morning when Pynchon set out by horse and buggy along the rough dirt trail that would take him to West Peak. Just beyond Lake Merimere, he stopped to examine an unusual rock formation.

All of a sudden, he saw a little dog standing on top of a boulder nearby. The friendly little fellow just stood there, wagging its tail, tongue hanging out, eagerly awaiting some attention from the human intruder. Although the animal didn't approach him, Pynchon was pleased to see it trot along by the side of his buggy when he continued on his way.

The little dog stuck with him the whole distance up West Peak and down into Southington, where the geologist had lunch. When he left the restaurant, Pynchon was happy to see the little dog waiting beside the buggy, wagging its tail.

Again it accompanied the scientist as he retraced his route, stopping now and then to examine another rock formation. When he stopped, the dog stopped. When he continued, the dog trotted along at his side.

About nightfall, Pynchon passed the spot where he and the dog had originally joined company. Shortly thereafter, he looked around and realized his companion was gone. He whistled and called, but the little animal did not reappear.

Several years passed before W.H.C. Pynchon returned to Meriden, Connecticut. This time he brought a good friend, a fellow geologist who had visited the area before. Both men were fond of the unusual landscape and eager to rediscover the fascinating geologic formations in the Hanging Hills.

In conversation, Pynchon recalled his diminutive companion from the earlier visit—the little black dog. His new companion seemed surprised. He told of how he, too, had seen what sounded like the same friendly little animal on two prior occasions.

Both men hoped they might see the sad-eyed little animal again this time.

It was a bright, cold, February morning when the two geologists began their journey up West Peak. In their buggy, during the first part of their trip, they watched for the dog. Both were somewhat disappointed when it did not appear.

After securing the horse, they continued on foot, commencing the rugged climb up the steep cliffs toward the summit of West Peak. Surrounded by dark volcanic pinnacles, and concentrating on each careful step, they had now forgotten all about the little black dog.

That's why they were so surprised when they looked toward the summit and saw the little dog waiting above, his dark form interposed between the climbers and the sky. Wagging his tail vigorously, he raised his head and seemed to bark a hello—but the men heard nothing. Perhaps too eager to greet their little friend, the men picked up their pace for the final ascent.

A sudden gasp issued from Pynchon's companion. A flurry of activity—waving arms and peddling feet—caught Pynchon's eye, and his friend tried unsuccessfully to recover his footing on a slippery rock.

Pynchon grabbed for him but it was too late. All he could do was watch as the other man slid down the steep slope, screaming for help. For a moment he was airborne, then he smashed against the rocks below.

It was the third time Pynchon's friend had seen the dog. It was the second time for Pynchon.

Perhaps if Pynchon had truly believed the legend of the Black Dog of West Peak, he would never have returned to the Hanging Hills of Connecticut. If he had just trusted his own account of the black dog sightings, he might have stayed away forever. But the lure of the landscape in this mysterious area proved fatally attractive to the geologist.

He came back alone a few years later. His plan was to retrace the same route he had climbed with his friend. But W.H.C. Pynchon was not to write the last chapter of the story. Almost in the same place his friend had plunged to his death, Pynchon slipped and fell and died.

Recording the story today, there is one detail I cannot legitimately include. I'd like to say that the geologist saw the little dog again, for the third time, before he took his fatal fall. But of course, there's no way I can know that for sure.

A GRIM FAIRY TALE?

BEFORE WRAPPING-UP THIS SECTION, I must include one last denizen of darkness and death.

Of all the strange visitors we've encountered so far, this one—at least to me—seems by far the most incredible. Maybe that's because I have always dismissed it as allegorical rather than literal. However, according to research done by Mark Chorvinski, there are frequent historic and contemporary sightings of this specter, and many of them occur in New England.

Like most people, I have always associated this black-clad creature with death, much like the banshee. Apparently, that is not always so.

But if it doesn't materialize to forewarn of doom, then what is it doing here? And if it is not what we think it is, then just what is it?

Have a look and see what you think.

Around 1970, when Diana Deans of Orland, Maine, was about 10 years old, she invited her best friend for a sleep-over. It was nighttime, but Diana remembers a beautiful full moon that lit everything outside with a kind of silvery light.

After a few hours of good-natured interaction, the two girls bedded down in the living room and—after much giggling and talking—eventually fell asleep.

For some reason, they both woke up at the same time.

Looking around for the cause, Diana chanced to glance out the living room window. Scanning the darkened yard and the road beyond, she suddenly perceived motion. Looking harder now, she saw a solitary figure, moving up the road toward the house.

But there was something odd about it. Something was not as it should be.

Diana continued to observe the figure, trying to determine what was strange about the sight.

The form of the creature, for all intents and purposes, appeared to be human. But the dress was eccentric. It wore a long black cape with a hood that fully covered its head. The person might have been perceived as some sort of medieval monk, except for one thing . . .

Whatever it was, was not walking. It was gliding along, weightlessly, moving horizontally a few inches above the road. There was no motion of moving limbs beneath the dark fabric.

Diana saw all this clearly in the light of the full moon. Doubting the testimony of her own eyes, Diana called her friend to have a look.

Her friend saw it, too. Both girls stared with mounting fear as the dark-robed figure continued up the road . . .

And turned into their driveway.

Now it was coming directly toward the house.

The girls moved quickly into the kitchen so they could get a better view from the window there. Even though they'd changed location, the thing had not. It was still out there, advancing toward the house.

Terribly frightened now, the girls ducked down below the kitchen windowsill. Frozen, frightened, they cowered there for what seemed a long time.

Eventually, a terrible tension forced them to stand up to see if the thing had gone.

What they saw frightens Diana to this day.

Now the figure was close enough for Diana to see its head. The dark hood was clearly visible. But inside, exactly where the face should be, there was nothing but total blackness. No face. No eyes. Nothing but the dark interior of the hood.

The girls ran back into the living room and hid under the blankets for a long time. When they dared to take another peek, the thing had gone.

Later, they told their parents about the odd midnight visitor. Not surprisingly, their parents accused them of having experienced a shared hallucination.

So what had they seen?

In 1991, Diana Deans told Mark Chorvinsky, "I didn't find out until years later what the grim reaper was. The thing we saw looked like [the grim reaper] without the scythe . . ."

What we have here is a classic gothic image: the hooded, faceless monk—the image of Death personified. This horrific apparition has been reported thousands of times, worldwide. It is probably fixed in each of our memories, assimilated from movies, comic books, Halloween cards, and a thousand other sources. But sometimes it seems to wander out of our "collective unconscious" and into the three-dimensional reality of New England.

Just what was it doing there? What was its interest in Ms. Deans's house? And what caused it to vanish, apparently without having accomplished anything? I find it noteworthy that the girls seemed to be fully awake when they saw the thing. They moved from room to room, changing the angle of perception, and the image didn't vanish.

While it is easy to dismiss such an experience as the by-product of sleep, in this case the girls were not only awake, but up and moving around. As another witness to a strange apparition once told me, seeing the thing "got our adrenaline going."

The argument is that one cannot have such an experience without becoming fully alert.

I once interviewed a woman in her twenties who saw the "reaper." As of this writing, she hasn't decided whether she wants to go on record with her name, but her story is certainly worth recording.

She was driving north on Vermont Route 22A, not far from the New York border. It was nighttime, around ten o'clock, but the visibility was good. She doesn't recall the fullness of the moon.

Anyway, somewhere above Shoreham her headlights swept past a solitary figure walking along on the right side of the road. She could see only its back, but it looked human. For some reason, she had the impression it was an elderly person, dressed in a long black robe, with a hood covering its head. Because it was late fall and cold outside, the hood didn't strike the driver as especially out of place.

As she drove past the figure she glanced to the right, curious about who might be out alone on a deserted road at that time of night.

Now she admits this next bit happened very quickly: when she got a look at the roadside form—which she had determined was definitely a person—she couldn't see any face within the enclosure of the hood. It looked empty. Though the material maintained the shape of a head, no head was visible.

She says that when the strangeness of the sight registered, fear surged. She pressed the gas pedal a little harder, racing forward a hundred yards or so. Then she looked back, expecting to see the solitary figure fading off far into the distance.

Instead, it was still in the same place in relation to the car, as if she had just barely passed it.

And she still could see no flesh within the folds of the dark material.

With that, she stomped on the gas pedal again and sped off. She didn't dare look back until she reached the relative safety of downtown Vergennes.

Obviously troubled as she related the details of her curious encounter, she kept trying to push explanations at me, as if attempting to shoehorn a natural cause into a supernatural event. "Maybe it was a black person," she said. "Maybe he was just so dark I couldn't see his face."

But she hadn't seen his hands, either. Just an apparently empty robe in the shape of a man. And regardless of race, for the individual to have kept pace with the car, he, she, or it must have been ambling along at a pretty good clip, maybe 40 or 50 miles per hour.

The Mysterious Men *in* Black

CERTAIN MYSTERIOUS VISITORS TO NEW ENGLAND SEEM TO DRESS UP FOR THE occasion. Wearing dark suits with broad-brimmed black hats, black ties, and shoes polished to an ebony sheen, they usually come in threes, arriving in big, black, American cars—usually Cadillacs.

Of course, we wonder who—or what—these visitors are, but perhaps the bigger question is: Where do they come from?

Wherever they originate, their initial point of entry into New England seems to have been Bridgeport, Connecticut. But similar enigmatic black-clad intruders have been visiting humankind for centuries. Often associated with the Devil, demons, vampires, dark-robed faceless phantoms, or evil in general, these terrifying tourists from beyond may show up unexpectedly, bearing warnings or threats powerful enough to have reduced more than one New Englander to demoralized silence.

What secrets are these menacing missionaries trying to protect?

In the early 1950s, a Bridgeport, Connecticut, man's unsettling encounter brought the mysterious Men in Black out of the Middle Ages and into mid-twentieth-century New England.

THE MAN WHO KNEW TOO MUCH

IN 1947, A WEST COAST PILOT NAMED KENNETH ARNOLD captured the world's attention when he spotted several flying disks over Mt. Rainier in Washington State. On the East Coast, Albert K. Bender, a factory clerk in Bridgeport, read about Arnold's adventure and became fascinated with this new phenomenon of UFOs.

He began to study the subject, conducted his own investigations, and eventually founded a research organization called the International Flying Saucer Bureau. With Bender as editor, the organization's newsletter, *Space Review*, was mailed to a growing number of subscribers.

In those days, UFO study was in its infancy. Most believers assumed the saucers were spaceships carrying visitors—or maybe enemies—from faraway planets. It was just a matter of time, people believed, until we'd know exactly what these visitors wanted and why they were coming here in such vast numbers.

So subscribers to *Space Review* were understandably surprised when Bender announced in the September 1953 edition that his research had led to the solution of flying-saucer mystery. "I went into the fantastic," Bender said, "and came up with the answer. . . . I know what the saucers are."

No doubt, disappointment followed surprise at Bender's second announcement. He wrote, "STATEMENT OF IMPORTANCE: The mystery of the flying saucers is no longer a mystery. The source is already known, but any information about this is being withheld by orders from a higher source. We would like to print the full story in *Space Review*, but because of the nature of the information we are very sorry that we have been advised in the negative."

More ominous was his accompanying warning that anyone engaged in flying-saucer research should be "very cautious."

Immediately following these puzzling proclamations, Bender stopped publishing his newsletter and dissolved the International Flying Saucer Bureau.

What had happened? Had this inquisitive Connecticut man actually discovered the secret of the flying disks? And if so, why wasn't he sharing it?

Some of Bender's acquaintances assumed he had simply run out of money but didn't want to admit to anything as unglamorous as bankruptcy.

But closer associates noticed that Albert was suddenly acting strangely. It was as if he were hypnotized, or lobotomized, or something. He suffered recurring headaches that would disable him whenever he tried to talk about UFO secrecy. No, Albert's friends knew there was a lot more to all this than an unsuccessful business venture.

Sure enough, about a month later Bender stated in a newspaper interview that he had been instructed to stop publishing *Space Review* by "three men in dark suits."

Prior to the publication of his last newsletter, he had mailed a letter to a friend. In it he spelled out his revelations about UFOs and asked for feedback. Instead of a response from his friend, three Men in Black showed up and returned Bender's unopened letter.

But this was no ordinary visit. It began as he was lying on his bed resting. Then, he writes, he became aware of "three shadowy figures in the room. The figures became clearer. All of them were dressed in black clothes. They looked like clergymen, but wore hats similar to Homburg style. The faces were not clearly discernible, for the hats partly hid and shaded them." Then the visitors proceeded with their cease-and-desist warning. Apparently, they were so intimidating that Bender actually feared for his life.

Exactly what did they say? And who sent them?

Though Bender never identified the "higher source," many people guessed it was some branch of the American military. Then, as now, a fair number of people—including many ex-servicemen—came to believe the government is involved in some sort of cover-up to keep the truth about UFOs away from the population at large. That their dark-suited agents would be dispatched to "silence" someone who knew the truth is no real stretch of the imagination.

Bender strengthened this "government intervention" idea in an interview with researcher Gray Barker. Barker asked him why he could not talk freely. According to Bender, one of the Men in Black told him, "I suppose you know you're on your honor as an American. If I hear another word out of your office you're in trouble."

"What will they do with you if you give out information?" Barker asked.

"Put me in jail and keep me shut up." Bender had done the only sensible thing; he got out of the UFO investigation business. But those who knew him were certain there was still more he wasn't telling.

This episode seems to be the first modern example of intervention by the seemingly sinister Men in Black. If we are to believe Mr. Bender, then a couple of things can *almost* be accepted as fact: First, that Bender knew something he wasn't permitted to share; and second, that there actually is something to know. To this day, we have no idea what that mysterious *something* is.

The whole Albert K. Bender incident might have been dismissed and forgotten if the mysterious Men in Black, or MIBs as they were soon to be called, hadn't started appearing to other people.

In time, what might have been agents of some military group—or a more covert CIA- or FBI-type organization—were perceived in a different way. They began taking on the air of mystical, maybe even supernatural, emissaries of some truly "alien" power.

In 1963, after a decade of silence, Bender finally wrote a book about his experience, but his disclosures were so outlandish that no prospective editor could accept them as factual. Consequently, no American publisher would take on *Flying Saucers and the Three Men*. Yet true or false, Bender's revelations were certainly indicative of the paranoia that would follow the Men in Black wherever they went.

When another UFO investigator Maurice K. Jessup committed suicide in 1958, some said he had failed to heed the "warning of the dark trio." This increased everyone's fear and elevated MIB status to folklore and modern myth.

Over time, a composite picture of these puzzling phantoms began to emerge. Generally, they appear following a UFO sighting. They arrive three at a time with the apparent intent of harassing, confusing, and intimidating the witness. Often they show up so promptly that it is impossible to determine how they could have heard about the event to which they're responding. Yet they possess names, addresses, and details about all those concerned.

Typically, witnesses say MIBs arrive in older-model cars that look brand-new. They wear official-looking black suits. While sunglasses hide their eyes, their dark skin is more difficult to conceal. They're said to look "Oriental," "Italian," or "like Gypsies."

When MIBs speak, it's in halting, yet carefully enunciated tones. They'll explain they work for some branch of the government and they'll flash official-looking badges to prove it.

In those rare cases when witnesses have the presence of mind to verify the IDs or to check the license plates on the cars, the names will be phony and the plates never issued.

Occasionally, their behavior is conspicuously odd, as evidenced in the story of how one puzzled over a ballpoint pen, and how another tried to drink Jell-O. Often they behave as if there is something medically wrong with them. They make abrupt exits, unexpectedly ask for water, take odd-looking pills, or appear to lose strength. They might walk with strange, mechanical gaits, or with peculiar caution, as if they are slightly off balance.

The mysterious strangers give the impression of coming out of nowhere, vanishing to the same place, often leaving the shaken witnesses feeling unaccountably nauseated, weak, or physically ill. Some individuals report needing psychotherapy for insomnia, eating disorders, or depression following an MIB encounter.

It certainly *appears* as if the macabre messengers' sole purpose is to silence people with important UFO-related secrets, but that is not so. The MIBs will just as readily harass individuals who are merely curious about the UFO question. For example, in 1969, an anonymous but seemingly sensible Massachusetts man started investigating cases of UFOs in his locale. Shortly, he was seeing black-clad characters almost everywhere. Big black cars waited in front of his house, apparently spying on him. At first, he tried to record evidence of these odd intruders, but soon his fear built until his symptoms resembled paranoia, then schizophrenia. A psychiatrist sent to examine the young man found him sitting with a loaded gun, "waiting for the Men in Black."

Observing this mental metamorphosis, one wonders if a diseased mind is required to perceive the inexplicable, or if a confrontation with the unknown sometimes results in mental collapse. It's a chicken or egg issue, but personally, I'd side with the chickens.

THE MAINE EVENT

ANOTHER OF THE MOST PUZZLING CONFRONTATIONS on record also occurred in New England. In this case, the character of the witness implies that insanity is not a prerequisite for dialogue with the Men in Black.

The date: September 11, 1976.

The place: Old Orchard Beach, Maine.

A 58-year-old medical doctor named Herbert Hopkins was acting as a consultant on a case of alleged UFO abduction. His practice was to use hypnosis to help the patient reconstruct the repressed events, and to tape record their dialogue during the sessions.

That evening, when he was at home alone, Dr. Hopkins received a phone call from the vice-president of the New Jersey UFO Research Organization, who said he was in the area. He told Dr. Hopkins that he'd heard about the abduction case and wondered if he might visit Dr. Hopkins to discuss it. Dr. Hopkins readily agreed.

Immediately after they hung up, Dr. Hopkins walked to the front door to switch on the porch light. The man was already climbing up the steps.

After Hopkins let his visitor in, he noticed how the man was dressed: a black suit with black socks, black shoes, black tie, and a white shirt. The clothing looked brand-new, and not at all wrinkled. The pants were sharply creased.

Upon entering, the man politely removed his black hat, revealing not only that he was totally bald, but also, Dr. Hopkins observed, completely hairless—no eyebrows or eyelashes.

The man's skin was deathly pale. His lips, by contrast, were brilliant red.

During the course of their conversation, the stranger never removed his gloves, but at one point he happened to brush a glove against his mouth. To Dr. Hopkins amazement, the man's lips smeared and the glove was stained with lipstick. In retrospect, Dr. Hopkins admits how strange it is that he didn't feel there was anything particularly unusual about the meeting while it was happening.

But things soon got impossibly stranger.

The man seemed to know everything about the UFO case, although very little information had been released. No matter what Dr. Hopkins told him, the man would nod and say, "Yes, that's the way I understand it."

During their discussion, the man paused and made the incongruous observation that Dr. Hopkins had two coins in his pocket.

Yes, said the doctor, that is true.

The man asked Dr. Hopkins to take one of the coins in his hand and to stare at it. At this point the doctor was starting to sense the escalating weirdness, but he went along with this seemingly harmless request, expecting, perhaps, an ill-timed parlor trick or something of the kind.

As Dr. Hopkins stared at the coin, it seemed to go out of focus, then it seemed to change color, and gradually it vanished entirely.

The stranger then ominously stated, "Neither you nor anyone else on this plane will ever see that coin again."

Eventually, the conversation got around to Betty and Barney Hill, the Portsmouth, New Hampshire, couple who were supposedly abducted by aliens in the White Mountains back in 1961. The man asked Dr. Hopkins if he knew what had happened to the Hills.

He wasn't sure about Betty, Dr. Hopkins told him, but he knew Barney had died.

"Yes," said the man, "that's the way I understand it. And do you know what he died from?"

Hopkins wasn't sure; he thought it was from a heart attack.

"That's not entirely the case," the man replied. "He died because he knew too much."

As the conversation continued, Dr. Hopkins observed that the stranger's speech was slowing down. Soon the visitor sluggishly stood up, saying, "My energy is running low. Must go now. Good-bye." And so saying, he crossed to the door and left, walking somewhat unsteadily.

Then Dr. Hopkins saw an abnormally bright, bluish light outside in the driveway. He figured it was the stranger's headlights and thought no more about it.

Alone again, Dr. Hopkins finally began to realize just how weird the whole experience was. The more he thought about it, the more terrified he became. Clearly, he had been threatened. When his wife and children finally got home, they found Dr. Hopkins in a locked house with all the lights burning brightly. He was terribly shaken, seated at the kitchen table with a gun beside him.

Ultimately, he complied with the two requests his unearthly visitor had made: he erased the tapes of the abductee's hypnosis sessions, and he withdrew his involvement with the UFO abduction case.

The next morning, someone noticed marks on the driveway. At first, the doctor thought they had been made by the visitor's car, but later realized that was unlikely: the marks were right in the center of the one-lane drive. By the next day, the marks were gone entirely.

Hopkins never saw his strange visitor again, and when he tried to contact the New Jersey UFO Research Organization, he found that it had never existed.

The list of questions posed by this odd encounter is too long to enumerate here. Among them, of course, would be the following:

Was Dr. Hopkins the victim of a tasteless joke or elaborate hoax? And if so, who was the trickster?

Just where had the strange man come from? All we know for sure is that he was not from the New Jersey UFO Research Organization.

And what caused the coin to vanish? Had the hypnotist himself been the victim of hypnosis?

Then again, was the whole episode a hoax perpetrated by Dr. Hopkins? If so, why would a respected professional invent such a bizarre tale? His only reward, one would think, would be the loss of respect.

Or was the deception perpetrated by some earthly—or perhaps unearthly—organization, the motive for which is impossible to guess?

WRAP-UP

THE MEN IN BLACK, or their ancestors, have been up to these seemingly pointless tricks for a good long while. Though they make threats, it has never been shown that they act on them. Their purpose seems to be to frighten and, by doing so, to influence human behavior toward some unknowable end.

Researcher John A. Keel has chronicled many cases of human contact with MIBs. He argues that they have worked their old black magic on such historical dignitaries as Julius Caesar, Thomas Jefferson, Napoleon Bonaparte, and even Malcolm X.

In his book *Operation Trojan Horse*, Keel quotes Malcolm X's description of such a contact while he was imprisoned, supposedly alone, in a locked jail cell: "As I lay on my bed, I suddenly became aware of a man sitting beside me in my chair. He had on a dark suit, I remember. I could see him as plainly as anyone I look at. He wasn't black, and he wasn't white. He was light-brown-skinned, an Asiatic cast of countenance, and he had oily black hair. . . . He just sat there. Then, as suddenly as he had come, he was gone."

And, after extensive research, Keel's conclusion about MIBs is implicit in his repetition of Albert K. Bender's warning: "[Parents,] schoolteachers and other adults should not encourage teenagers to take an interest in the subject [of UFOs]."

Although most meetings with MIBs result from some level of UFO involvement, they've been reported following other bizarre phenomena like water-monster sightings and various types of creature confrontations.

Humankind has long associated black with evil, so if someone, or something, were trying to scare us, the choice of costume color would be easy. The appearance of Men in Black is clearly related to descriptions of the Christian devil, witches, vampires, and the lesser-known "Brothers of the Shadow," who try to prevent eastern occultists from discovering the great truth.

In conclusion, we must say the great truth about MIBs is as elusive as the MIBs themselves.

A SOLUTION AT LAST?

ALTHOUGH THE ADVENTURE OF ALBERT K. BENDER is only a small smudge on this black picture, it is where this chapter began and it is the event that launched a modern cycle of MIB mysteries.

Today, after nearly half a century, at least the Bender portion of the MIB mystery may have been solved.

Though some might still be tempted to dismiss Bender as a crackpot and his story as a hoax, that may not be the case, according to researcher Michael D. Swords. In a recent article in the *International UFO Reporter*, Swords points out an interesting correlation between two seemingly unrelated events.

First, in August 1953, Joseph Barbieri witnessed a small fiery object plunge out of the skies above New Haven, Connecticut. He watched it crash through a 20-gauge steel billboard, leaving a 12-inch hole. It then changed course, soared through some treetops, and vanished into the wild blue yonder.

Meteors don't do that. They fall. Period.

So obviously this was something other than a meteor.

Upon examining the perforated billboard, an investigator saw and removed metallic pieces of the object. These particles were analyzed and found to be almost pure copper.

Interestingly enough, this Johnny-on-the-spot was not a policeman or military officer—he was one of Bender's men, August Roberts. Roberts delivered the fragments to Bender at the International Flying Saucer Bureau, and then Bender sent them away for analysis.

The second event occurred during the next month, September. That's when Bender backed out of the UFO business forever, following his confrontation with the Dark Trio.

Swords put the two events together and came up with the following scenario:

It is fact that in January of 1953 the CIA pulled a bunch of scientists together to discuss all available Air Force data about UFOs. The head scientist, H.P. Robertson, recommended that all sightings be debunked in an effort to discourage public interest. He also recommended that civilian UFO groups should be watched.

Whether Bender's IFSB was "watched" is a matter of conjecture, but, as Swords points out, they were involved in a very ambitious project to track and plot UFO routes around the globe, hoping to determine their point, or points, of origin. That effort alone, according to Swords, would be enough to provoke CIA interest.

That, coupled with beating the military to the meteor fragments, might have been enough to provoke CIA anger. After all, something powerful enough to blast a hole in a steel sign, bounce off the treetops, and continue on a low-level trajectory out of sight "sounds," Swords says, "suspiciously missilelike to me."

And missiles—domestic, foreign, or intergalactic—should be the province of the government, not some group of civilian hobbyists.

Swords concludes, "I suspect that the Bender affair was an intelligence game or experiment to see how effectively operatives could manipulate the fledgling UFO 'research' community."

Apparently, the three men told Albert something so menacing or scary that he would never speak out about UFOs again. To this day, Bender, now living in California, has held his silence.

And by so doing, perhaps gave birth to a modern myth.

Prosaic or preternatural? That, of course, is the big question. And, in the final analysis, perhaps it doesn't really matter.

A Vermont woman's experience seems to be a metaphor for the whole MIB phenomenon: She had been pestered by occasional MIB visits after a UFO sighting in the northern part of the state. When she thought she recognized one of the MIBs on a street in downtown Burlington, she decided to follow him. She told me she watched him walk into an alley. Although she never lost sight of the entrance, when she got close enough to see the alley's interior, she realized it was dead-ended. And empty. The man had apparently vanished.

When *the* Devil Came *to* Provincetown

To misquote Albert K. Bender, "We've gone into the fantastic. . . ."

But have we come back with an answer?

Probably not. But before we escape the mysterious land of Men in Black altogether, let's take a little detour to one of New England's more popular vacation spots, Provincetown, Massachusetts. There, in 1938, the puzzled citizens played host to a black-clad phantom who seemed to combine the most sinister qualities of the MIBs with the superhuman capabilities of a comic-book hero. In fact, someone dubbed him with a name worthy of such a hero; they called him "The Black Flash."

He, she, or it seemed to come out of nowhere, worked its pranks, then magically eluded all serious attempts at capture. But I'm getting ahead of myself . . .

To many, Provincetown—located way out on the nail of Cape Cod's beckoning finger—may seem like part of a surreal world during the height of the tourist season. But back in 1938, the busy season was a little less busy, and during the off-season the area couldn't have felt much more desolate and remote.

In any region as isolated as this, stories accumulate. And storytellers who entertain and challenge their listeners do a lot to ease the passing of long winter months. Local yarn-spinners are a venerable part of the New England heritage. They tell of ghost ships, haunted houses, and strange beasts that come from the sea. But there was nothing in the folk tradition or history of the area to prepare the population for the arrival of Provincetown's "Phantom Fiend." And everyone who saw him described him the same way: he was gigantic, swift, and ugly. But perhaps most relevant here is that he was always dressed in black: his clothing, the hood covering his head, and the long cape that flapped like hideous bat wings as he sprinted across the sand dunes or vaulted impossibly over 8- and 10-foot barriers.

Starting around Halloween of 1938, people began talking about the phantom. Mostly, the tales originated with children who had briefly spotted something black and reptilian far off among the dunes or peering at them from behind trees or big rocks. The children were frightened, but their parents tended to toss it off, saying it was just some Halloween prankster or eccentric summer tourist who'd stayed around after the season ended. It was easy to dismiss what the children said about pointy ears and glowing silver eyes. After all, children do imagine things, don't they?

By the second week of November, townspeople were forced to reevaluate all the assurances they'd given their children. That's when Maria Costa had a run-in with the phantom right in the middle of town. She was on Commercial Street, near the Town Hall. As she prepared to cross the road toward the coffee shop, something caught her eye. Sure enough, some large creature was moving about in the shadows outside a closed-up shop. Maria stared, but the thing didn't vanish into the gloom. Instead, it jumped right at her as if it were on springs, spreading its cape like vast black wings.

Maria froze, too startled to scream. The dark, menacing presence loomed over her like a giant. If she had been able to move, she could have reached out and touched it.

Then it was gone.

Later, Maria told the police, "He was black, all black with eyes like balls of flame. And he was big . . . maybe 8 feet tall." And, most unsettling of all, he made sort of a buzzing sound, like a monstrous insect.

Over the next few weeks, more and more people saw the phantom. His favorite tricks were to leap at someone from behind a tree or to drop down into somebody's path from a rooftop or tree limb. In one case, a local man chased the creature but was quickly outdistanced by the phantom's seemingly superhuman swiftness. Reluctantly, the Provincetown police allowed as maybe—just *maybe*—there was something to this phantom business after all. Still, whatever it was hadn't broken any laws, nor had it harmed property or people.

But the next year, all that was to change.

First, it added a dramatic new trick to its repertoire.

A terrified teenage boy burst into the police station, his pale face slick with tears. He'd been on his way home from the library when the phantom met him head on. "It jumped out at me from nowhere," he said, "and spit blue flames into my face."

On another occasion, Charles Farley's dog cornered the phantom in the yard. Farley went out, shotgun in hand, to experience the craziest confrontation of his life. He saw a tall black monster with what looked like long silver ears. "I thought it was some kind of wild animal," Farley said, "so I shot it."

But it didn't react like any wild animal; the thing just laughed and vaulted over the 8-foot fence and out of Farley's yard.

What sort of creature laughs when attacked with a shotgun?

At this point, the Provincetown police chief knew he had a real mystery on his hands.

Many people were convinced they had something supernatural loose in their community, a gigantic black monster with glowing eyes that defied gravity, breathed fire, mocked gunfire, and seemed to be able to vanish at will. And whatever it was could be in two places at once; sometimes people reported sightings on both sides of town just moments apart.

Meanwhile, the police and other no-nonsense types were putting together a list of human suspects. But there were few tall, athletic high-jumpers with a penchant for practical jokes.

The phantom returned year after year, making his occasional nighttime attacks on the wary townspeople. No one was ever apprehended. And the few prime suspects were cleared when World War II started. All those under suspicion went off to fight; the phantom stayed in Provincetown.

In the early forties, a local fisherman named George Loboas had his run-in with the phantom on the town common. Loboas was known for his great strength and his willingness to use it, so he wasn't too frightened when the black shape leapt out at him. Reflexing into a defensive posture, George struck out at the thing. The phantom grabbed George's fist and squeezed so hard it brought the fisherman to his knees. All the while its preternatural laughter resounded like thunder.

Fear gripped the whole community in its icy claw. The police were baffled and the citizens of Provincetown felt like prisoners in their own homes.

A colorful local pool shark called "Eightball Charlie" refused to stay off the streets. He often boasted that he'd like nothing better than to meet the phantom some night.

And that's just exactly what happened.

It was a dark fall night with a freezing wind off the ocean. As Charlie walked home, he was ultra-aware of all the motion around him. Long tree limbs swayed in the wind's arctic breath. Bushes rustled and litter skittered along the empty street.

As he was climbing the hill near his home, a shadow moved into the road in front of him. Charlie stopped in his tracks, staring in disbelief at the interloper's size. The phantom spread his cape like a giant vampire bat. Silver glowing eyes stared back at Charlie from the creature's hooded head.

Unwilling to back down from man or monster, Charlie cried out, "You better get out of my way or I'll smack you one."

It was then that the thing attacked. It rushed Charlie before he could react and slapped him in the face so hard it knocked him down. Somehow, he got to his feet and ran home, the terrifying black shadow close at his heels.

The Provincetown Phantom showed no favoritism among the people it chose to terrify. It would as readily jump out at women and children as it would the village's brawny young men and respectable elders. Although physical contact was rare, the phantom seemed to take great delight from in-your-face confrontations and the victim's inevitable hysteria.

Then, on a chilly November evening in 1945, the phone rang at police head-quarters. It was the first of several rapid-fire phone calls reporting the phantom skulking through the Bradford School's fenced-in yard.

Sgt. Francis Marshall headed out fast, thinking this might be the first real break in the case—he knew the schoolyard had a 10-foot fence all the way around it. And there was only one way in or out. If he hurried, Marshall would be able to trap the Phantom.

With their headlights off and their sirens silent, two cruisers pulled up to the entrance of the schoolyard. One officer stayed outside the fence while three others—flashlights in hands—converged at the entrance. Then they entered, one by one.

"I've got him!" somebody yelled.

And there he was, right in a corner, squeezed into a tightening triangle of fence and four policemen advancing in a line.

At this point Sergeant Marshall got his first and only good look at the phantom. Later, he would say that he was sure the terrifying face was some kind of silver-painted mask. And the creature was big, though perhaps not as big as dozens of terrified witnesses had reported.

Now, as Provincetown's finest closed tighter around him, the phantom held his ground. Hands on hips, he glared back at them. When Sergeant Marshall warned him not to move, the phantom just laughed. In a final demonstration of superhuman bravery and skill, the black-clad figure turned and, with one mighty leap, soared over the 10-foot fence and vanished. Nothing remained but the echo of a scornful laugh fading into the Provincetown night.

There were a few more scattered sightings of the phantom after that, but the ultimate confrontation came on a foggy December afternoon a few weeks later. The four Janard children—Al, Joey, Elanore, and Louie—were playing in the yard of their home on Standish Street. Suddenly, little Elanore announced that a bear was crouching on a sandy hill nearby. Knowing there were no bears on Cape Cod, Al—who had endured a terrifying confrontation with the phantom once before—recognized the strange creature that watched them from the hill. Vaguely visible amid the thick covering of fog, the black figure began crawling downhill, directly at the children.

Since their parents were away, the four young Janards had to face the fiend alone.

They raced into the house and armed themselves with knives, rolling pins, and whatever else they could find. Suddenly, they froze as the doorknob began to turn, its metallic grate seemed to fill the house. Fearing the phantom would be on top of them any second, the children tried to conceal themselves, all the time aware that the door was not locked.

The phantom continued to rattle the doorknob and to make heavy breathing sounds, but for some reason he didn't come in. Louie grabbed a bucket and tiptoed up the stairs. He filled the bucket with hot water from the sink, and sneaked out an upstairs window onto the roof above the front door.

When he was able to see the black figure below, he took aim and dumped the water, then ducked back inside.

His brothers and sister heard the splash and a startled gasp.

And then, the Black Phantom Fiend was gone, retreating, wet, cold, and defeated, into the December night. And—as far as I know—he was never seen again.

So just exactly what was this thing that visited the village of Provincetown? Could it have been some quasi-material visitor from a parallel dimension? An interplanetary traveler, supernatural trickster, or an emissary of the Devil?

To this day, no one can say for sure. Perhaps the phantom was one of a long line of colorful Yankee eccentrics. Or perhaps more likely, an organized cluster of bored villagers who wanted to give their neighbors something to talk about during those long winter months between tourist invasions.

Whatever it may have been, the mysterious stranger is little more than a memory today. But when you stop to think about it, there is a certain irony here. Isn't it strange that the Black Phantom of Provincetown, like the Wicked Witch of the West, was finally defeated by a brave child wielding a bucket of water?

A FLOCKING OF PHANTOMS

I AM INDEBTED TO ROBERT CAHILL, Salem resident, writer, and longtime ghost-chaser, for the wonderful story of the Provincetown Phantom. Though it is a fascinating saga, it is by no means unique.

In some ways, Provincetown's Black Flash seems like a lone surviving member of those weird, frolicsome colonial guerrillas that harassed the residents of Cape Ann in 1692. Like them, he did no one any serious bodily harm.

But the annals of New England strangeness contain a few more of these pesky phantoms. And not all of them are predisposed to kindness.

The grandfather among them might be an apparition that frequented the Newhallville area between New Haven and Hamden, Connecticut. This aggressive specter, called the "Newhallville Ghost," first materialized in the fall of 1881. Shortly, the whole area was overcome with dread.

For the most part, the thing confined its mysterious activities to the area around

Shelton Avenue and Division Street, where it was spotted almost every night. Those who got the best look at it said it was from 8 to 12 feet tall and could easily leap over fences, no matter how high the barrier might be.

A typical confrontation occurred when an attractive young woman, Jennie Burton, and her companion were coming home from a day in New Haven. After getting off the horse-drawn trolley, they headed down Division Street, going to their Dixwell Avenue home.

The "ghost" appeared to them, looking like a man wrapped in a yellow-white material that might have been a dirty tablecloth. The phantom held up its hands and wiggled its fingers as if it were clawing the air. Its hands and face glowed with "phosphoric radiance."

This ghastly sight provoked screams from Jennie's companion, while Jennie passed out and fell to the ground. As passersby came to the women's aid, the Newhallville Ghost did its vanishing act.

The next night, the ghost reappeared on Dixwell Avenue, between Ivy and Brewster Streets. It approached Mrs. Meeker and Mrs. Hindsley, but stopped about 60 feet in front of them. Again, it was dressed in a dirty cloth.

Though universally known as "the Newhallville Ghost," apparently no one thought it was supernatural. Otherwise, they reasoned, why would it have to leap over those 10-foot fences? Why not just pass through them? Some concluded the ghost was a man trying to frighten the people who had treated him badly. Others thought it was a rejected lover seeking revenge on the woman who had rejected him.

In any event, armed expeditions were regularly organized to go out ghost-hunting. They searched for the culprit in fields, woods, vacant buildings, and sheds. But the Newhallville Ghost had done what ghosts do best: it disappeared.

Seven years later, Milford, Connecticut, was plagued by a similar entity. Or maybe the Newhallville Ghost had simply relocated and added a few more tricks to his repertoire. Again, the "spirit" confined its activities to one portion of the town. According to an issue of the *New Haven Evening Register* dated September 21, 1888, ". . . the chap from the supernatural regions has frightened two young women almost to death."

One saw it at a distance and ran home screaming.

The other was not so fortunate.

She was walking to her Broad Street home between eight and nine o'clock at night, when, without any warning whatsoever, she felt something tugging at her clothing. Her first thought was of the ghost. When she looked, that's what it turned out to be!

"The sight was about as overwhelming to the nervous system as any such fearful spectacle could be . . . he was eight feet tall . . . equipped with eyes about as large as tennis balls and red as fire . . . rolling in the sockets. . . ."

Although the hideous apparition was absolutely silent, the woman screamed to high heaven. This triggered another flurry of grappling at her clothing, ripping her skirt and top. Perhaps when her clothing tore, she was able to free herself. She and the ghost fled in different directions.

Armed groups of men took off after the thing, suggesting the good people of Milford suspected this of being a flesh-and-blood phantom. But somehow it managed to vanish in the manner of a real live ghost.

Unfortunately, some of New England's phantom fiends have not been quite this nonviolent. For example, between February 1925 and June 1928, Bridgeport, Connecticut, was held in the grip of terror by a "Phantom Stabber." Generally he did his dirty work in the daytime, but occasional nighttime forays became part of his M.O. He was completely out in the open when he did his damage, striking in the streets, in parks, and public buildings, including a library.

A somewhat theatrical stabbing was staged in a department store in front of hundreds of people. According to the *Herald Tribune*, "The stabber who has terrorized Bridgeport for the last thirty months suddenly appeared this afternoon and claimed his twenty-third victim in a crowded downtown department store. The victim was Isabelle Pelskur, fourteen, 536 Main Street, a messenger girl employed in the D.M. Read store. The girl was stabbed in the store where she was employed.

"The stabbing occurred at 4:50, just two minutes before closing time. . . . Already some of the store's doors had been locked, and a large crowd of shoppers were being ushered from the store. The employees were leaving their counters, and the victim had started up the stairs from the arcade side of the first floor to the women's dressing room.

"The girl had scarcely ascended more than half a dozen steps when she was attacked by the assailant who lunged his sharp blade into her side, causing a severe wound."

He got away without anyone having seen him.

The wounds he inflicted were rarely serious; they seemed designed more to cause general panic than to do any significant harm.

In November of 1930, a more harmful fellow operated in Boston. He used a "noiseless weapon" with which he seriously injured two men and a woman over the course of two weeks. Small-caliber bullets were removed from the wounds.

The sinister nature of these frightening attacks and the scary idea of a noiseless weapon rattled the people of Boston so thoroughly that policemen armed with riot guns lined the roads south of the city. Though they had been ordered to catch the "silent sniper," the attacks continued until February 1931. As usual, no one was caught.

Wild *and* Wily Wanderers

FOR MORE THAN A CENTURY, THE PEOPLE OF WINSTED, CONNECTICUT, have played host to a most unusual tourist. No one knows where he stays, nor can anyone say where he goes when he leaves. But all who have met him will remember him forever.

As far as we know, this mysterious stranger showed up for the first time back in August of 1895, when a local dignitary, Selectman Riley Smith, was heading over to Colebrook on business.

Mr. Smith, accompanied by his faithful bulldog, was in no particular hurry for his meeting. Along the way, he stopped to admire the scenery and occasionally paused to pick berries on the roadside. As he munched contentedly, his dog—normally a brazen little beast—began acting up. It growled, yipped uncertainly, and eventually whined as it dashed back to the safety of its master's side.

Wondering what had spooked his companion, Smith looked around. Immediately, he understood the dog's discomfort.

Something huge was thrashing in the undergrowth. As Smith squinted into the shadows trying to see what it was, a creature crashed out of the bushes. The sight of it left Selectman Smith slack-jawed while his bulldog cowered in terror. For there, standing before them on the road between Winsted and Colebrook, was an oversized manlike monstrosity, better than 6 feet tall, sky-clad, and hairy all over.

Although Selectman Smith was frightened and surprised, his visitor seemed more alarmed. The wild man gave a fearful cry, about-faced, shot back into the woods, and vanished.

Following this incident, Winsted's naked nuisance was frequently spotted in the area. People all over Litchfield County were buzzing with tales of the latest sighting.

Who was this mysterious visitor? He'd never identified himself. Nor had he registered at any local inn or campground. But folks had to call him something. So they dubbed him the "Winsted Wild Man."

His story appeared in the August 21, 1895, edition of the *Winsted Herald.* A larger paper, the *New Haven Evening Register*, reported it too, but dismissed the topic a month later with a sarcastic editorial.

Soon, renewed community contact with the primitive specimen revitalized journalistic interest. In October, the *Register* discussed the Winsted Wild Man in another article, saying, "The humanitarians of the staid old village of Winsted are getting up an expedition for the capture of an alleged wild man, who is roaming the plains in nude condition."

This hunting expedition was to be led by Lucius Merritt, who had seen the wild man once himself. He described it as savage-looking and covered with red bristles. Apparently, none of the townspeople were quick to accompany Merritt into the bush.

Anyway, the reporter, who couldn't quite get his tongue out of his cheek, ended by saying, "On the coldest nights [the wild man] comes from his lair and pursues his avocation of scaring people with quite as much energy as on the balmy evenings of summer."

Despite Lucius Merritt's best efforts, the wild man was nowhere to be found. It is difficult to say whether he dropped out of sight, left the area, or was simply exorcised from the pages of local newspapers.

But wherever he went, residents of Litchfield County had not seen the last of their vexing visitor.

By July 24, 1972, the Winsted Wild Man must have been getting along in years. That's when two teenagers spotted him near Crystal Lake Reservoir. As David Chapman and Wayne Hall chatted at Chapman's home on Winchester Road, the early morning silence was suddenly disturbed by a wicked commotion.

According to Hall's colorful description, "It sounded like a frog and cat mixed together, a really weird sound." He claims it was "like when a frog blows up and makes a lot of noise."

Looking out the window toward the lake, both boys saw exactly the same thing:

a figure about 8 feet tall and covered with hair. They were able to see its limbs and head, but couldn't discern any facial features.

The wild man seemed in no hurry. He lumbered out of the woods, ambled across the road, and, after puttering around some, eventually vanished into the shadows around Albert Durant's barn.

Dave and Wayne watched him going about his business for a good 45 minutes. They gave him the best eyeballing that distance and dim morning light would permit. Both were absolutely sure it was not a bear.

Hall described the strange figure like this: "It was kind of stooped, but more upright. It was hairy. I would say black. It never crouched down; it was always upright. Once in a while it would reach up and scratch its head."

No doubt, it left the boys scratching theirs.

In 1974, the creature shambled out of the woods again.

It was early in the morning of September 27. Winsted Police Officer George Corso was in his cruiser, moving along Main Street, when two terrified men flagged him down.

Breathlessly, the men explained that they, along with their lady friends, had been parking near Rugg Brook Reservoir. As one of the men got out of the car, the creature put in his appearance. It stepped from the woods, saw the automobile, and began walking directly toward it. They estimated it was 6 feet tall, weighed at least 300 pounds, and was covered with dark hair.

The men asked Officer Corso to accompany them back to the reservoir. When he agreed, one man insisted that the police car be securely locked. Corso had no trouble with that; he could see the man was truly terrified. As they passed the site of the earlier confrontation, one of the men cried, "There it is!"

Corso spun the cruiser around to get a better look, but by then there was nothing to see. Later, he returned to the spot, looking for evidence. Unfortunately, there was no trace of the mysterious visitor.

Did Officer Corso believe the men's story?

"They were terrified," he had to admit. Even if the wild man wasn't real, the men's terror was absolutely genuine.

WINHALL'S WOODMAN

So where did the Winsted Wild Man go after he stepped out of the car headlights and vanished? Quite possibly, he emulated another Connecticut Yankee wild man, Ethan Allen, and headed north to the Green Mountains. It looks as if he may have moved from Winsted, Connecticut, to Winhall, Vermont.

The details of this strange story came to me in a letter from a Brattleboro, Vermont, woman, Arlene Tarantino.

In the summer of 1985, Arlene managed an office for a local developer. On her day off, she grabbed a book and headed out into the Winhall woods. At an isolated spot known as Pike's Falls, she found a pleasant place to sit and read. Everything was ideal until she heard something crashing through the bush. Motion caught her eye as a form whipped past. It moved like lightning, violently disturbing the leaves in its path. Finally, whatever it was leapt through the bushes, landing about 15 feet away.

Arlene froze, her sense of reality momentarily short-circuited. For there, standing directly in front of her, was something out of a nightmare.

His body was thin and youthful, with "muscles . . . like ropes wrapped around his skeleton." Yet his face looked old, almost ancient. His "cheeks were . . . wrinkled in a long thin fan of heavy creases." His gray eyes were clear and sharp, but vacant.

Though his straggly body hair seemed abnormally long, it did nothing to conceal that he was completely naked. His gnarled legs, she recalls, were positioned in an apelike crouch, making it difficult to estimate his height. Her best guess is that he was about 5 to 5½ feet tall, weighing, maybe, 120 pounds.

Arlene says he moved like a chimpanzee moves, using all fours, yet he traveled "as fast as you could imagine. . . . If you've ever seen a dog run so fast that it almost falls sideways, this is the speed [he] attained."

Fearing danger, Arlene remained perfectly still. Eventually, she broke eye contact, letting her gaze drop to the book on her lap. Although she doesn't remember what happened next, she feels she may have been immobile, possibly entranced, for as much as 40 minutes. When she finally looked up, the visitor was gone.

As a belated sense of terror mounted, Arlene did the only sensible thing—she got up and ran away.

Today, more than a decade later, the curious encounter still affects her. She's convinced what she saw was a human being—not a bear and not a monster. She suspects he might still be out there, some kind of feral person, a lost soul who doesn't even realize he's human. She has even given him a name: "Woodman."

Although Arlene's initial fear quickly changed to compassion, she was never to see her strange visitor again. And though she has tried, she has never been able to locate any other witnesses.

Nonetheless, encounters of this type are far from rare. And they've been going on for a long, long time.

THE INDIAN DEVIL

IN THE EARLY 1800s, for example, an experienced woodsman named Hugh Watson was working near his camp on the shore of Telos Lake, some 20 miles northwest of Mt. Katahdin in Maine. Gradually, an uncomfortable feeling began to intrude; it was as if he were being watched, maybe even followed. It could be a mountain lion, he thought, maybe even an Indian. The possibility of robbers even crossed his mind.

Since he had long ago learned to trust his wilderness instincts, Watson slowly and quietly headed back toward his camp.

He stopped abruptly when, from a distance, he saw a shadowy group of large men milling around his campsite. Watson jumped into some bushes to hide and wait for the uninvited visitors to leave.

Eventually, they wandered off. Watson hid a while longer before making a cautious return to camp. When he arrived, he saw that his gear had been thrown all over the place. Someone had ransacked all his belongings.

Later, in conversation with other men, Watson learned who the intruders were and how lucky he was not to have challenged them.

By 1866, Hugh Watson had become an old man. Still, he willingly agreed to lead the Robbins brothers, Zeke and Cluey, on a hunting trip far into the area now called Baxter State Park.

As the trio pushed farther into the thick nineteenth-century wilderness, the old man's survival instincts clicked in again. He knew the feeling; he'd had it before: something was out there. Watching. Waiting. Maybe even hunting them.

With eyes darting furtively back and forth, Watson scanned the trees, the pools of shadows, and the trail ahead. But, not wanting to alarm the younger men, he said nothing.

Apparently, the boys had noticed Watson's demeanor changing as, gradually, he became more sullen and withdrawn. That night around the campfire, they finally voiced their concern, asking what was wrong.

He told them his story from so many years before. He recalled the sudden sense of alarm. The dark forms surrounding his campsite. His ransacked belongings. He told them everything . . . everything except what the intruders had been.

Zeke and Cluey thought the old man was just trying to frighten them with a scary campfire tale. Still, sleep came slowly that night. And with the morning light, the whole story was forgotten.

A few days later, in the evening, Cluey left the campsite to fetch water from a nearby brook. There, on the far side of a remote stream, he saw something dark, man-like, and gigantic. It was kneeling at the water's edge, catching fish and eating them live. In the twilight, Cluey could see the thing was covered with dark red hair. "But it didn't see me," he said.

That night Cluey stayed awake, listening to weird noises outside their camp. The sounds were like footsteps, faint, stealthy footsteps, way off in the darkness. Sometimes they seemed close by, sometimes far away.

Whatever was making the sounds, the boy realized with some alarm, was not a solitary creature. There were several of them out there!

Fearing a family of bears, Cluey rested his hand on his firearm. He sat up, looked around. Again he saw the giant hairy thing, dark against the moonlight. In a moment it was gone and all was quiet.

Next morning, he told his companions about the two odd incidents.

While his brother, Zeke, smirked a little, Hugh Watson wasn't laughing at all. "That's the *Pomoola* you seen," Watson said. "That's the Indian Devil."

And to this day the belief in this creature is alive and well. Way up in the northeastern part of Maine, perhaps making its home on Mt. Katahdin, the creature—called *Pomoola* by its native neighbors, and the "Indian Devil" by the whites—is said to be half man and half beast. It is a colossal creature, covered with reddish brown hair. For centuries, he, she, or it has harmoniously cohabited with the Penobscots. According to their lore, it is a gentle giant, but if disturbed or provoked, it can turn instantly savage.

With that in mind, Watson and the Robbins boys broke camp and left the area that very day.

The same creature—or more likely, one of its descendants—was spotted in September of 1988. It was about halfway up Katahdin, seated at the edge of the forest, pulling up roots.

A whole troop of boy scouts from Massachusetts saw it. So did six out-of-state campers. All agreed it had a dark, triangular-shaped face, broad shoulders, and reddish brown fur. "It made frightening sounds," one of the scouts said.

Another boy contributed an interesting detail. He said, "It stunk like rotten eggs." This acrid smell must have been quite potent; reportedly, it lingered for a long time after the creature vanished into the trees.

We can be certain that many stories of confrontations with these hairy enigmas are never spoken of at all. Some are passed along by word-of-mouth. And sometimes they become very public when the media gets hold of them.

Here's an example of one from the old days. It ran as a front-page article in the *New York Times*, dated October 18, 1879. All in all, it's typical of many nineteenth-century news stories that appeared in New England papers with alarming regularity.

A WILDMAN OF THE MOUNTAINS
Two Young Vermont Hunters Terribly Scared

POWNAL, VT., OCT. 17—Much excitement prevailed among the sportsmen of this vicinity over the story that a wild man was seen on Friday last by two young men while hunting in the mountains south of Williamstown. The young men describe the creature as being about 5 feet high, resembling a man in form and movement, but covered all over with bright red hair, and having a long straggling beard, and with very wild eyes.

Although I draw no conclusions about the identity of this "wild man," I note that it was spotted not far from the location where, a century later, Arlene Tarantino saw her fleet-footed "Woodman."

BOWERS & FRENCH

ARLENE'S STORY NEVER FOUND ITS WAY INTO THE NEWSPAPERS, but similar tales have often received front-page treatment. You've seen the tabloids. "I Was the Wild Man's Secret Love Slave" or "A Hairy Monster Healed My Child!"

Even more "respectable" papers habitually treat monster stories with some derision, or dismiss them as fluff. Reporters automatically become disrespectful, sarcastic, eager to show they've not been hoodwinked by a hoaxer.

But more courageous journalists are apt to approach the subject with genuine, open-minded curiosity. Such was the case when Walter Bowers, Sr., met Scot French.

Mr. Bowers had lived all his life in Webster, New Hampshire. In late September of 1987, he was making the most of his recent retirement by enjoying one of his life-long pleasures—bird-hunting.

While trudging across a field near Mill Brook in Salisbury, he was suddenly overcome by the sensation that he was not alone in the woods. Was another hunter nearby? Or maybe some big game lurked just beyond the stand of trees?

But Mr. Bowers couldn't shake the feeling. It intensified. Soon he was sure he was being watched. Looking around, he caught sight of a gigantic figure standing in plain sight, right in the middle of the nearby field.

"This thing was BIG," Mr. Bowers told Scot French of the *Concord Monitor*. "I would say at least 9 feet. Maybe more, maybe less; I didn't stick around to do any measuring."

Even faced with his startling visitor, Bowers, an experienced woodsman, remained exceptionally observant. His description leaves little doubt about what he saw. "The whole body was covered with hair . . . kind of grayish color. . . . The hands were like yours or mine, only three times bigger, with pads on the front paws like a dog. Long legs, long arms . . . like a gorilla. But this here wasn't a gorilla. . . . I'm tellin' ya it would make your hair stand up."

Mr. Bowers lit out of there, repeatedly glancing over his shoulder. He was relieved to see the hairy giant running in the opposite direction, heading for the swamp.

Disturbed and puzzled by what he had seen, he finally reported the incident to Salisbury Police Chief Jody Heath. He didn't want Heath to take any action, he simply wanted to find out if it was all right to shoot the beast if it ever threatened him.

Heath promised to find out, but Walt Bowers knew the policeman was humoring him. He got the same treatment when he phoned the local game warden. "He just laughed at me," Bowers said. "He said it was probably a bear or a moose."

Remember, Walt Bowers was 55 years old at the time. He'd been hunting those woods all his life. In that time, he'd killed four bears and knew damn well what a moose looked like. He was certain they never walk around on their hind legs like a man. "If a man can't tell the difference between a moose and a thing like that," Bowers said, "he hadn't ought to be hunting . . ."

In time, Mr. Bowers found his way to Scot French at the *Monitor.* Mr. French was interested and curious, so Bowers agreed to take him to the spot where his sighting occurred. "It don't bother me any to go out with you," he told the journalist, "but I'm not going to go unarmed." So, with his .357 Magnum strapped to his side, Walt Bowers led Scot French into the wilds of Salisbury.

During the hike, Bowers speculated that creatures like the one he'd seen probably occupied caves in the swamp. Maybe, he suggested, they routinely come out in the morning to "look for apples, or corn, or whatever it is they eat."

He also said he suspected more people see the creatures than will admit to it, " 'cause they don't want to get laughed at."

But Scot French wasn't laughing.

"I believe him," French wrote in his column. And then he posed a couple of questions worth considering: "Why would Bowers, a retired caretaker at the New Hampshire Veterans Home, make up such a story?" And, "Why would he subject himself to such ridicule?"

Yes, why indeed?

OLD SLIPPERYSKIN

PRESUMABLY, SCORES OF WITNESSES down through the years are not all seeing the same creature. No, it would certainly appear that we, like our New England forefathers and mothers, are sharing the region with some hidden race of feral phantoms. We might wonder just exactly who—or what—we have in our midst?

Let's see if we can figure it out.

Perhaps the first *recorded* sighting of our mystery monster was in Vermont, near Lake Champlain. In 1759, during the French and Indian War, Maj. Robert Rogers (of Northwest Passage fame) and his rangers were returning from their attack on the St. Francis Indians.

Then, just south of Missisquoi Bay, something attacked *them!*

One of the rangers—a scout named Deluth—described the creature in his journal. He said it looked like: ". . . a large black bear, who would throw large pine cones and nuts down upon us from trees and ledges. . . ."

Smart bear! Yet this canny creature was no stranger to local Native Americans. They even had a name for it, *Wejuk,* meaning "Wet Skin."

Vermont's earliest settlers recorded many similar run-ins with preternaturally intelligent bears. One notable specimen was repeatedly encountered in the wilds of Vermont's fabled Northeast Kingdom. In the late 1700s and early 1800s, the townships of Morgan, Maidstone, Lemington, and Victory were repeatedly invaded by a fearsome oddity known as "Old Slipperyskin."

The creature was said to resemble a huge bear, but unlike any *known* bear, it always walked upright, like a human being. It was said to have a mean disposition. Sometimes it even sought revenge against individuals who had offended it. It might fill their sap buckets with stones, terrify their children, or worse.

Then, it had a way of disappearing by carefully backtracking in its own prints, leaving a trail that appeared to end abruptly and mysteriously.

In her *History of Lemington, Vermont*, Marion M. Daley writes:

"The story is told that an old bear once terrorized this part of the country for many years and committed wholesale destruction. He was a mean animal, and evidently had a grudge against humans. He destroyed their fences, ripped up their gardens, frightened their cows and sheep, tromped through the corn fields and caused no end of mayhem. The settlers came to refer to the bear as 'Slipperyskin,' for the reason that he managed to elude every trap that was set for him. He was a huge bear, the stories relate, and he always ran on his hind legs and never on all fours. Before a hunter could lay his gunsights on him, the old bear would vanish into the woods silent and swift as a drift of smoke. He is said to have left tracks as big as wagon wheels. His legs, in fact, were compared with spruce logs, and for what it's worth, it is told he squeezed the sap out of the maple trees when he felt inclined. For maliciousness and cunning, it was claimed he would never be compared, except to humans. He seemed to enjoy himself immensely, frightening people and livestock, kicking over manure piles and throwing stones into machinery left in fields. Where the old bear came from and why he eventually disappeared entirely is a mystery."

Mystery, indeed. Or folk tale? Or Indian legend? Then again, maybe it's something else? A specimen, dead or alive, would answer the question once and for all.

Around 1815, Vermont Governor Jonas Galusha promised to get rid of Old Slipperyskin. Known as an excellent hunter, the governor organized a hunting party and entered the Maidstone woods, where the beast had last been seen.

Galusha—so the story goes—had covered himself with the scent of female bear.

Then, gun in hand, he stalked the pesky critter alone.

Shortly, the governor came whooping and bellowing back into camp screaming, "Outta my way boys, I'm bringin' him back alive!"

Old Slipperyskin was in hot pursuit. The hunters scattered; and not one of them thought to shoot the "bear."

According to one account, however, a specimen of one of these hair-covered oddities—or perhaps one of its offspring—was actually captured back in January of 1855.

Earlier, I mentioned J.W. McHenry of Waldoboro, Maine, who investigated after hearing loud, high-pitched screams coming from the woods nearby. He saw an 18-inch creature covered with long black hair. Supposedly, McHenry chased it, caught it, and kept it as a pet. Could it have been an underage member of Old Slipperyskin's extended family?

These stories—hovering between tall tales and historical hyperbole—have enormous charm, so it's easy to overlook the fact that today we have no idea of what Old Slipperyskin and company actually were.

The core facts seem to be these: it resembled a bear and walked like a human; it was apparently miffed because people were starting to intrude on what for centuries had been its own private domain. It was vindictive, occasionally hostile, and—so it would seem—highly intelligent.

But the real identity of Old Slipperyskin may not be lost in legend because—as we have seen—sightings of this hairy enigma continue to this day.

Before we hazard a guess about Old Slipperyskin's identity, let's take a look at a slightly more contemporary case.

BRIDGEWATER REVISITED

OUTDOOR ENTHUSIAST, PHOTOGRAPHER, and former security guard, Joseph M. DeAndrade of Bridgewater, Massachusetts, has an interesting sideline. Following the footsteps of Lucius Merritt and Governor Galusha, he leads occasional hunting parties in search of big hairy monsters.

In 1978, Mr. DeAndrade experienced a personal encounter with the beast. Although his was brief, it lasted long enough to change his life forever.

Now in his early forties, he's determined to discover just exactly what he saw. "I saw it across a pond in the daytime," he says. "It walked like a man but real slow, like Frankenstein. I turned my head to tell my friend with me, then it was gone."

His theory is that the creature makes its home in the mysterious depths of Hockomock Swamp at the heart of the so-called Bridgewater Triangle. Armed with a camera instead of a gun, Mr. DeAndrade searches the swamp for the solution to this age-old enigma: Just what are these gigantic hairy man-beasts?

The results of his safaris have been predictably unproductive. But during a 1985 expedition, he and his companions heard fearsome wails—"horrifying, evil, hungry."

Alas, as is so often the case with this ephemeral phantom, the hunters came back empty-handed.

WHAT'S IN A NAME?

WILD MAN. WEJUK. Old Slipperyskin. Pomoola. Indian Devil. I don't think they are all different creatures. More likely, we're looking at a variety of labels for the same thing. Those who study such anomalies call this formidable creature by another name; they call him Bigfoot.

But in New England?

Usually, we associate Bigfoot sightings with the Pacific Northwest. Or we think of the Yeti, the "Abominable Snowman" of the Himalayas. However, an acquaintance of mine, the late Dr. Warren Cook of Vermont's Castleton State College, kept track of East Coast Bigfoot encounters for years. He chronicled over 150 New England sightings. Investigators like Joe DeAndrade and researchers like Bill Green of The New England Bigfoot Research Center continue the tradition.

Of course, they chronicle only the *reported* sightings. I wonder how many people see a Bigfoot and don't tell anyone simply because the experience is too weird, or because they don't want to suffer the inevitable ridicule?

For example, what would you have done in the shoes of Mrs. Neota Huntington of Durham, Maine? She phoned the police after a 400-pound "ape-man with shaggy black fur" frightened her three children.

Her daughter Lois panicked and fell off her bicycle, injuring her knee. Then, Mrs. Huntington said, "It stood there by the side of the road, just looking down at Lois and at the other two, ages ten and eight, who were paralyzed with fear. . . ."

After a few moments the creature nonchalantly wandered off into the woods.

"I called the police," Mrs. Huntington said, "but nobody seemed to believe me or the kids."

But Sgt. Fred Bird of the Connecticut State Police was a little more open-minded when he investigated a similar report one rainy Monday night in August of 1982.

In the chapter called "Barnyard Tales and Terrors," I told how farmhands Fuller and Buckley walked into the Ellington dairy barn, where they worked, and ran into a huge, hairy creature. This 7-foot, 300-pound specimen fit Bigfoot's description to a "T."

Apparently as scared of them as they were of it, the creature ran away.

We are tempted to dismiss the whole episode as a joke until we recall Sergeant Bird's comment about pranksters who spook animals: "You play a practical joke like that around a farm and you're liable to wind up dead."

Good point.

Of course, people don't like to get spooked, either. Take the case of Vermonter James Guyette. In April 1984, he was driving north on Interstate 91 around six o'clock in the morning. Within sight of the Hartland Dam, James spotted a "huge hairy animal-man," swinging its arms as it walked along the roadside about 100 yards away. It was tall and lanky, he reported, and definitely walking upright on two legs. The creature moved down the bank beside the interstate heading west, away from the Connecticut River. Later, when telling his wife about the encounter, Guyette started to cry.

And in New Hampshire, in the Squam Mountain area, a pleasant evening drive turned to terror for John Oswald and his family. Something gigantic leapt out of the bushes and into his headlights. As he told the State Police, "It was a furry creature seven feet tall. It was strong looking, with big shoulders and a big nose. It's face was triangular shaped. Once it saw the car it backed away and bolted into the woods."

In Hollis, New Hampshire, there were two independent sightings of what was probably the same creature. On the night of May 7, 1977, Gerald St. Louis and two 12-year-old boys were on their way to set up a booth at a flea market. In order to be fresh, chipper, and on time the next morning, they camped out near the market site.

Their parking area seemed ideal; it was surrounded by woods and completely private. No buildings, vehicles, or other people were anywhere in sight.

At about ten o'clock, Gerald opened the truck door to go outside. But something was there waiting for him.

"I saw it face-to-face," he said. "It was all hairy, brown colored, and eight or nine feet tall, with long arms and long hair. Thank God for the lights that came on when I opened the door; they startled the creature and it ran toward a fence about four and a half feet high, and it jumped over it with ease. I could see it standing there in the distance, just looking at us. I drove out of there so fast that I left everything I was going to sell the next day behind on the ground."

About 300 yards away, Jeff Warren and Stanley Evans were sitting in their own truck. They too were flea marketers with the same plan for an early arrival.

All of a sudden, their truck started shaking as if they were caught in an earthquake. Looking around, both saw a large, hairy animal. Moments later, they were barreling down the road, shaking with fear and trying to figure out what had happened to them.

Maybe it was a competitor trying to scare them off. If so, it didn't work. Jeff and Stan were at their flea-market booth the next day.

And Gerald St. Louis was at his.

When, eventually, all three got acquainted, they had plenty to talk about. The men compared notes and checked for signs of the mysterious creature. Whatever it was had vanished, leaving behind some 17-inch footprints and three puzzled flea marketers.

Just outside Augusta—Maine's capitol—Debbie and Donna Adams had a curious encounter on Old Camp Road in Manchester. They spotted a 7-foot creature covered "with brown fur, and markings of white on its chest and stomach." It was standing behind a tree, watching a farmer cut wood. As it watched, it swayed rhythmically back and forth.

One of the girls screamed, apparently startling the creature. When it turned to face them, the girls both screamed. The terrified duet apparently scared the creature, who momentarily acted confused. "At first it didn't seem to know which way to go, but then it crossed the road and ran into the woods."

The farmer heard the yelling, but saw nothing. When the police arrived, they found no sign of the hairy visitor.

BIG FOOTNOTES

SO WHAT'S GOING ON HERE? The skeptic in me asks, can so many witnesses be hallucinating? At the same time, the persistence of evidence—anecdotal and physical—suggests they are not.

For example, at about 8:30 on the evening of September 20, 1985, Al Davis and his family ran into something highly peculiar behind their house in West Rutland, Vermont.

Al heard a big animal thrashing through the underbrush, coming toward him. Thinking one of his neighbor's cows had gotten loose, he stepped off the trail. However, the sickening odor that wafted by wasn't from any cow. In fact, Al had never smelled anything like it. He described it as "swampy."

Then he saw the source of the odor. Al eloquently described his resultant fear: "It was like someone pulled back the hammer of a gun and pointed it at me."

As the lumbering creature passed under a street light, its silhouetted form looked like a gorilla. But it walked upright, like a human being. "It had a distinct swaying motion of the shoulders, and had real long arms," he told Bob Trebilcock for *Yankee* magazine.

Other members of the family saw it, too. Sixteen-year-old Bob Davis even threw rocks at it. Ed Davis heard it grunting and screeching.

Examining the spot the next morning, they found distinct tracks in the compacted gravel of the road. Dr. Warren Cook and a Rutland schoolteacher named Mr. Loomis took castings that were 14 inches long by 7 inches wide.

It should be no surprise that the extremely haunted Hockomock Swamp in Massachusetts would be visited by Bigfoot. But what are we to make of this case, reported in the April 9, 1970, edition of the *Boston Herald*?

A big hairy "thing" kept popping up in Bridgewater. State and local police used attack dogs to search the swamp for two days and nights. All the while, residents kept phoning in more sightings of the giant bearlike animal.

Whatever it was, wildlife officials assured everyone it was not a bear. Bears hadn't occupied that area for well over a hundred years.

Repeatedly frustrated, the police began to suspect it was nothing at all. Then an event occurred that was "somewhat" convincing. Two policemen in a cruiser got the fright of their lives. One said, "Something began to pick up the rear of our car. I spun the car around and got my spotlight on something that looked like a bear running around the corner of a nearby house." The puzzled policeman refused to speculate whether he had seen a Bigfoot. But whatever it was left behind some very big footprints.

Another swamp. This one in Sudbury, Vermont. One morning in February 1951, lumbermen Rowell and Kennedy returned to work and discovered a canvas-covered oil drum had been moved. Someone, or something, had removed the 450-pound drum from its place on the tractor and carried it several hundred feet toward the woods. When they checked the ground near the tractor, they found dozens of huge prints—20 inches long and 8 inches wide—which Rowell was able to photograph.

Some people find it terrifying to speculate about what kind of rude beast might be skulking by night along the little-used roads outside Agawam, Massachusetts, near the Connecticut border.

During the 1970s and '80s, a hairy monster or a hirsute wild man over 7 feet tall put in numerous appearances. Police reports kept piling up.

On one occasion in the mid-seventies, the hairy visitor left a trail of clearly visible footprints embedded in the ice and frozen into the muddy bank of the Westfield River. They measured 27½ inches by 8 inches, suggesting whatever made them must have weighed around 700 pounds.

Though that is certainly a big foot, no one could be sure the prints were made by a Bigfoot.

My friend George Earley was living in Connecticut at the time. As a writer and investigator of Fortean phenomena, he decided to look into the matter.

"It had become something of a media event," he told me. "TV people flying overhead, photographing the scene, a 'monster hunter' from New York City coming up, looking, pontificating, and sleeping out on the scene to film the critter if it came back. It wasn't until mid- or late January that I had a free Saturday to get up there."

When he arrived in town, Mr. Earley asked the local police for directions to the site. "The road started off paved, as I recall, with some houses on it, then became dirt and terminated in a circle where some building lots had been scraped out.

"Apparently when the 'monster' slogged through, the area was slushy: soft enough to take prints and hard enough that they didn't collapse before they froze.

"But . . . there were no tracks when I got there, just big holes where someone either tried to chip the tracks out, or where they had been deliberately obliterated. I think the latter, though I can't prove it. I think the cops or the neighbors or both destroyed the tracks because of all the media fuss and gawkers coming to look at the site."

He followed the craters until they went into—or came out of—the woods.

Those woods, Mr. Earley observed, were made up mostly of healthy saplings set so close together that he had to squeeze between them. He quickly realized that something big enough to have 27-inch-long feet could not have passed through the woods without tearing up some trees.

He also examined the ice on the river that had allegedly been broken by the stomping of Bigfoot's heavy feet. "No heavy creature required," he told me, because, "the breakage was at a point where a little stream flowed into the bigger one. That means the ice was pretty thin, owing to the flowing water."

At that point, Mr. Earley had seen all he needed to. He concluded that this particular incident was most likely a hoax.

A couple of weeks later, the town police phoned him. They said the case was closed and offered to give him the details before they went to the press.

"Remember," he told me, "this all happened during the Christmas vacation period in 1976—the year the *King Kong* remake was released. So I wasn't too surprised when I drove up and was shown a pair of large plywood feet that had been screwed to the bottom of a pair of boots.

"The perpetrator was a 16- or 17-year-old kid who, under the influence of the *King Kong* movie, made the feet and went stomping out in, if I recall correctly, an area where his girlfriend lived. He never dreamed his joke would get so much attention."

But for every entertaining hoax, embarrassing misperception, or embellished yarn, a fair number of cases remain mysterious.

The pseudonymous Daniel Blanchard, for example, is one of the few people to meet Bigfoot more than once. In November 1977, while hunting in Cornish, Maine, Daniel chanced to look up. He saw that many small trees along the trail were broken. Examining the breaks more closely, he noted a few red hairs lodged in some of the splintered wood. As he studied the wounded branches, he caught a glimpse of something rushing along the trail in front of him.

He didn't get a good look at it, just saw a big, dark shape. Yet for some reason, he felt ill at ease, as if the dark presence were somehow threatening.

This apprehension was immediately reinforced when he heard the growl. It began as a low, throaty rumble, then escalated in volume and pitch, turning into a scream. The strange sound ended as a kind of whistle. Upon reflection, Daniel says it was the loneliest, saddest sound he'd ever heard.

Later, on August 15, 1982, Daniel was bass fishing on Forest Lake in Cumberland, Maine. He turned his boat into a small, isolated cove. As he sat quietly, a big hairy creature stepped out of the woods, knelt down by the water's edge, and began to drink. Daniel estimated the creature was nearly 7 feet tall and must have weighed 400 pounds. After it returned to the woods, Daniel waited awhile, then went ashore, where he found footprints on the beach. They measured 19 inches long, 10 inches across, and 4 inches at the heel. What could it have been if not a Bigfoot?

During October of 1976, a Rutland, Vermont, businessman (who won't reveal his name) was taking photographs for a land-development project in northeastern Rutland County. When his pictures were developed, one showed what appeared to be the upper torso and head of a gigantic gorillalike creature.

Dr. Warren Cook sent the photographic negative to a California lab for analysis. They could discover no evidence of tampering or trickery. When Cook visited the spot in question, he searched for a tree stump or rock formation that could account for the strange photographic phenomenon. Finding nothing unusual, Dr. Cook concluded he possessed what might be the first authentic photograph of an actual Yankee Bigfoot.

SO WHAT THE DEVIL ARE THEY?

SIGHTINGS CONTINUE. Some are mistakes in perception. Some, of course, are hoaxes. But the others, what of them? The sheer number of encounters is absolutely mind-boggling. Giant, hairy, manlike creatures have been reported for hundreds of years in every state except, as far as I know, Rhode Island.

Of course, none of this anecdotal evidence, nor the castings made from hundreds of footprints, can be considered conclusive. No proof can be accepted until we've found a body. Or captured a live Bigfoot. Or killed a specimen.

But hold your fire!

After studying North American Bigfoot sightings for years, Peter Byrne, director of The Bigfoot Research Project, says, "We do know—and of this we are certain—whatever or whoever they are, they are harmless and inoffensive creatures, with absolutely no historical record of violence or aggression towards man. We also know—and again we are certain—that like our planet's higher life form, man, they are the only primates to walk upright. We also are cognizant of the fact—from highly credible eyewitness reports—that size and hair covering apart, they look oddly like us, or at the least like a primitive version of us."

If Byrne is right and Bigfoot is like us, then most likely it is one of two things: some form of primitive human who, against all odds, survived into the twentieth century; or maybe it's a highly evolved, manlike ape. Dr. Cook came to believe Bigfoot is *Australopithecus*, the first true hominid, now considered extinct. Other researchers favor *Gigantopithecus*, a creature that lived in China some 500,000 years ago. Both share a family tree with human beings though neither is, strictly speaking, human.

However, buried in all this narrative, we find a couple of interesting clues that might lead us to look at Bigfoot in a different way. Over and over again, witnesses have mentioned the creature's revolting odor and his unique vocalizations.

Byrne identified its cry as one of its most distinctive features. He says, "The unearthly screech of a Bigfoot cannot be confused with that of any other creature."

To give you an idea of the powerful impact of that cry, consider the 1984 case of a Chittenden, Vermont, man who was awakened by loud screaming in his dooryard. Normally, this longtime hunter (who wishes to remain unidentified) wouldn't be afraid of much, but, as he told investigator Ted Pratt, "I just couldn't get out of bed. It was a horrible scream. It lasted five to seven seconds."

Daniel Blanchard heard Bigfoot's wail in 1977. As you recall, he said it was the loneliest, saddest sound he'd ever heard. By contrast, Joseph DeAndrade and the members of his expedition described the sound as "horrifying, evil, hungry."

And then there's the odor.

Witnesses from West Rutland, Vermont, described a "swampy" smell. When the troop of Boy Scouts spotted it on Mt. Katahdin, one said, "It stunk like rotten eggs." The powerful stench lasted for hours after the creature made its exit.

These details lead us to a more mysterious side of Bigfoot's nature, a side that suggests the creature might not be natural, but rather supernatural.

Its bansheelike wail has the power to paralyze and provoke mind-numbing terror. Its extraordinary olfactory presence, or rotten-egg stink, is a familiar detail in many ghost, UFO, and creature manifestations all over the world. Quite possibly, it's the smell of hydrogen sulfide, the "brimstone odor" occultists and clergymen have for centuries associated with demonic encounters.

So our thinking has come full circle. Natural to supernatural. And that's exactly what the Native Americans were telling us centuries ago.

Think about it: the Bigfoot phenomenon is not limited to New England. In spite of the fact that they're known to every Indian tribe in North America, and that sightings have been documented all over the world for centuries, we've never found a body or killed or captured a specimen.

Doesn't that seem odd? If they're real, why no bodies? No bones? No live specimens in our zoos, labs, or neighborhoods? Why just enough evidence—footprints, hair, fuzzy photos—to keep us interested and to keep us guessing?

All we can say for sure is that Bigfoot is a mystery. But it might be more of a mystery than most people realize. My guess is that a hundred years from now we'll have exactly the same amount of evidence as we had a hundred years ago. And Bigfoot will still be running wild and unclassified, a permanent resident of the hills and forests of Weird, New England.

PART VI

DAMNED YANKEES

"Mercy should have known better than to hire anyone from the Nooseneck Hill country, for that remote bit of backwoods was then, as now, a seat of the most uncomfortable superstitions."

— H.P. LOVECRAFT
The Shunned House

The **Hungry Dead**

*"Mr. William Rose dug up the body of his
daughter and burned her heart, for she
was drawing energy from other members
of the family."*

—The Providence Journal, *1874*

*reported in the village of
Placedale, Rhode Island*

HEARTLESS CREATURES

IN 1990, TWO CHILDREN PLAYING at a newly developed construction site in Griswold, Connecticut, made a horrifying discovery.

As they took turns sliding down the steep bank of a recently opened gravel pit, one of them suddenly began screaming. The terrified child found himself fighting off an avalanche of skulls and bones—and they looked human.

When their panic subsided, the frightened children ran off to tell their parents who, in turn, summoned the authorities.

Local police were worried. They feared they might have stumbled onto the dumping ground of some unknown serial killer. So the investigation began.

According to procedure, several officials were automatically summoned to the site, among them the state archaeologist from the University of Connecticut, Dr. Nicholas Bellantoni. For Dr. Bellantoni, this investigation would be unexpectedly unnerving. Imagine how he felt when his first excavation disclosed a coffin with the letters N.B. upon it—the doctor's own initials, outlined in brass tacks.

The shock of this curious coincidence diminished a bit when the doctor made his next discovery: another coffin marked "J.B.—55," positioned within a field-stone crypt. But there was still another oddity: some of the bones were on top of the fieldstone, outside the crypt. How could that be? Had the grave's occupant tried to escape?

The next revelation answered that question, but posed one of its own. Dr. Bellantoni discovered the crypt and wooden casket had been broken into, violated. Someone had deliberately mutilated the remains of the body. Its rib cage was split open. Long leg bones, femora, rested where the chest should have been, with the skull positioned on top in the familiar skull-and-crossbones configuration.

Why? Who would do such a thing?

Subsequent investigation began to disclose that the playful children had accidentally stumbled upon proof of something previously only hinted at in New England history—our ancestors had actually waged war against vampires.

Of all the creatures of the night, there is none that generates more terror than the vampire. Yet, as monsters go, it is strangely popular in contemporary American culture. Part of the vampire's allure, I think, is that in spite of ourselves, we envy him. While we may hate his evil nature and dread his potential to destroy us, there is something attractive about the vampire's seductive charm, and something desirable about his exemption from death.

At least, that's what we may think if we were raised on the charismatic creatures defined by Bram Stoker and his erudite progeny.

Our colonial ancestors, however, saw the vampire in a very different way. While the European bloodsucker might have been a charming aristocrat, its American counterpart was a loathsome parasite from the darkest sewers of hell.

In retrospect, we might call 1990 "The Year of the Yankee Vampire" because it marks the occasion when the suspected horde of New England vampires finally came to light. Before the grisly Griswold excavations, some vampires lay safely buried in the dusty pages of old newspapers, while others reposed forgotten in ancient town histories and medical records. Even when rediscovered, most stories were ignored by modern researchers; they seemed so far-fetched and fantastical.

And that has always been the vampire's best protection, hasn't it? If no one believes in him, he remains unchallenged.

HEARTBURN

PRIOR TO THE GRISWOLD EXHUMATIONS, we had flimsier evidence on which to start a vampire hunt—just rumors, folktales, and campfire stories. The tales were fun to swap, but who could really believe them? For example, what would you conclude if you were to read the following headline while sipping your morning coffee?

VAMPIRISM IN WOODSTOCK

That's exactly how Vermont's most famous—or at least most long-lived—case of vampirism came to the public's attention.

The remarkable events were reported in the *Boston Transcript* during the first week of October 1890. A more complete accounting appeared as a front-page story in Woodstock's own newspaper, the *Vermont Standard*. The article recalled events that supposedly occurred in the 1830s after a local man named Corwin had passed away, apparently of consumption.

His body was buried in the Cushing Cemetery. Some time later, his brother—presumably also named Corwin—began wasting away. Of course, the living Corwin displayed symptoms of his dead brother's contagion, but common wisdom offered a more ghastly alternative. Perhaps the dead Corwin had come back as a vampire, his spirit rising from the grave by night to feed on the blood of his living brother.

To find out for sure, town fathers ordered the body disinterred. A horrifying discovery convinced them they were dealing with the supernatural. Dr. Joseph Gallup, the town's leading physician and head of Vermont Medical College, observed that "the vampire's heart contained its victim's blood" (though how the good doctor achieved this bit of forensic wizardry remains a mystery).

Alas, there was but one way to stop the spread of evil: concerned parties would assemble on Woodstock's green to perform an exorcism.

Predictably, most of the town's population turned out for the event. Dr. Gallup and Woodstock's other physicians built a fire in the middle of the green, heated up an iron pot, and cooked the undecayed heart until it was reduced to ashes.

Then they buried the pot and ashes in a hole 15 feet deep, covered it with a 7-ton slab of granite, and, before refilling the hole, sprinkled everything with bull's blood for purification.

Finally, they forced the dying Corwin to swallow a hideous concoction of bull's blood mixed with some of his brother's ashes. They believed this medicine would break the vampire's curse and stop the victim's body from wasting away.

Unfortunately, we never learn if Brother Corwin survived the disease, let alone the medicine, but the town fathers were convinced they had cured Woodstock of vampirism forever.

As far as I can tell, they were right.

Keep in mind that the above article was written in the 1890s, reporting events that supposedly took place more than half a century earlier. Certain details suggest the whole thing might have been nothing more than a Halloween spook story. For example, the anonymous author goes on to say that a few years later, some curious townsmen tried to find the buried pot. After they had dug down 15 feet, "They heard a roaring noise . . . as of some great conflagration, going on in the bowels of the earth, and the smell of sulphur began to fill the cavity. . . . " Understandably alarmed, they refilled the hole and scurried away.

Although this sort of questionable detail might be a deliberate hint that the story is a put-on, the modern reader can't help wondering if there could be a drop of truth to some of this bloody business.

Researchers have found that Dr. Gallup, all his colleagues, and most of the townspeople mentioned in the newspaper article were real.

On the other hand, Woodstock's records—birth, death, church, and property—show no indication of a man called Corwin. And there is no Corwin marker in Cushing, or any other local cemetery.

Although people have tried, no one has been able to locate the 7-ton granite slab, much less the iron pot of ashes supposedly buried somewhere under Woodstock's scenic boat-shaped green.

Still, there is much of interest in the piece. If it is fiction, can it be based on fact? And if so, how does one fillet the fact from the fantasy? As we will see, many of the details conform to actual New England practice.

HUNTING THE DEMON VAMPIRE

THERE IS A LOT OF CONFUSION about which may be the oldest recorded instance of vampirism in New England. One of the earliest also occurred in Vermont. In 1793, there was a terrific public uproar in the town of Manchester, where locals claimed the "Demon Vampire" was at work.

In March of 1789, Capt. Isaac Burton married Miss Rachel Harris, a fine, beautiful, and above all healthy, young woman.

Shortly after the wedding, Rachel's health began to fail. The illness was easily diagnosed: consumption. Rachel's constitution continued to weaken until February of 1790 when she died.

Nearly a year later, Captain Burton remarried. His new bride was Miss Hulda Powel, another "healthy, good-looking girl."

Soon Hulda too began to show the dangerous symptoms: loss of vitality, unnatural pallor, fever-flushed cheeks, and a persistent, bloody cough. By February 1793, she was in a bad way. Captain Burton and his wife's despairing relatives were ready to try anything to save her.

Some well-intended villagers whispered the unspeakable: maybe a vampire had been responsible for Rachel's death and now maybe it was having its evil way with Hulda. Another villager, Timothy Mead, suggested it might help to make—as an old account puts it—a "sacrifice to the Demon Vampire."

And now there was hope; maybe they could save dear Hulda after all.

When they dug up Captain Burton's first wife, they found that a year in the grave had left her in a sorry state. Undaunted, Mead, Burton, and company removed all that remained of her heart, liver, and lungs. Then Mead presided over a ceremony that involved burning the unfortunate woman's organs in a blacksmith's forge. Everyone hoped the morbid ritual would appease the Demon and "effect a cure of the sick second wife."

Predictably, the bizarre ceremony inspired so much interest and curiosity that, according to one source, "from five hundred to one thousand people" attended. That's quite a few, considering the population of Manchester was only about 1,200 souls at that time. But as we'll soon see, vampires are great for tourism.

Anyway, despite the enthusiastic show of community support, all efforts failed. Hulda Burton died on September 6, 1793, a second victim of the Demon Vampire.

THE STUKELEY CASE

ANOTHER EARLY CASE TOOK PLACE in the tiny state of Rhode Island. For years, the vague line separating folklore and reality has been especially blurry here. Some sources say the events occurred as early as 1770; others merely state "around the time of the American Revolution."

Until recently, it was known as the "Stukeley case." Some writers call the victims the "Stukeley family," others identify them as simply "the Stukes." The most recent report I've seen is apparently the most precise, or at any rate the least vague. It is based on the work of Rhode Island folklorist Michael Bell as reported by Paul Sieveking in *Fortean Times*. Through archival research, Bell identified the family as "Stutley and Honor Tillinghast of Exeter, Rhode Island." The date? Again very precise: 1799.

As traditionally told, the story begins with a farmer's prophetic dream.

The farmer, known to everyone as a clever and industrious father, good churchman, and excellent provider, ran a prosperous farm in rural Rhode Island. He and his wife had fourteen children who, against the odds of the era, survived, healthy, strong, and successful, into adulthood.

Just when life seemed ideal, the father was troubled one night with an especially vivid dream about his apple orchard. Exactly half the trees were dark, twisted, and dead. He woke up with a terrible uneasiness. A dream that lucid must mean something. What, exactly, could it portend?

When Sarah, the couple's oldest daughter, became ill, there was no reason to equate her misfortune with the strange dream. In fact, the dream was all but forgotten as Sarah grew sicker. When she eventually died, she was buried in the family cemetery nearby.

Then the second daughter sickened. Eventually, she too perished. But before she died, she had complained repeatedly that her dead sister, Sarah, had come to her in the night. The apparition had entered her room, advanced to her bedside, and pushed on her chest, making it difficult to breathe.

Deaths continued.

By the time their fifth child was buried, the farmer finally understood the dream's deadly message. But there was another puzzle: what should he make of the fact that each dying child had complained about midnight visits from Sarah?

Shortly after the demise of the sixth child, the seventh began to report the same prophetic symptoms of preternatural fatigue. And before the child passed away, the farmer's wife had begun to weaken after several late-night reunions with dear dead daughter Sarah.

While conferring with neighbors, the farmer came to believe that Sarah somehow was responsible for the deaths. Either by instinct or education, many villagers knew what had to be done. In order to stop the spreading evil, the men trouped to the cemetery and dug up the six dead children. Five were in the ghastly condition of any decaying corpse. But one of them, the first to die, was perfectly preserved. Sarah's eyes were wide, her hair and nails had grown, her limbs were supple, and, upon inspection, she was found to have fresh blood in her arteries.

The neighbors cut out Sarah's heart and burned it right there in the cemetery. And just to be sure, they did the same with the hearts of the other five siblings.

The seventh victim died nonetheless, apparently too far gone by the time the evil was destroyed. But the wife recovered, never to be bothered by Sarah again.

In the end, the farmer's dream had come true: he and his wife had indeed lost half their orchard.

Evidently, there is some truth buried in all this. According to Sieveking's article, Stutley and Honor Tillinghast actually had fourteen children, four of whom died of consumption. Sarah, age 22, was the first to go. When the fifth child took ill, all the dead siblings were disinterred from the family plot on Pine Hill (today Historic Cemetery 14, near Route 102).

The true condition of the bodies, especially Sarah's, is a matter of conjecture. But we can be sure any suspicious corpse was subjected to loathsome exorcism rituals.

RAY'S HOPES

S O FAR WE HAVE WITNESSED HOW TO DIAGNOSE VAMPIRISM, and we've learned the ritual used to combat it. As you may have noticed, to the Yankee, vampirism was very much a family matter.

In this next case, we'll look in on the family of Henry B. Ray of Jewett City, Connecticut. The Rays had been native to the region throughout the nineteenth century. As a struggling farm family, they had plenty to worry about without the addition of vampires. In fact, Henry and Lucy Ray and their five children probably weren't thinking about vampires at all when Lemuel, their second-oldest boy, took sick during the winter of 1845. The strapping 24-year-old began the all-too-familiar wasting away.

In March, he was laid to rest.

The grieving Rays did the only thing they could; they struggled to get family life back to normal. But now all was uncertain; the specter of death loomed everywhere. Who would be the next to feel its icy breath?

In just four years, the father, Henry, began to experience the first symptoms of what he feared might be consumption. All too soon, with his family clustered around him, clutching their Bibles and praying, Henry too slipped into unconsciousness and passed away.

Two more years passed. In 1851, before the family had fully adjusted to the father's death, 26-year-old Elisha began the coughing that would never stop. He weakened, wasted, and eventually fell. Even by nineteenth-century standards, the Rays were dying far too rapidly.

The family had experienced unrelenting grief since 1845. In 1854—less than a decade later—one of the two remaining sons took ill. Henry Nelson Ray, aged 35, was terrified. He knew full well what was coming.

On May 8, 1854, in an effort to save Henry, the desperate family decided to take action. It is uncertain who, if anyone, first uttered the word "vampire," but subsequent behavior clearly illustrates what the family believed.

With so many recent deaths recorded in the family Bible, the Rays concluded that young Henry's wasting illness was caused by his dead brother. The wisdom of the time dictated that the first to die was the first to return. Surely, Lemuel Ray had become a vampire. It was he who rose from the grave, extending his own life by draining the vital essence of his siblings.

In a scene reminiscent of a Hollywood horror film, the Rays, accompanied by a small group of friends, marched down Main Street. Carrying shovels, matches, and fuel oil, they entered the Jewett City cemetery.

Just to make certain, the vampire-hunters dug up not only Lemuel's corpse, but also the body of his brother Elisha. For some reason, they spared their father the "resurrection" and ensuing indignities. There, right in the village cemetery, they burned the dead brothers' corpses. And then, presumably, they partook of the disgusting related rituals that routinely followed.

Did the ceremony work? Apparently so.

However, there is just one odd factor to consider: of the seven members of the afflicted family, only Henry Nelson Ray is without a recorded date of death. There is no death certificate, no town records, nor does he have a gravestone in the family plot.

Now I don't want to jump to any conclusions, or start any rumors, but could Henry still be alive? Is it possible the Ray family destroyed the wrong vampires?

CORPSE KILLERS

MORE DEATHS IN MORE FAMILIES. Rhode Island again. The vampiric events in the timber and farming town of Exeter may be the most recent in New England history.

Chestnut Hill Cemetery, right behind the Baptist Church, contains the grave of Rhode Island's most famous vampire. In fact, Mercy Brown probably has become the most famous native vampire in all America.

The pattern is familiar: Mercy's family members began to take ill and die of "the white death." Among them, the first to feel the fatal symptoms was Mrs. Brown. Her suffering ended mid-winter, on December 8, 1883, at the age of 36. Just six months later, their eldest girl, Mary Olive, followed her mother to the grave.

This left George Brown with one son and four daughters.

Edwin, the son, did not live with the family; he had his own place in West Wickford. According to all reports, he was a rock-ribbed, able-bodied sort, never sick a day in his life. Edwin worked in a store to support his new family and to maintain their independent life. But the young man had to resign in the early 1890s when he experienced the first debilitating symptoms. Rather than move home to Exeter with his family, Edwin headed for Colorado Springs, where mineral waters and a healthy climate might facilitate recovery.

While Edwin was away, things were getting worse back home. His 19-year-old sister, Mercy, became ill. On January 12, 1892, her remains were carried down the well-worn path to the grave.

In Colorado, Edwin began to realize he was losing the battle. He returned home to spend the remainder of his days among the people he loved. As his condition worsened, his despondent father met with a group of neighbors to decide what, if anything, could be done to end this family curse.

The manner in which family members had suffered and died clearly suggested a vampire was at work. Proof would be easy to obtain: all the graves must be opened and the bodies examined to see which member of the family was playing host to the demon vampire.

After agreeing to the necessary action, they equipped themselves with the tools of the trade. Everyone paraded along Purgatory Road to the graveyard.

The exhumation might never have come to public attention if the family hadn't sought official sanction for their vampire extermination plan. They approached the district medical examiner, Dr. Harold Metcalf, "a young and intelligent graduate of Bellevue." He discouraged them at first but ultimately relented, agreeing to examine the bodies.

Standing with Dr. Metcalf beside him, Edwin Brown watched in horror as friends opened the graves of his mother and sisters.

According to the doctor, they found "just what might be expected from a similar examination of almost any person after the same length of time [in the grave]."

The vampire-hunters, however, saw things differently.

Leaving George and Edwin Brown with their friends to rebury the corpses, Dr. Metcalf made his exit.

Those who remained conducted their own examination. All agreed that Mrs.

Brown and Mary were appropriately decomposed. But Mercy Brown . . . well, that was something else entirely. She was relatively intact. What's more, she was now lying on her side. Obviously she had moved . . .

There could be no doubt: it was within her bosom that the vampire dwelled. Indisputable proof came when one of their number—history fails to record his name—opened Mercy's chest to reveal a heart still wet with blood!

The self-styled surgeon cut out the organ and burned it atop a rock by the side of the grave. Then the bodies were returned to the earth.

After her heart had been consumed by flame, Mercy's ashes were gathered to make the notorious prescription that should cure the failing Edwin.

Edwin—no doubt with tremendous reluctance—consumed the revolting mixture. Apparently, he didn't ingest enough of it though. On May 2, he, like his mother and two sisters, perished in spite of all efforts made to save him. However, all was not in vain: the evil had seemingly been destroyed. After Edwin's death, Demon Consumption left George Brown's family alone.

A century after her death, Mercy Brown still holds the title "Queen of New England's Vampires." Over the years, her sad story has been written with many variations. Even H.P. Lovecraft inserted a loosely disguised Mercy into his horror tale *The Shunned House.* He wrote, "Mercy Dexter's once robust frame had undergone a sag and curious decay, so that she was now a stooped and pathetic figure with hollow voice and disconcerting pallor. . . ."

Mercy has occasionally even found her way onto several nationwide television programs concerned with such things. Her grave, now a popular landmark, is visited regularly by hordes of curious tourists. In fact, she is responsible for a veritable cottage industry in Exeter. In time, thanks to Mercy Brown, vampires may be to Rhode Island what witches are to Salem, Massachusetts.

Today, Mercy Brown and her family still have relatives in the area. Exeter resident Lewis Peck, whose grandmother was a Brown, recalls being repeatedly warned not to play near Mercy's gravesite. And he was instructed never to touch her gravestone. Sometimes he tells of the strange light he saw one night back in the 1960s. It seemed to rise from Mercy's grave and soon became so bright it looked almost blue.

When he informed other family members about it, they were not surprised; they told him the light had been seen many times before.

Surely, at least to residents of Exeter, Rhode Island, Mercy is still among them.

LIVING MEMORY

EORGE R. STETSON WAS PERHAPS THE FIRST to study the notion of Yankee vampirism. His 1896 article, "The Animistic Vampire in New England," ran in *The American Anthropologist*. There, he demonstrated that the Yankee vampire was still very much a part of living memory at the turn of this century.

One tradesman he interviewed, a mason, had lost two brothers to consumption. "Upon the attack of the second brother his father was advised . . . to take up the first body and burn its heart, but the brother attacked objected to the sacrilege and in consequence subsequently died. When [the mason] was attacked by the disease in his turn [the] advice prevailed, and the body of the brother last dead was accordingly exhumed, and 'living' blood being found in the heart and in circulation, it was cremated, and the sufferer began immediately to mend and stood before me [Stetson] a hale, hearty and vigorous man of fifty years."

THE WALTONS

HE ABOVE STORIES, THOUGH PERHAPS LITTLE KNOWN, have been around for a long time. We can easily infer that belief in the consumptive vampire lasted at least into the first decade of the twentieth century.

And with that we've come full circle.

So now let's return to the events described at the beginning of this chapter and ask, Okay, so what was the big deal about the bones those kids found in the Griswold, Connecticut, gravel pit in 1990?

What those children found was an ancient unmarked cemetery. Archival research showed that it had belonged to a family known as the Waltons. Though now extinct, the Waltons had lived on the land during the eighteenth century, the last family member dying about 1840.

When Dr. Nicholas Bellatoni examined their coffins, he found everything reasonably well preserved. The human remains—29 bodies in all—were sent off to the National Museum of Health and Medicine in Washington, D.C. There, Dr. Paul Sledzik made a lot of interesting inferences about J.B. and the disheveled state of his remains. Apparently, J.B. and the other forgotten New Englanders had succumbed to a horror that is recorded nowhere better than in their bones.

J.B., Dr. Sledzik discerned, had died of consumption at age 55. His ribs were sufficiently scarred to indicate a long battle with the disease. Such scarring also indicated that toward the end of his life, he was often racked with terrible coughing fits interrupted by bloody expectoration. Dr. Sledzik also noted a crippled leg. Healed fractures on J.B.'s collarbone and ribs suggest that he had limped about in an oddly hunched manner.

In life, he must have been a rather unhandsome sort, grotesque enough to be remembered when people began screaming, "Vampire!"

J.B.'s corpse was thoroughly disturbed. This suggests he'd been held responsible for the White Death evident in many of the 20-odd neighboring bodies. His tomb had been invaded and his corpse mutilated some ten years *after* he died.

In short, J.B.'s case is important because it *proved* there was a strong tradition of vampirism in New England, dating from colonial times and continuing almost to the present.

Perhaps the vampires were not real, but the vampire-hunters most certainly were. As we explore the various chronicles of New England horror, we might be tempted to ask which is worse, the imaginary vampire or the corporeal ghoul? A ghoul, you may recall, is a grave-robber, an evil spirit or demon believed to plunder graves and feed on corpses. Not only did these early New Englanders invade the sanctity of the tomb, they also mutilated bodies. And, as we have seen, they actually consumed parts of the deceased as a kind of homeopathic inoculation.

THE WHITE DEATH

THESE STORIES OF OUR NATIVE VAMPIRES AND GHOULS are good examples of how early New Englanders resorted to folk beliefs about ghosts, witchcraft, and Satanism to come to grips with unexplained events like mysterious illnesses and deaths.

It is not hard to imagine why consumption—or tuberculosis, as we now call it—came to be associated with vampirism. Tuberculosis was the plague of the nineteenth century. In New England alone, the death tolls were staggering. Transmission was facilitated by everyday living conditions: large families, often poorly nourished, who shared crowded quarters for long periods. It was quite normal for the disease to run through families. Highly contagious and generally fatal, tuberculosis was so lethal one physician called it the first disease "to deter practitioners from attempting a cure."

Its vernacular names—consumption and The White Death—tell much about how it affected the victim.

As "The White Death" progressed, there was indeed a transformation: the infected person's skin became alabaster pale, ghostly, and translucently thin. A network of light blue veins became visible beneath its surface. There was often a feverish reddening of the cheeks, fainting spells, anemia, weight loss, and an increasingly fragile demeanor. Oddly, due to certain romantic notions of the time, these symptoms made the victims, especially young women, strangely alluring, while their health and strength were consumed by the disease.

It was probably easy for early New Englanders to imagine this wasting away—this process of being *consumed*—as the result of a vampire's parasitic kiss. No doubt, the resulting mysteriously heightened feminine beauty was evidence of the infernal transformation from victim to vampire.

A seemingly incongruous component of the disease contributed to its mystery: consumptives occasionally experienced surprising bursts of energy. Many were known to have powerful sex drives. These attributes suggested the individuals were clinging to life in a manner that could survive the grave.

As Dr. Sledzik explains, "When someone died of consumption it was believed they could come back from the dead and drain the life force of their living relatives. In order to stop this, family members would go into the grave and somehow attempt to kill the person again."

When relatives opened the coffins of recently dead consumptives, the corpses, formerly thin and frail, were often found to be bloated with pale flesh. Fingernails seemed to have grown into claws and, perhaps the most damning evidence, blood was often found in the mouth. There are even accounts, Dr. Sledzik says, of bodies jerking and gurgling as the remains were mutilated.

The stake-through-the-heart approach to dispatching vampires was a European tradition, not practiced by New Englanders. Here, as we have seen, the technique was to remove any remaining flesh and burn it. Decapitation was also a popular deterrent. Or, as we have seen with J.B., simply causing some disruption to the body was thought to be enough to kill a vampire.

Today, while walking through historic New England graveyards, it's hard to keep from wondering how many similar rituals went unrecorded. And how many heartless corpses rest beneath our feet?

WHO'S TO BLAME?

RHODE ISLAND IS KNOWN FOR MANY WONDERFUL THINGS, including Mercy Brown and her vampire associates. But should we blame the Ocean State for inflicting vampirism on the rest of New England? Did Rhode Islanders bring the vampires here?

Yes, so it would seem.

In tracing the dissemination of Yankee vampire beliefs, Prof. Faye Ringel, in her entertaining and informative *New England's Gothic Literature*, demonstrates how the whole scourge of vampires and ghouls most probably stems from Little Rhody.

According to her linguistic detective work, the parts of Vermont where corpse-killing occurred were settled by families from eastern Connecticut. And that vampire-infected section of eastern Connecticut had been settled by people from Rhode Island's South County—where the earliest instances of New England vampirism are recorded.

So if Rhode Island was vampirism's port of entry, where did it come from? Europe, most likely—but there is another possibility. Professor Ringel says, "It seems likely . . . that the vampire belief originated spontaneously in New England, in response to the increased incidence of and dread of consumption. . . ."

If that is the case, then at some point New Englanders simply started using an imported term to label an existing belief. Those energy-sucking revenants that preyed on consumptives suddenly became vampires.

According to the *Oxford English Dictionary*, the word "vampire" entered the English language in 1734. It had relocated to America as early as January 21, 1765, because on that date the *Hartford Courant* reprinted the OED definition of "vampyre," adding, "such a notion will probably be look'd upon as fabulous but it is related and maintained by authors of great authority."

There is no subsequent evidence to suggest that the word entered colloquial American usage until well into the nineteenth century. That, of course, does not certify that the word "vampire" wasn't whispered among New England townspeople as they diagnosed what they believed was the true cause of consumption.

It is fitting, then, that we close this section with a final visit to Rhode Island.

In West Greenwich, not far from Exeter, is the burial spot for Nellie Vaughn, who died in 1889 at age 19. Although, as far as I know, the word "vampire" has never been uttered in connection with Ms. Vaughn, local folks will be quick to tell you that there's something a mite peculiar about this particular gravesite: no grass will grow there. And, to compound the mystery, no lichen will take root on the headstone. It is as if some supernatural power were keeping the stone clean so its ominous inscription can be easily seen. It reads, "I am waiting and watching for you."

Old Man *of the* Mountain

One of the most gleefully gothic tales to come out of northern New Hampshire takes place amid the White Mountains, in the little town of Benton.

Hikers on the slopes of Mt. Moosilauke have for years reported seeing a mysterious caped figure in the woods. A camper might glimpse a dark form disappearing behind a tree. A picnicker might get a more complete look at a black-clad individual with long white hair vanishing around a bend in the trail. Others might spot a wrinkled hand or pant leg pulled quickly out of sight.

In most cases, there is nothing especially odd about these encounters. Most are so unremarkable that the observer might mention it in passing, if she mentions it at all.

But others who spot the furtive shape find it most peculiar indeed. They might respond in some atavistic way, suddenly experiencing a motiveless feeling of dread, or an overwhelming urge to flee. Observers might instinctively realize there is something not quite right about this mysterious old man of the mountain.

And—if we can believe the stories—perhaps there is good reason to be afraid.

In the 1970s, for example, a Dartmouth student took off by himself for a solo climb on the headwall of Jobidunk Ravine. When he didn't return in a timely fashion, his friends went out looking for him. They found him just where he said he'd be, but he was in a bad way. He was wandering aimlessly, as if lost, a glazed look locked on his face. And when he spoke, his friends realized he was in a kind of shock or delirium.

A quick examination revealed cuts, bruises, and a fractured skull. His rescuers put him on a stretcher and transported him to the Ravine Camp. From there, an emergency vehicle moved him to the hospital in Hanover.

In time, the boy recovered, though he was curiously vague about what had happened to him. But eventually, the story came out. He told one of his friends that while he was climbing on a ledge, a hand shot out through an opening in the rocks, and shoved him!

OLD STORIES

PEOPLE WHO HAVE HEARD these stories might wonder if we're dealing with some sort of eccentric hermit, or maybe a ghost.

That the encounters have been occurring for nearly 200 years might favor the "ghost" explanation, but when all the details are known, we might decide the caped, white-haired phantom is a human being after all.

In the late eighteenth century, the Benton family was among the first settlers of the New Hampshire town that now bears their name. And young Tom Benton proved himself an able lad in the town's one-room schoolhouse. He surpassed all his classmates, even the older ones, and soon had acquired a vast knowledge exceeding even that of the teacher.

The bright young man caused a bit of talk in the village. Eventually, his abilities came to the attention of a well-to-do judge from Plymouth. He took Tom under his wing after persuading Mr. and Mrs. Benton to allow their son to live in the city with the judge and his family. There Tom could take advantage of a far better school and would have the benefit of the judge's extensive library.

Tom proved to be something of a prodigy, continually astonishing the judge and his colleagues. Of course, the judge wanted the boy to follow his footsteps and read the law. But Tom's interests and aptitudes tugged him in a different direction. Tom wanted to study medicine.

At that time, the best medical school in the world was in Heidelberg, Germany. The expense would be enormous. Tom's parents couldn't afford anything like that, and the generous judge wasn't able to foot the bill himself.

Then again, there was a tremendous need for doctors in the north country, and surely there was no better candidate for the position than young Tom Benton. So the judge arranged a fund-raising campaign that would divide the cost of Tom's education among the families who would eventually make use of his services.

Of course, Tom agreed to the arrangement; he had no wish to live anywhere but New Hampshire. And soon he embarked on his first ocean voyage, crossing the Atlantic.

THE GERMAN PATRON

AT THE UNIVERSITY OF HEIDELBERG, Tom's progress was briefly delayed because he didn't speak German. He quickly proved as adept with languages as he was with everything else, and soon he was progressing more rapidly than his native classmates.

An elderly instructor took an interest in this brilliant American boy, and worked very closely with him.

Tom learned, however, that there was a sinister cloud over his elderly mentor. Although the man's classes were well-attended, his colleagues seemed to avoid him. The old man had been a brilliant young doctor, Tom learned, but he had done something that got him ostracized. Tom couldn't find out exactly what, but it had something to do with blasphemous experimentation.

Perhaps because they were both outsiders, Tom and the professor struck up a cautious friendship.

Tom was often invited to the professor's home for dinner. Their evenings would pass rapidly with challenging discussions of chemistry and theology, as well as animated debates about theoretical and clinical medicine.

Tom's curiosity about his new friend was satisfied all too soon. The old teacher passed away and expressly left Tom a small inheritance: a sum of money, a few books, and an old, locked trunk.

Upon finishing his four years of study, Tom returned home to honor his obligation to his benefactors.

Very soon people of the Baker River Valley knew that their investment had paid off. Tom's skills in diagnosis and treatment were extraordinary. His reputation as a healer quickly spread far and wide. People from hundreds of miles away began seeking him out. Offers for lucrative positions in big city hospitals poured in, but Tom remained loyal to his neighbors.

Life was good as Tom enjoyed a few years of spectacular success. He even became engaged to the daughter of a wealthy and influential local landowner. For a while, Tom's future looked as bright as his past.

Then—around 1816—something happened.

Stories differ on exactly what it was. One source holds that Tom's fiancée jilted him in favor of another man. According to a second account, Tom's beloved fell ill with typhoid and, in spite of all his best efforts, she died.

In either event, Tom suffered greatly from the blow. Perhaps his reaction was way out of proportion because he had never before experienced failure or disappointment. Anyway, he began missing appointments, failed to make his rounds at scheduled times, and began to appear more disheveled and sickly.

As the years passed, Tom became progressively more withdrawn. He lost all interest in his practice. Then, he left his fine house and moved into a decrepit dwelling on the slopes of Mt. Moosilauke.

Soon, people were describing him as a hermit.

The loss of Tom's fiancée, his subsequent depression, and the collapse of his medical practice might have caused many people to wish to end their lives. Tom, on the other hand, sought to prolong his. And perhaps he had discovered a way to do it.

One of the few possessions Tom carried with him into the woods was the locked trunk the old German physician had willed to him. He spent days poring over its contents: records, notebooks, journals, medical texts, and more. They were the very documents the dead doctor had used in his blasphemous research. The old man had been searching for the secret of eternal life.

And Tom picked up where his benefactor had left off.

THE NIGHTMARE BEGINS

MANY OF TOM'S OLD FRIENDS wondered what had become of him. They'd see him from time to time in the local stores, but he'd never stop to talk. Sometimes he wouldn't even nod hello.

Folks brave enough to seek him out to ask for medical treatment were abruptly turned away.

Then, a group of inquisitive youngsters decided to find out what Dr. Tom was doing all by himself out there in the woods. They sneaked out to his place one dark night and peeked in the windows. What they saw frightened them terribly.

There was Dr. Tom, his white hair in wild disarray, his clothing old and rumpled, and a look of maniacal determination on his face. He was bending over a table cluttered with beakers and tubes and vials. "Gosh," one of the boys said, "he's got a whole laboratory in there."

Animals started dying all over the region.

A milk cow was discovered dead in her stanchion. Bloated sheep dotted the green pastures like balls of snow. Healthy horses were found dead in their stalls.

The deaths might not have seemed out of the ordinary if there hadn't been so many of them. And they all had one factor in common: each animal had a fresh wound behind its left ear.

Odd events continued all up and down the Baker River Valley. The corpse of a young man vanished from the back of an undertaker's wagon. Eventually, a search party turned up the missing cadaver. They found it discarded in some bushes near Warren. Another unfamiliar corpse was right beside it. Both were naked; both had wounds behind their left ear.

When the searchers stopped at Dr. Benton's place, they found it deserted. A cursory search disclosed no indication of where the doctor might have gone. Over the next few days, repeated checks proved he had abandoned his cabin.

Had he vanished, too?

Would they soon discover his discarded cadaver in the forest, unmarked except for a small wound behind his ear?

Maybe.

But from time to time, hunters or hikers would see him in some wooded part of the 30-square-mile Moosilauke area. He was consistently described as wearing a black cape with his long white hair trailing down his back. He had gotten old, they said.

STORMING THE SUMMIT

ONE COLD NOVEMBER DAY AROUND 1825, a Benton woman was hanging laundry outside her house. The normally mundane activity was suddenly horribly changed when she heard her daughter scream. She spun around just in time to catch sight of a black-caped figure carrying her little girl off into the woods. The woman's husband lit out after the kidnapper while the woman ran to the neighbor's to get help.

Soon, a group of armed men followed the two sets of footprints in the direction of Little Tunnel Ravine. At that point, they had to proceed on foot. But at least now there was hope: the ravine would slow the villain's progress until he reached a dead end.

Already, there was a lot of speculation that the kidnapper was Tom Benton. They'd know for sure soon enough.

But their optimism collapsed when the footprints abruptly ended. The cluster of men milled around in bewilderment, wondering how such a thing was possible.

It was then that they heard laughter coming from above their heads. Looking up, all saw at once the dark silhouette of a man standing on a cliff far above them. Yes, it was Dr. Benton, clutching the struggling girl to his chest.

As the men watched in horror, Dr. Benton lifted the child above his head and returned her to his pursuers by hurling her off the cliff toward their outstretched arms. Unfortunately, no one was able to catch her.

As years passed, people continued to see a caped phantom in the woods. Fortunately, kidnapped children and dead farm animals seemed to be a thing of the past.

However, stories and speculation continued.

Then, in 1860, two adventurous entrepreneurs from Warren—Darius Swain and James Clement—decided to build a hotel on the top of Mt. Moosilauke. It would be a low stone building, called Prospect House.

Trouble was, no tradesmen would hire on to build it; they didn't want to stay on the summit overnight. Compromises were made, but progress was slow because the laborers insisted on going up and down the mountain every day.

On the fourth of July, they had their gala grand opening. More than 1,000 people made the trip up Mt. Moosilauke on foot, on horseback, and by the wagonload. The Newbury Brass Band entertained and there was dancing and much self-congratulatory oration. Clement and Swain thought they had it made.

But as darkness approached, not one single guest checked into the hotel. As folks drifted away, they talked about how Doc Benton might still be lurking up there on the mountain.

Business never picked up. By fall, in an effort to rescue their investment, Clement and Swain knew they somehow had to prove their hotel was safe. In order to do so they hired a couple of brawny loggers to stay at Prospect House through the winter. The owners promised to keep them supplied with firewood, food, and drink. They also installed a telegraph line for easy communication with the base.

A month went by with no incident. Then a massive winter storm descended on them. Wind howled and snow fell for three solid days with no let-up. This was an ill-timed tempest. It struck just as supplies were running low, leaving the men stranded, cut off from town.

One of the loggers tried to summon Swain on the telegraph, but the lines had been blown down.

With their supply of whiskey running low, the men knew they had to take action. Repairing the telegraph line would be far easier than hiking down the mountain, so they flipped a coin to see who would go.

By nightfall, the weather had settled to a point where it would be safe to leave the building. The loser suited up and prepared to do battle with the snow.

They agreed that if the first man wasn't back in 20 minutes, the second man would go out and find him.

Ten minutes passed. Then 15. At the 20-minute mark, the second man began putting on his heavy clothing, gloves, and boots. He took his lantern and left the safety of Prospect House to face the savagery of the storm.

As he followed the telegraph line, a blast of arctic air extinguished his lantern. But he felt his way along as the moon ducked in and out of the heavy storm clouds.

At length, the man tripped over something in the snow. His partner.

He struggled to drag the unconscious man back to Prospect House. After positioning the logger beside the woodstove, he tried every trick he knew to revive the unconscious man. Heated blankets, warm water, he even tried slapping him, but nothing worked. It was weird, for the man hadn't really been outside long enough to freeze to death.

Upon closer examination, the logger discovered it wasn't the cold that had killed his friend. It looked as if he'd hit his head, or maybe something had struck him. There was a small wound behind his left ear.

Then the surviving logger remembered all the stories about Dr. Benton. Panic hit him like a blow from an ax. He abandoned his dead friend and ran screaming out into the snowy evening.

By the time Swain finally made his way to the summit, the man's tracks were covered. There was no way to determine which way he'd gone. In any event, the second logger was never seen again.

Swain was able to blame the loggers' demise on the storm, but local people had their own ideas about what had happened. As a last desperate move, Clement and Swain hired twenty men with guns to pass one whole night at the summit. This they did with much revelry. They played cards, drank, and sang. No one slept and everyone survived.

Hotel business picked up, possibly due to the twenty loggers, possibly due to changing the hotel's name to the Tip-Top House.

In time, it became so successful they had to expand. Additions were built in 1881 and another in 1901.

There were still occasional sightings of a dark figure with long white hair. But the mountaintop had become very busy, and Dr. Benton had never been one for crowds.

Yet to this day, whenever a tragedy occurs on the mountain, there are people who feel Dr. Benton had a hand in it.

A man named Park built a gravity railroad for logging on the mountain. When the empty train sped into Warren as a runaway, a group of men followed the tracks up to find out what had happened. They found the body of Mr. Tomaso, the brakeman. But his corpse was so far from the tracks that he couldn't have been flung all that way by the centrifugal force of a runaway train. And if he had fallen from the train, more damage should have been done to his body. As it was, there was only that one wound behind his left ear.

On October 24, 1942, four Dartmouth students hiking up Slide Ravine spotted an odd tower on the top of Moosilauke, a tower none of them had ever seen before.

Strange, they thought. How could it just spring up overnight like that?

As the puzzled young men got closer, they realized what they were seeing was a freestanding chimney. The Tip-Top House had disappeared!

When they were closer still, they realized what had happened: there had been a fire and the hotel had burned to the ground. But the oddest thing was that no one had seen the flames. Most likely, the place had been struck by lightning. The whole thing must have been consumed while the summit had been shrouded in fog.

Then again, Dr. Benton might have had something to do with it.

Today, something or someone is still heard and occasionally seen on Mt. Moosilauke. Even if the witnesses know of Dr. Benton's escapades, they can't say for sure if what they have seen is, in fact, Dr. Benton.

But if someone were to get close enough to positively identify him, would it be possible to discern whether he was a ghost or a man?

Perhaps he still haunts the slopes in spirit form, playing his wicked tricks and causing damage from time to time.

Or maybe, by kidnapping pets and people to experiment on, he eventually found the secret of prolonged life. Maybe there really is an impossibly old man, strangely agile for his years, prowling the slopes of this haunted mountain.

What has he been doing up there for all these years? Perhaps now he's trying to discover some arcane formula that will finally permit him to die.

SHACKLED IN SECRECY

THE STRANGE SAGA OF DR. TOM BENTON is among my all-time favorites. I first heard it from a friend, a Dartmouth College graduate, who spent some time on Mt. Moosilauke.

Sadly, there is precious little in print about the good doctor and his misdeeds. The chief literary source is Katherine Blaisdell's ambitious, multi-volume *Over the River and Through the Years*.

Yet in the oral tradition, the story has been told for decades, first to guests at the Tip-Top House, later to folks staying at Ravine Lodge. Today, the lodge and much of Mt. Moosilauke are owned by Dartmouth College.

At the risk of sounding more than normally gothic, I should say that the people I've contacted at Dartmouth seem "strangely reluctant" to talk about Dr. Benton. One person associated with the outing club promised he'd send me some material, and didn't. Another individual repeatedly failed to return my phone calls.

What may seem secretive or protective is probably more proprietary. Incoming Dartmouth freshmen are routinely shuttled off to the lodge as part of their orientation. During the day, they are exposed to the great outdoors, and at night around the fireplace, to a ritualistic presentation of Dr. Benton's opus. Dartmouth alumni help perpetuate the tale.

Dartmouth has always been an institution shackled by tradition. Apparently, they want to keep Dr. Benton in the oral tradition and out of books such as this one.

THE ETERNAL YANKEE

ALTHOUGH THE STORY OF DR. BENTON is not a classic vampire tale, the two traditions have much in common, especially in the area of longevity.

Perhaps the best-known attribute of vampires is that they live forever—providing no one pounds a stake through their heart or reconfigures their bones. But vampires, like those they prey on, are said to be victims. They do not choose their eternal life sentence; instead, it is thrust upon them by fate, or by the design of another vampire. On some level, they probably bless the person or ghoul who finally lays them to rest.

Dr. Benton is typical of another variety of eternal Yankee—a human being with immortality on his mind. He deliberately seeks the path to eternal life, be it magical, medical, chemical, or even diabolical. Though they may be few and far between, certain lonely New Englanders, like the alchemists of old, have single-mindedly pursued what most people dismiss as impossible.

In addition to Dr. Benton, I have tracked down another man with a similar goal. Possibly a relocated kinsman of Dorian, Ephriam Gray from Malden, Massachusetts, tried to fabricate his own fountain of youth. Whether he succeeded remains a mystery, as we will see in the next story.

A **Picture** *of* **Ephriam Gray**

IN ACTUALITY, THE PICTURE OF EPHRIAM GRAY IS MORE OF A BLURRY SNAPSHOT. Of all the stories in this book, this is the one about which I have the least information. I chose to include it because I like it, and because it far exceeds my "passing strange" standard. It comes from a yellowing photocopy that has been in my files for years. There is no note to identify the source, though it appears to be from a magazine or book rather than a newspaper. I'm not even sure how it got into my files, which may add to the mystery.

So if Ephriam's story is not a fixed part of the folk memory of the Malden area, I want to do my small bit to reinsert it.

Apparently, there was always something a little odd about Ephriam. Though known to be highly intelligent, he nonetheless exuded a certain undefinable air that caused neighbors to avoid him. Folks simply didn't like him, but no one could state exactly why.

Predictably, Ephriam became sullen and rude. He made no overtures toward comradeship, finding it easier to avoid the people who avoided him. Eventually, he earned the reputation of being not only a recluse, but also a man of mystery.

It wasn't just his behavior; there were other mysterious aspects to Ephriam. For example, as far as anyone could tell, he didn't have a profession, yet he never was without considerable funds. In fact, he was wealthy enough to employ a single male servant.

The two men lived together in a big dark house on a side street near the center of town. Ephriam had no wife and was never seen in the company of women.

He never appeared at any of the town social events, he took no interest in politics, and what religion he practiced was a mystery to all his neighbors. As time passed, it became rare to spot him on the streets at all. Shopping and other chores were taken care of by the manservant.

But Ephriam was still around; people passing his house at any hour of the day or night were likely to see him silhouetted against the shade of an upstairs window, apparently engaged in some mysterious activity.

What was he doing up there?

If anyone was brave enough to inquire, the questioner would be met with a curt, dismissive grunt. In time, people learned never to ask.

One might have thought that such a misanthrope would be destined for a life of obscurity, but not Ephriam—he actually got a good deal of attention. But not until some time after he'd died.

Certain people speculated that he had killed himself, though not intentionally. For years men, women, and children passing his house had remarked on terrible odors wafting from inside. This noxious chemical stench was occasionally so pungent that anyone near enough to inhale it became ill.

Whatever the damn fool had been up to in there finally caught up with him. After all, he'd been breathing those same chemicals for years. It was bound to have an effect sooner or later.

So no one was surprised or brokenhearted that day in 1850 when the servant showed up in the Malden Police Station with the news that Ephriam Gray had died of natural causes during the night.

Perhaps the more curious of the townspeople were glad to hear the news; now they could find out what he'd been up to all those years.

News of Ephriam Gray's last will and testament spread rapidly. He had no relatives. He left nothing to the town or to charity. The eccentric recluse had bequeathed all his worldly possessions to his devoted servant. But there was a condition attached: the servant was to see to it that nothing was done to Gray's body prior to burial. No autopsy, no cuts, no sewing, no embalming.

And why not? the funeral director demanded. This was a strange request, highly irregular. The servant explained that Gray had been racing against time, trying to develop a chemical formula that would guarantee eternal life. If he had lived longer, he might have done it. Instead, he attained only partial success. His formula, Gray was convinced, would maintain his corpse in perfect preservation for years.

Of course, the servant had a certain investment in seeing this request carried out. If the formula worked, it could replace formaldehyde and all other embalming chemicals. Marketing Mr. Gray's potion could make the servant a rich man.

Since there was no way to legally prohibit it, Ephriam Gray was laid to rest in the Malden Cemetery. The servant died soon afterwards and gradually Gray's extraordinary claims were almost forgotten.

Twenty years after Gray's death, a student physician at Harvard Medical School heard the story from a friend who had come from Malden.

Intrigued, a small group of curious young doctors made the short trip from Cambridge to Malden. That night, they stole quietly into the darkened cemetery and eventually located Gray's tomb.

With two standing guard, the others opened the crypt.

To their surprise and possibly horror, they viewed the corpse of Ephriam Gray. He looked very much alive. His cadaver displayed none of the symptoms normally associated with death and two long decades in the ground.

Satisfied, and now eager to leave, they closed the tomb, resealed everything, and returned to Boston, not knowing quite what else to do. None of them had any problem keeping their midnight activities a secret; grave-robbing, especially for medical reasons, was a serious offense. If caught, they could expect no sympathy from judge or jury.

The lad from Malden made some discrete inquiries, but learned only that Ephriam Gray's formula was lost. The servant had passed away without telling anyone its whereabouts.

And there the whole story might have ended. By today, all would have been forgotten, if not for one thing: the tomb was opened again.

Just after the beginning of the twentieth century, the Malden Cemetery was relocated to make space for a road-building project. The relocation went smoothly until the crew got to Gray's tomb.

When they opened it, they found he was gone!

Impossible. How could it be?

The astonished authorities launched a major investigation. After many weeks of questioning, examinations, and head scratching, their findings were frustratingly inconclusive.

Police and medical experts kept coming back to one annoying detail: there was no way the body could have been removed without anyone knowing it. The seal the medical students had used to reclose the coffin remained unbroken.

Yet Ephriam Gray had vanished.

The question, of course, is where was he?

Could it be that he had, in fact, found the secret of prolonged life? After all, he was very specific about how his body should be maintained after death. Could it be that following a 20-year period of hibernation, he got up and walked out of the tomb?

Or is it more likely that the contingent of Harvard students disguised a medical grave-robbing by feigning curiosity about the state of the cadaver? Could they have taken Gray's well-preserved corpse, then resealed the tomb?

After all, who would have been the wiser?

No one. No one at all.

Whatever the truth is about Ephriam Gray—and even if there is no truth at all—the story still raises some spine-tingling questions about life and death and the vagaries in between.

This speculation has nothing to do with ghosts. For me, the unsettling, though admittedly remote, possibility is that after more than two decades in some kind of hibernation, Mr. Gray somehow got up and walked away from his tomb.

Impossible, of course. That is the stuff of horror stories and better left to the likes of Hawthorne and King. But still we must ask: Do people ever get up and walk out of the grave?

Maybe there is an answer in the stories of the following New Englanders.

PART VII

GRAVE
SOJOURNERS

"The boundaries which divide Life from
Death are at best shadowy and vague.
Who shall say where the one ends,
and where the other begins?"

— EDGAR ALLAN POE
The Premature Burial

The **Publick Universal Friend**

IN 1776, THERE WERE BIG DOIN'S IN LEDYARD, CONNECTICUT.

No, people were not flocking into town to join the American Revolution or to approve the Declaration of Independence. They were coming to see a miracle—the woman who'd come back from the dead.

In spite of the more primitive communication systems in those days, word about such wonders was sure to travel fast. No doubt, most curiosity seekers knew the full story before they arrived in town.

The object of their search was a 24-year-old woman named Jemima Wilkinson. She had been born in Cumberland, Rhode Island, in 1752, and raised in a large Quaker family.

Although she was considered more than normally good-looking, Jemima had from an early age seemed a mite peculiar, at least to some. She was predisposed to illness, shunned ordinary housework, and claimed an almost preternatural aversion to dirt. On the other hand, she showed more than a routine interest in matters religious. Even as a youngster, she spent hours reading the good book, studying Quaker history, and pondering weighty theological concerns.

She was able to quote chapter and verse with the best of them. Biblical diction so influenced her day-to-day speech that some found it hard to distinguish between quotations and ordinary conversation, an idiosyncrasy that would serve her well in later years.

When Jemima was in her teens, her mother died while giving birth to her thirteenth child. Shortly after that, the Wilkinsons moved from Cumberland to Ledyard, Connecticut. There, Jemima apparently attracted attention on two levels: some folks talked about her because she seemed a bit odd, but young men talked about her because she was a very handsome young woman. Local men pursued the pretty, dark-haired newcomer with passion and purpose. But Jemima wasn't interested; none of her suitors suited her.

She might have spent the rest of her years as a sickly, Bible-spouting old maid if providence hadn't intervened.

At age 24, Jemima Wilkinson took sick and died.

Jemima's grieving family laid her out in the parlor, as was the custom in those days. Folks gathered around to reminisce about her good points and to give her a proper Quaker send-off. They placed her in a pine box and hauled her to the graveyard. Just before they placed her in the ground, someone—perhaps a relative or spurned suitor—asked to gaze upon her one last time. There, right at the graveside, someone lifted the lid of Jemima's coffin.

Instead of seeing a pale visage with permanently closed eyes, the mourners were taken aback to see that Jemima's cheeks were rosy and her eyes wide open.

And then the miracle happened.

Jemima Wilkinson sat up and stepped out of her coffin.

Immediately, she started talking about how at the moment of death she had been visited by two "archangels descending from the east, with golden crowns upon their heads, clothed in long white robes, down to the feet."

"Yes," she said, "I have passed through the gates of a better world, and I have seen The Light." She continued with a vivid, and apparently convincing, description of heaven, and how the angels had sent her back to earth with a mission: she was to be the second "Redeemer." As of this day, the day of her resurrection, she would begin the moral regeneration of the world.

In recognition of the fact that she had literally been "born again," the divine powers-that-be had awarded her a brand-new Spirit. Therefore, she had to be called by a new name. From that moment on she was no longer Miss Jemima Wilkinson; henceforth, she was to be addressed as the "Publick Universal Friend."

Today, we might call Jemima's revival a "near-death experience," an illness-induced hallucination, or an out-and-out fraud. But in those religion-charged times, a return from the dead was a fairly big deal.

Needless to say, the local minister was interested in Jemima's angelic visitors and her tour of heaven, so he asked if she would be willing to speak publicly, in church, about her experiences.

She agreed, of course.

As the story goes, she preached like one inspired. She also looked especially pretty in the pulpit. According to the Marquis de Barbe-Marbois's contemporary description, "This soul sent from heaven has chosen a rather beautiful body for its dwelling, and many living ladies would not be unwilling to inhabit that outer shell."

Folks from all over southern Connecticut came to look at her and to hear what she had to say. The men found Jemima to be an eyeful, but no one went away without getting an earful. She passed along everything the angels had told her. They promised she would live for 1,000 years and predicted she would become the leader of all spiritual affairs for the new country of the United States of America.

The pretty prophet was invited to speak at many churches throughout Rhode Island and Connecticut.

According to biographer Herbert Wisbey, "Jemima Wilkinson evidently had some sort of a messianic complex that helped to create a sublime self-confidence, which, with her evident sincerity, contributed to her effectiveness as a preacher."

But other things were convincing as well, like her apparent supernatural abilities. In East Greenwich while she was preaching to a group of thirty-five people, she said, "One of you will not live to see another day."

Sure enough, that night a black servant boy who'd been in the audience doubled over and fell dead. Whether it was chance, or, as some scoffers believed, poison, the immediacy of the event enhanced Jemima's reputation as a seer.

During her travels, Jemima began to accumulate a following. Known as the "Jemimaites," the zealous crew and their decorative demagogue settled in New Milford around 1780. There they built a house of worship.

Lots of stories grew up about the lovely Jemima and her followers. Many had to do with her gift of prophecy. But the Publick Universal Friend also became renowned as a miracle worker.

In Swansea, Massachusetts, Jemima declared that as a demonstration of her divine power, she would replicate the First Redeemer's extraordinary feat of walking on water. The coming miracle was well advertised and thousands congregated at Mount Hope Bay to witness things firsthand.

Jemima appeared before them looking quite lovely in long flowing robes. After subjecting the masses to a lengthy religious harangue, Jemima proceeded with the demonstration.

Needless to say, she sank like a stone.

She blamed her failure on the scoffing, unbelieving throng, and stomped away wet and angry.

It is unlikely that she tried this demonstration more than once, but there are other versions of the story that take place in various locations around New England. An alternate ending has Jemima forcefully punctuating her sermon with the phrase, "Do you have faith?"

The crowd would answer, "Yes, we have faith!"

The question-answer ritual was repeated over and over—"Do you have faith?" "Yes, we have faith!"—until Jemima had worked the crowd into a near frenzy. Then, when she was just about to "take the plunge," she stopped her sermon, posing for the last time the critical question, "Do you have faith? Do you believe I can do this thing?"

"Yes, we believe!"

"That is good," Jemima is said to have replied. "If you have faith, you need no evidence." With that, she gathered up her robes and marched triumphantly, and dryly, away.

Yet another variation has Jemima's followers clandestinely building a wooden walkway just a few inches below the surface. This would permit The Publick Universal Friend to appear to walk on water, thus demonstrating her divinity. However—legend has it—non-believers just as secretly removed a few of the planks in The Friend's platform, invoking a soggy demonstration of her mortality.

In yet another story, The Publick Universal Friend tries her hand at reproducing another of her precursor's miracles—raising the dead.

The event was advertised. A crowd gathered. But then a skeptical observer stepped forward and asked for verification that the deceased was really dead. He then volunteered to run the corpse through with a sword.

And with that offer, the miracle occurred—the corpse got up and ran away.

Judge William Potter had a grand mansion called "Old Abbey" in Kingston, Rhode Island. The judge's daughter Susannah was deathly ill and Jemima offered to cure her. The judge and his wife, Penelope, willingly agreed since local medical doctors had been of no help whatsoever.

Before Judge Potter knew what was happening, the Publick Universal Friend and her entourage of "Jemimakins," as they were now called, moved into Old Abbey right along with the Potter family. Then all hell broke loose.

In spite of Jemima's reassurances, Judge Potter's little girl passed away. Undaunted, the would-be miracle worker offered to bring the poor child back from the dead. It might take a little while, of course. Such miracles were not easy to accomplish. But Jemima didn't see that as a problem; she had plenty of time. After all, she was going to live 1,000 years.

Unfortunately, as an old account says, "The laws of nature were inflexible."

The death of the child only prolonged Jemima's stay at the Potters' house. Long before the little girl could be restored, the judge—or maybe his wife—began to lose faith in their resident healer.

The nature of Judge Potter's relationship to Jemima Wilkinson has always been a matter of discussion. One story has Mrs. Potter discovering them together in the judge's bedroom. The Publick Universal Friend quickly explained that the poor man wasn't well and she was just trying to ease his physical and spiritual discomfort.

"Minister to your lambs all you want," Mrs. Potter told the preacher, "but in the future, please leave my old ram alone."

By the time Jemima and her Jemimakins were banished, she had managed to finagle thousands of dollars from the man. Another generous donation was soon to be forthcoming from the state of Rhode Island. While Jemima and company were staying overnight at the State Treasurer's house, a quantity of money miraculously found its way from the state treasury to Jemima's coffers.

Soon after that, perhaps in a moment of divine inspiration, Jemima decided to pick up and leave the area. New Englanders were losing faith in her anyway, and there were plenty of souls to be saved elsewhere. So off she went, heading west.

Her followers provided her with a well-padded easy chair for the trip. It was painted garishly with her initials—P.U.F.—emblazoned on both sides. She climbed aboard, the Jemimakins picked her up, and everyone headed off to the promised land of New York State, where religious eccentricity has always been almost a virtue.

Fortunately, the Lord had provided her with plenty of money to buy land and build her "Little Jerusalem." There she presided for the rest of her life, ministering to her lambs and eventually earning a reputation as a "sincere, kindly, benevolent woman."

We must remember that public figures like Jemima Wilkinson have, in reality, two identities—one in history, the other in folklore. Though her religious crusade was then, as now, rather amusing to many people, she was nonetheless an astounding historical personage.

She was the first native-born woman to found a religious society and was—along with Universalist John Murray and Shaker visionary Mother Ann Lee—one of the three great religious innovators of the Revolutionary period.

Though impoverished and self-educated, she managed to gather a wealthy, well-schooled following. With her vision, strength, and conviction, she actually led a group of people into the primeval American wilderness to set up a religious community.

As Herbert Wisbey says in his biography of the Publick Universal Friend, "Jemima Wilkinson deserves to be ranked with the small group of outstanding women of the colonial period."

Oh, by the way, her prediction about living 1,000 years turned out to be a little bit off. Jemima "left time," i.e. experienced her second death, in 1819 at the ripe old age of 67.

Danville's Divine Comedy

IN THE RANKS OF THOSE NEW ENGLANDERS WHO HAVE RETURNED FROM THE dead, Jemima Wilkinson can be classified as a sanctified superstar. Especially when she's compared to an obscure Vermonter named John P. Weeks.

Like The Publick Universal Friend, John P. Weeks died—but he just wouldn't stay dead. And all the strange events following his demise on July 16, 1838, are true. To prove it, a corroborating document exists, written in Weeks's own hand. It bears the signatures of thirty-one Vermonters. Fifteen of them were eyewitnesses to the miracle, including four church deacons, three ministers, and three medical doctors.

Even today, townspeople still swear the following events actually happened.

At the time of the marvel, John P. Weeks was a 26-year-old farmer and a lifelong resident of North Danville, Vermont.

In the blistering heat of that fatal summer, Weeks took sick with a painful disease, diagnosed as "inflammation of the bowels," or, as we would call it today, appendicitis.

For six days he writhed on his bed in nearly unbearable agony. Three doctors from the surrounding towns examined him, but offered little optimism. They'd seen the illness before and knew it was usually fatal. There was nothing anyone could do for him.

So day after day, everyone watched as John's misery continued.

His wife, along with their relatives and friends, wept helplessly at his bedside. The doctors tried unsuccessfully to ease his torment while local ministers took turns praying for his soul.

On Saturday, the sixth day of his ordeal, everyone abandoned what little hope they had left. They watched powerlessly as John P. Weeks closed his eyes and faded into unconsciousness.

At last, the stillness of death settled over him.

After the doctor confirmed the bad news, John's family began the process of "laying him out." Some heated water to wash his body, while others began removing his clothing.

You can imagine everyone's surprise when all of a sudden John sat up in bed and called for his pants.

Before the mourners' unbelieving eyes, the dead man climbed out of bed, then walked unsteadily to the door. There he stood transfixed. He seemed to be watching something no one else could see. At length, he raised a hand and began to wave.

In time, Mr. Weeks recovered completely from his illness. He survived two wives, fathered fifteen children, and lived to the age of 70.

Over the years, he told time and again the story of the miracle in which he had participated. He even wrote a narrative account, describing all the things that happened to him between the time the doctor pronounced him dead and the moment he sat up looking for his trousers.

"While I lay in this situation," he wrote, "I looked towards the east door of the house and saw a great reflection of light . . . lighter than the sun. I then saw two Angels advancing toward me, and the nearer they came, the brighter they shone. . . . One of them touched me with his finger and my spirit left my body. . . . The other angel sat and watched over my body while my spirit was absent from it. . . .

"One of the angels left the house and I followed him, floating in a path of light."

Weeks said that when he looked down at himself, he saw no flesh or blood. All he saw was his own spirit, formed in the familiar shape of his body.

Then he noticed that his angelic guide carried "a small trunk in his arms, about five inches each way." Naturally, John wondered what the mysterious box might contain.

As if he were some Yankee version of Dante Alighieri, Weeks followed the angel through what he called "The Valley of the Shadow of Death."

Looking around in this shadowy, sinister region, Weeks saw "a multitude that no man could number, in a dark, lost condition. They were weeping and wailing and trying to climb out of this place, only to fall back again."

Next, Weeks ascended a bright and glorious path about 3 feet wide, to the land of Paradise. Upon entering, the angel put down the mysterious little box. Weeks expected it might contain a golden crown to be placed upon his head. But the little box remained closed.

Weeks describes "the beautiful plains of Paradise" as only a Vermont farmer might: "The land," he wrote, "is perfectly level, grass perhaps half an inch high, no trees, nor stumps, nor stones."

He went on to discuss the climate, which he says, "was delightful . . . no clouds, no storms, no winds—the air neither too hot or too cold, but always agreeable."

The layout of Heaven seems to resemble that of a typical New England small town. In the same way that Vermont has a Danville, a North Danville, West Danville, and South Danville, Weeks's Heaven also is similarly subdivided.

He described a "Second Heaven" that lies to the east of Paradise. East Heaven is filled with genderless angels singing songs of praise.

And, he said, there's even a "Third Heaven," above, but clearly visible from, the Second Heaven. Mostly it's made up of God's golden throne ". . . ten thousand times brighter than the brightest gold," and more singing angels.

Weeks wanted to stay in Paradise, but, alas, his work on earth was not finished.

Leaving the mysterious little trunk in Heaven, the angel led John back to North Danville. On the way, they detoured through Hell again, just to give him a second glimpse as a reminder. As they watched the tortured throngs, the angel instructed John to be sure to warn all sinners not to come to that place of torment. When John agreed, they headed directly back to earth.

There they found the second angel still watching over John's lifeless body. The angel touched John's body three times and his spirit returned to it. The sensation, John said, was like entering an icy-cold room.

And that was the exact moment John P. Weeks sat up and demanded his pants.

He then rose and walked haltingly to the door, following the two departing angels. They paused at the threshold long enough to assure him he'd get completely well.

Sure enough, John P. Weeks recovered—just as the angels promised. And he kept his promise to them. He spent the rest of his life telling people about his tour of Heaven and Hell and warning sinners about the hot and hopeless place he had seen on his way from North Danville to Paradise.

"All this is true," Weeks wrote, "and Heaven is my witness."

All true? Maybe.

Real? Certainly. To John P. Weeks the experience was every bit as real as the sickness that brought it about. The episode changed his life, provided a calling for his remaining 44 years.

And when he died for the second, and presumably final, time, I suspect he bypassed the hopeless regions altogether. I have every confidence he soared directly to his little farmhouse on the outskirts of North Heaven where, at long last, he got to examine the contents of that mysterious little box.

Dr. Dixon's Dilemma

DR. ROBERT DIXON HAD A REAL PROBLEM ON HIS HANDS.

Apparently, a family right in the center of town was keeping a dead woman in their house. That's what the constable had told him, and that was definitely against the law.

Trouble was, the family insisted that the corpse would soon be up and walking around again. As a trained physician and medical examiner of Damariscotta, Maine, Dr. Dixon thought it unlikely that anyone would return from the dead. But like it or not, it was his job to go to the house, examine the body, and determine whether Mary Howe was dead or alive.

And he had to do it right now; the town constable had ordered him to.

Dr. Dixon had known the Howe family for a long time. They'd moved there after the War of 1812, when Col. Joel Howe, Jr., came up from Massachusetts, looking for a little peace and quiet. Because he brought five daughters and four sons with him, the Howe family caused quite a jump in the town's population.

Anyway, after the colonel passed away, his survivors had established Howe's Tavern. It became a popular local spot and, as a stagecoach stop, brought a lot of business into town. In fact, it became *the* place to stay for traveling dignitaries, and as such, a source of pride for all Damariscotta.

In spite of certain benign eccentricities, the Howe family members worked hard enough. The young women were intelligent. And the young men displayed that certain aptitude for invention often referred to as "Yankee Ingenuity." Lately, their so-called "perpetual motion" machine was causing quite a bit of talk. Far less, however, was being said about their second project: a mold for minting their very own half-dollars.

Sister Mary was a strange one, too. Not long ago, she'd got the notion into her head that she could fly. Apparently, she climbed to the top of the stairs, spread her arms, and flew directly to the floor below, banging herself up pretty good and breaking an ankle. That was the last time that Dr. Dixon had seen her.

Sometime before Mary's flight, all the Howes—right along with many towns-people and lots of folks all across the country—became interested in Spiritualism. They even tried their hands at contacting the dear departed. Of all the children, Mary was the one who showed exceptional aptitude as a medium. She was able to slip eas-ily into trances and converse with entities no one else could see.

When word of her extraordinary ability got out, many friends and neighbors came around to consult with her. Others dropped in to satisfy their curiosity or just for the entertainment value.

In time, thanks to all the travelers passing through Howe's Tavern, word about Mary's seances began to spread beyond Damariscotta. Pretty quick, people from all over New England showed up to avail themselves of her extraordinary gifts. Conse-quently, rooms at the inn were rarely vacant.

Eventually, the two enterprises—innkeeping and communicating with spirits—proved profitable enough so the family could relocate. They moved out of the inn and into a house they'd bought up the street. There Mary continued conducting her seances and inspiring a lot of gossip.

As with all spirit mediums at the time, there was no way to be absolutely certain whether Mary Howe was on the level. It was all a matter of belief, and Damariscotta, Maine, like any New England town, was divided on the matter of belief.

In later years, resident skeptics felt vindicated when Charles Crooker and his crew began renovating the inn. They discovered all sorts of perplexing and mysteri-ous devices. Oh, maybe the odd contraptions were the product of Edwin's Yankee ingenuity. He'd always wanted to be a successful inventor like Uncle Elias, who'd come up with the sewing machine. But the wires and pipes and tubes were suspicious. Some said the "spirits" might have spoken through them rather than through Mary.

Of course, along with the detractors, Mary had plenty of enthusiastic supporters. Many of her feats, they argued, just couldn't be explained. For example, in his arti-cle in *Yankee* magazine, Harold W. Castner tells about the time his grandmother at-tended one of Mary's seances just to "see the show." While she and several others sat around a table in the darkened seance room, Mary slipped into a trance.

Unbeknownst to anyone present, one of the sitters had a relative visiting New York City. Suddenly—perhaps hoping to catch Mary off guard—she asked if Mary could see when the relative would be coming back home to Damariscotta.

Mary mumbled in her trance, finally saying something like, "Yes, yes, I see him. But wait! I see lights. Many lights all around him. Oh . . . oh. He . . . he will not return. When all those lights appear, he will . . . die!"

No one had any idea what she was talking about. Later, however, her odd prediction proved to be true. At the exact time the lights of Brooklyn Bridge were turned on for the first time, the man died of a heart attack. Even the skeptics had to raise an eyebrow at that one.

As Mary Howe's mediumistic skills improved, the duration of her trances lengthened. And public curiosity about them increased.

No one, however, has satisfactorily explained exactly what triggers a medium's trance. And no one knows what happens internally when trances occur.

Some believe the trance somehow fine-tunes mental acuity, allowing the medium to see and hear things not normally perceptible. Others think that the medium vacates her body, in effect "loaning" it to whatever spirit wants to "take the controls." If that is the case, what happens to the medium's consciousness when it leaves the entranced body? Does it merely sleep? Or does it fly off to explore distant realms during a so-called "out-of-body" experience?

But what if consciousness abandons the body and no one else takes over? Does the body remain unoccupied for a while?

Maybe so. And maybe that was what happened to Mary Howe.

Maybe, just as her brother Edwin maintained, she was not dead at all. Maybe she was merely sleeping that day as Dr. Robert Dixon headed up the street toward the Howe home.

All the doctor knew was that two weeks ago, Mary had slipped into one of her trances and didn't come out. When people called at the house, Edwin had showed them in as if nothing were out of the ordinary. And really, according to him, it wasn't. Sister Mary had gone into trances like this many times before, he assured everyone.

But by the time she had lain there a week, people were beginning to wonder. By the time two weeks had passed, word had found its way to the authorities. It was then that the constable ordered Dr. Dixon to go find out what's what.

So bracing himself for an uncomfortable confrontation, Dr. Dixon extended his hand and rapped on the door.

Edwin opened it, smiling cordially as if all were perfectly normal. He showed Dr. Dixon where Mary was in repose. Oddly, although it was summertime, a fire was burning in the room.

Not far from the stove, Mary Howe was lying on the couch, laid out like a corpse.

Why, Dr. Dixon wondered, was the body surrounded by stones?

Edwin explained that he had heated the stones and placed them around his sister's body so it would not lose heat.

Dr. Dixon had to admit Mary didn't look dead. There were none of the expected signs of physical deterioration. As Edwin pointed out, her cheeks looked natural, her flesh remained supple, and her limbs could be easily moved. She'd been lying there two weeks, yet there was no trace of rigor mortis. Perhaps more remarkable, Dr. Dixon could not detect the slightest hint of a putrefaction odor.

But upon closer examination, the doctor discovered that Mary wasn't breathing at all. That, coupled with the fact he could find no heartbeat, brought him to the only possible conclusion—Mary Howe was dead.

Now it was Dr. Dixon's turn to issue an order. He found the constable and told him to seize the body and bury it.

In spite of Edwin's protests, the constable, a local minister, and the undertaker showed up, prepared the corpse, and carted it away.

But many people disagreed with the decision. Lots of folks in town had seen Mary go into trances, some lasting several days, some as long as a week.

Yet even though prolonged trances were nothing new for Mary, the authorities buried her anyway.

Though it wasn't an easy job.

Hillside Cemetery was almost directly across the street, but its owner, Benjamin Metcalf, wouldn't let them bury her there; he thought she was still alive.

They had to transport her to Glidden Cemetery in nearby Newcastle. There they found a plot, but couldn't find anyone who'd agree to dig the hole. The determined trio had to do it themselves.

After that was done, the undertaker's assistant couldn't be persuaded to help lower the poor woman into the earth. At length, the constable, minister, and undertaker had to do that themselves, too. Then they had to fill in the hole.

Though the town was sharply divided, everyone—especially the authorities—hoped and prayed Mary Howe was really gone, for now a resurrection would be very poorly timed.

And so there she lies to this day, her trance, one way or the other, long ended.

But the haunting part of all this is obvious: Today, more than a hundred years after the burial, we don't know for certain whether Mary Howe was buried alive.

And speaking of hauntings: since the day they buried her, many people have avoided passing by the cemetery at night. Some claim to have heard moans, sobs, and cries coming from deep within the earth. Others swear they have seen dim lights and misty forms pass fleetingly among the tombstones after dark.

In his entertaining book *Inside New England*, Judson Hale tells about the foggy November day when he visited Glidden Cemetery. He knew the whole story and wandered around trying to locate Mary Howe's grave. Perhaps he did not realize it had never been marked, an omission undoubtedly designed to keep Edwin Howe from finding and digging up his sister's body.

The ruse worked on Judson Hale, too, although his motives were quite different. He poked around in the cold for a while but was unable to find a marker. Though his efforts didn't disclose Mary Howe's headstone, perhaps he did locate her grave, for he writes, "I truly thought I heard a moan. . . . One soft, short moan."

Troubled *at* Midnight

PEOPLE HAVE REPORTED MUCH MORE THAN MOANING IN THE EVERGREEN CEMETERY in downtown New Haven, Connecticut.

Admittedly, New Haven can be a pretty scary place. Few people, however, would list the grave of Mary E. Hart as the source of their fears. Yet, if you can believe the stories, the ancient cemetery where she resides might be one of the most dangerous places in the city.

It's enclosed by a tall wrought-iron fence whose spiked posts should warn anyone in their right mind to KEEP OUT! But, because of a whole canon of legends that have grown up around Mary Hart's grave, brave souls occasionally venture there after dark—more often than not, to their own detriment.

For example, some people tell of two college students from Southern Connecticut State who, on a dare, visited Mary's grave at night. Their proof would be to make a rubbing of her tombstone. Not only did they never return to their fraternity, they were never seen again.

Then there's the tale of the two young men who decided to demonstrate that there really was nothing to all these Scary Mary stories. They camped out overnight near her grave. When morning came, they boasted that they'd finally laid the legends to rest. But the next day, one died in a traffic accident and the other was left paralyzed after falling down a flight of stairs.

And who can say how many more tales of midnight adventures end with Mary's terrified victims helplessly impaled on the deadly spikes of that wrought-iron fence?

A fair number of similar shudder stories appear in David Philips's *Legendary Connecticut*. They are inspired, so it would seem, by a whole cycle of legitimate mysteries surrounding the life, death, burial, and perhaps the afterlife of the woman interred under that massive pink-granite tombstone. An ominous epitaph adds sinister suggestion; in bold, black relief it proclaims: "The People Shall Be Troubled at Midnight and Pass Away."

This provocative inscription has inspired a nickname for the grave's occupant: the deceased Ms. Hart is more commonly known as "Midnight Mary."

No one seems to know exactly what the words mean or why they were carved there. The rest of the inscription reads:

> *At high noon*
> *Just from, and about to renew*
> *her daily work in her full strength of*
> *body and mind*
> *Mary E. Hart*
> *having fallen prostrate:*
> *remained unconscious, until she died at midnight,*
> *October 15, 1872.*
> *Born December 16, 1824.*

To compound the mystery, no one knows who erected Mary's monument, or when it was put there, or why it looks brand-new in spite of its age.

But the real puzzle, of course, is that weird heading, "The People Shall Be Troubled at Midnight and Pass Away."

The enigmatic phrase has been interpreted as a curse directed at anyone who might lurk around Mary's tomb during the witching hour. And plenty of tales like those above have grown up over the years to reinforce the notion of a curse.

Was a curse actually part of the story, as people have come to believe? Or was it a warning carved there in the late nineteenth century to scare away vampire hunters and those accursed medical grave-robbers?

One story has come to be accepted as fact, and it really may contain some elements of truth. It asserts that Mary Hart was an unremarkable factory worker who lived quietly in the Winthrop Avenue area. At the relatively young age of 47, Mary suffered a "shock"—what today we call a stroke. Death followed—if we can believe the inscription—at midnight. Soon afterwards, she was rushed to her grave.

But, according to those who "know," Mary was not a victim of apoplexy. Instead, she had some rare variety of narcolepsy, or catalepsy, or one of those sinister diseases so feared by the Victorians—diseases that could replicate death.

Perhaps the grieving Harts were too quick to confine their loved one to the earth, for that night—perhaps at midnight—Mary's aunt experienced a disturbing dream. She saw Mary awaken in the black solitude of her coffin. Then the aunt psychically witnessed Mary's terror, panic, and ultimately her crazed kicking, clawing, and thrashing.

The dreamer awoke with Mary's screams ringing in her ears.

Within hours, the family had reassembled at the graveside. Cemetery laborers rapidly uncovered the grave and opened the coffin.

There could be no doubt.

Mary Hart was obviously dead.

But the condition of her contorted body made it equally obvious she hadn't been dead when they lowered her into the grave.

To ease their minds and consciences, the family erected the elaborate tomb with its succinct, though not quite factual, cover story, a revisionist bit of history intended to justify their deadly mistake.

Opened Graves

WHEN WE HAVE FINALLY DECIDED WHAT TO MAKE OF THE PRECEDING STORIES, we might turn our attention to the few that follow.

The first perplexing episode takes place in Greensboro, Vermont. It's rather a slow-moving tale, taking over a century to unfold. And it hasn't ended yet.

The events began in the 1880s, when the body of a man was buried in the Greensboro town cemetery. As far as we know, the corpse lay undisturbed for almost 100 years. Then one night in 1968, somebody opened his grave.

Phantom or physical, the intruder dug down to the coffin, carefully collecting all the displaced dirt on a nearby tarpaulin. Then he or she left the scene.

When, in daylight, the deed was discovered, no one could offer any explanation for what had, or hadn't, happened. All the mystified townspeople could tell is that the coffin was exposed, but apparently hadn't been tampered with.

Why would someone open a 100-year-old grave?

And why, for heaven's sake, would the culprit dig it up so carefully?

No one had the slightest theory.

Perhaps more to the point, *who* would do such a thing? No one could suggest a suspect. The grave's occupant had no descendants living in Greensboro; only a few old-timers could even recall the family.

Charles Morrissey, former director of the Vermont Historical Society, made a few faint stabs at some possible motives. Maybe, he speculated, there was a gold nameplate fastened to the coffin, and maybe the digger was trying to find it. Or maybe the digger had found an old letter or diary telling of a bag of money secretly stashed in the grave at the time of burial.

To this day, as far as I know, no one can explain this graveyard mystery. To me, it sounds as if something was interrupted. If so, and if the deed had been allowed to run its course, perhaps the outcome would have been no less confusing.

In a similar vein, take this more recent and apparently similar case from Lyme, New Hampshire.

On a Thursday morning in June 1993, sexton William H. LaBombard got a big surprise when he stopped to make a routine check of the Gilbert Cemetery off River Road. He discovered a rectangular hole about 5 feet long, deep as a grave, and exceptionally neatly excavated.

What had happened here?

Had someone dug a new grave? Or maybe opened an old one? More likely the latter, because this cemetery hadn't been used in many years. Also known as First Cemetery, it is where Lyme's original settlers—beginning in 1766—had been resting in peace until that Thursday morning.

The point is, why would someone dig up a historic grave? Most people quickly suspected it was the work of pranksters. However, according to Steve Marshall, the historical curio collector who brought the story to my attention, several factors argue against it:

First, the tiny graveyard is hard to find. Few people know about it; it's not easily seen, and it doesn't even appear on the town lister's map.

And second, once on the scene, how did the intruder know where to dig? There are no headstones or markings on most of the graves. So how would the robber know which way to orient the hole. East-west? North-south? That would be difficult with no frame of reference.

Third, once the digging began, how was it possible to create such a perfectly rectangular hole? An unmotivated digger would have found it nearly impossible to dig through the tough weavework of thick roots. More difficult still, there was hardly enough room inside the hole to effectively wield a shovel or ax.

But here's the kicker:

Although loose dirt was carefully piled around three sides of the hole and strewn carelessly around the fourth, there were no footprints to be seen anywhere.

Surely this was no run-of-the-mill grave-robbing.

But if it wasn't a prank, then just what was it?

Rest *in* Peace

I'D LIKE TO CLOSE WITH A STORY I'VE BEEN HEARING IN ONE FORM OR ANOTHER all my life. It has to do with an elderly couple, Harley and Gladys Spooner, who lived in the town of Cavendish, Vermont.

Over the years, Gladys had earned a reputation locally for being something of a shrew. Not a week went by that she didn't give somebody a piece of her mind.

However, when she passed away in the summer of 1919, her funeral was especially well attended. I guess people paraded by the open casket just to make sure Gladys was gone.

Anyway, Harley, her mousy little husband, sat through the whole service with his gaze cast down at the floor. It was as if he didn't dare meet his wife's eyes even in death. Then, after the minister said the final "Amen," Harley was the first person to leave the church.

The pallbearers closed the box and hauled Gladys out to the wagon that would transport her to the cemetery.

Perhaps in a big hurry to get her into the ground, the undertaker pressed the horses a little too hard. As they went around a corner, the wagon struck a rock by the side of the road. The impact caused the casket to bounce out of the wagon and break open. The corpse lay sprawled in the road.

Everyone stood aghast as Gladys picked herself up, dusted herself off, and asked the driver for a ride home.

There she lived to torment her husband for another three or four years.

At her next funeral, everything went as before, but this time, after loading the coffin onto the wagon, Harley Spooner took the driver aside and whispered, "Now you take care not to hit that rock again this time."

PART VIII

A
NEW ENGLAND
GHOST TOUR

That Harrison heard what sounded like a woman in tears meant very little. It could as well have sounded like a moan, or a rattling chain, or slamming door, or anything at all—anything the spirit wanted it to sound like.

— SHELDON HATHAWAY
Dark Twilight

Bridges *to* Nowhere

IN THE OLD DAYS, THE SPIRITUALISTS DESCRIBED A PLACE WHERE SOULS WENT to live after they had shuffled off this mortal coil. They called this postmortem metropolis "Summerland" because the sun was always shining, the temperature was temperate, and everyone got along well, like one great big functional family.

Christians believe in a similar place called Heaven, and there are one or two other names for the spot as well.

But apparently, sometimes the soul doesn't go anywhere after the body dies. It stays right here, haunting after death the same places it haunted during life.

Another notion holds that the spirit world and our world occupy the same place at the same time—they are but separate dimensions of the same reality. If that is true, then there may be places where the two dimensions intersect, points of passage from one world to the other.

And perhaps the Gold Brook Bridge is such a place.

To begin our Ghost Tour, let's cross that bridge into The Other New England.

EMILY'S CROSSING

To THE EYE, THE GOLD BROOK BRIDGE in Stowe, Vermont, is not unlike any of the myriad covered bridges that span New England waterways. Some sources say this one-lane, 50-foot structure is the oldest covered bridge in the country. Its builder, John N. Smith of Moscow, Vermont, designed it with many unique features and bragged it would last forever. Maybe he was right; today, as a historic structure, it is guaranteed perpetual care.

What better place for an eternal spirit to take up residence?

Though its formal name is the Gold Brook Bridge, some call it the Stowe Hollow Bridge. But to most locals it will always be "Emily's Bridge," because Emily is the ghost who haunts it.

Scores of people have had run-ins with Emily. Some are willing to talk about it. Some won't. Perhaps it depends on the nature of the encounter—they range from benign to terrifying.

On the least menacing end of the scare spectrum, we find tourists with cameras. Often, photographs taken on the bridge don't come out when there's no good reason for it. Or the photographer might discover that an otherwise perfect print includes puzzling, blurry blemishes that weren't there when the photo was snapped.

For example, I recently spoke with Vermont historian Howard Coffin, author of *Full Duty: Vermonters in the Civil War*. He told me about the time he and his friend Richard Smyers—both employees of U.S. Senator Jeffords's office—were visiting the bridge. Mr. Smyers snapped a series of photographs. When the pictures were developed, one showed a vague shape that both men were certain had not been present when the picture was taken. Though the shape is indistinct, one interpretation is that it is the image of a woman.

Other witnesses actually see things on the bridge, things they cannot explain, like flashing white lights with no visible source.

Sometimes the point of contact is not the eye but the ear. Certain visitors swear they can hear an eerie voice from nowhere, uttering words that can't quite be understood. When the voice is understood, it sounds like a woman crying for help.

These two types of encounters combined in the early seventies. Lifelong Stowe resident Ed Rhodes told me about the time he and a friend were chasing thunderstorms. Finally, parked in the shelter of Emily's Bridge, they waited for the storm to pass. While sitting in the dark, Ed's friend became unaccountably scared. "Let's get out of here," he said. "I heard somebody hollering for help."

The friend started to drive away, but Ed said, "Wait a minute. Maybe somebody really needs help."

When they turned around, Ed saw "little tiny specks of light, like strobe lights. But the funny thing was, the light did not illuminate the interior of the bridge."

Sometimes the contacts are a little more physical. Hats can be whisked away when the air is absolutely still. Or people can experience warm spots in the dead of winter or inexplicable chills in the blistering midsummer heat. One man even saw hand prints materialize on the foggy windshield of his car. A neat little trick since there were no hands visible while the prints appeared.

Judging by these reports, you might think Emily is simply trying to get people's attention. But there are more menacing encounters, terrifying dramas played out in the dark interior of the bridge. Perhaps these actions reveal Emily's true nature.

For years—until it was stolen—a quaint "Speed Limit" sign on the bridge read, "Horses at a walk. Motor vehicles, 10 miles per hr." At such conservative velocity, horses and automobiles were easy prey for Emily's attacks. Sometimes animals crossing the bridge at night were slashed by sharp invisible claws that left long bloody gashes.

When cars replaced horses, Emily continued her attacks. Her phantom claws ruined more than one perfect paint job.

Not long ago, a local man named Vaughn was at Stowe Hollow, sitting in a car with some friends. As he peered into the dark cavern of the bridge, he saw a filmy white light shaped like a woman. Everyone was convinced it was Emily. The shape approached the car as the people inside scrambled to lock their doors. For a while, the form hovered there as if it were simply observing them. Then it began to move again, slowly circling the vehicle. At some point, Vaughn says, it reached out, grabbed the door handle, and began shaking the car. One can't be certain if the shaking was attributable to the ghost's strength or terrified passengers quaking inside.

So who is this strange lingering soul who hasn't quite made it across the bridge and into the afterlife?

Sadly, we don't know much about her. While many accounts say that Emily died by her own hand, most agree her tragedy occurred on that bridge around 1849. Judging from her postmortem activities, Emily's spirit seems angry, maybe even insane.

But why? In 1981, a woman tried to make a different kind of contact with Emily—psychic contact. Hoping to get the real story, she went to the bridge one night, lit incense, and tried to communicate with Emily's restless ghost. But Emily was in no mood to explain herself; she didn't answer.

However, the psychic claims that she picked up another set of vibrations. Around 1876, she said, the townspeople had lynched someone on the bridge—but it was a man, not a woman.

Did he have anything to do with Emily? We can't say for sure. But there *is* a young man in the story.

The best-known history of the haunted bridge holds that Emily was a young Stowe woman who fell in love with a man who, for whatever reason, failed to pass muster with her family. Forbidden to marry, the love-struck youngsters decided to elope. They planned to meet on the bridge at night.

The appointed hour came and went, but the young man never showed up. Shattered, Emily hanged herself from a rafter. And her desperate, angry ghost has haunted the bridge ever since, perhaps waiting for her lover to return.

There are variations of the story, though all involve a failed rendezvous and Emily's violent death at the Stowe Hollow Bridge, alone and unloved.

But we've already met one man who shows great affection for Emily—Ed Rhodes. His relatives were among the first settlers of Stowe. From his window, Ed can look out on four generations of family farms.

He first heard about Emily's Bridge when he was a kid. The story piqued his interest, sparked his imagination, and has turned into a lifelong preoccupation. More than anyone else, Ed Rhodes is Stowe's resident Emily expert. Though he has never met her face-to-face, he believes his encounter in the early seventies was close.

His most recent brush with Emily was in the fall of 1995, while he was showing the bridge to a newspaper reporter and photographer. As they stood on the bridge, Ed says, he distinctly felt an odd sensation along his spine. It was like a sudden cold chill, an out-of-place shudder. Perhaps it felt like static electricity, or moving air disturbed by an invisible body passing close by.

Ed works as a tour guide, giving foliage tours on the local trolley. Unfailingly, he includes Emily's bridge on his itinerary. To enhance his presentation, he digs into Stowe's historical records, searching for details about the real-life Emily.

But so far no one, psychic, scientist, or historian, has been able to prove that Emily actually lived. Or died. We must remember, however, that in the old days, families routinely buried their dead at home. Records—particularly death records—were not always file. And sometimes families might choose not to talk about a death—especially a suicide.

Today, Ed Rhodes believes his search for Emily may be starting to pay off. Downtown, in the old Stowe graveyard near Main Street, there is a tiny white monument. Ed says, "It's a simple stone, eighteen by nine inches, the first stone on the right as you go down the steps behind the Memorial Building."

The date on the stone would be the right era—1843. The name on the stone is "Little Emeline." Could that be Emily's grave, if not her final resting place?

"I don't know," says Ed, "but I like to think that that's our Emily. It is possible."

But then again, anything's possible on the backroads of Eldritch, New England.

HARTFORD RAILROAD DISASTER

THE STOWE HOLLOW BRIDGE is not the only Vermont location that disproves an old myth that ghosts cannot cross running water.

If we were to hop a train in Stowe and travel east, we would eventually find ourselves on a haunted railroad trestle. Here we see another example of what's beginning to look like a ghostly pattern: disasters seem to create ghosts.

That is certainly true in Hartland, Vermont, the site of one of the worst railroad disasters on record. It occurred more than a hundred years ago on and under a bridge spanning the White River.

The year was 1887. At ten past two in the morning, the Montreal Express stopped briefly in White River Junction, Vermont, before continuing north from Boston. Running more than an hour late, it may have been moving a little faster than necessary as it approached the Woodstock Bridge, a high wooden trestle four miles outside town.

That February night was arctic-cold—18 degrees below zero. Oil lamps illuminated the interiors of passenger cars, while woodstoves fought the terrible chill. Conductor Sturtevant of St. Albans, Vermont, was still taking tickets from sleepy passengers as the train began rumbling across the bridge. In all likelihood, it was

Mr. Sturtevant who first understood the significance of a dull bump and grinding sensation.

Something was wrong.

Sturtevant pulled the bell and Engineer Pierce hit the brakes.

But by then it was too late. The last car in line, a sleeper, hit a defective section of track and jumped the rails. It tipped, toppled, and ultimately tumbled over the edge, pulling two more cars along with it. When a coupling broke, all three dangling cars plunged off the trestle, descended 43 feet, and smashed against the solid ice surface of the White River.

On impact, stoves and oil lamps erupted into flame. Fanned by the night wind, the blaze ignited the cars. In minutes, towering tongues of fire torched the wooden trestle. Soon tons of timber collapsed beside the crushed cars. Trainmen and passengers who had escaped the fall worked atop the ice, trying to save anyone they could. But the inferno burned so hot the rescuers couldn't get anywhere near the other trapped passengers.

Brakeman Parker, who'd made a last-minute leap to safety, ran the four miles back to town, hoping to get help. By the time he brought rescuers to the scene, nothing could be done. Exhausted men and women stood helplessly watching the flames, tortured by the horrifying screams of the dying.

The most severely injured were carried some 400 feet to the nearest building. Ironically, it was called the "Paine House," after its owner, Oscar Paine. The more able survivors were transported to the Pease Hotel in Hartford.

Of the 79 passengers aboard, 31 were dead, burned beyond recognition. Five railroad men also died. And hundreds of lives were forever changed by this tragedy of fire and ice.

Today, nothing remains of the Hartford Railroad Disaster. The granite abutments are still there, of course, but modified to support the new 650-foot bridge.

But dark stories linger . . .

I recently interviewed Stephen Marshall, a local tour guide with a special interest in the supernatural. Steve told me how he, personally, has experienced the unpleasant odor of burning wood, more than a hundred years after the fire. And he told me about the dark specter of a uniformed man, believed to be the shade of Conductor Sturtevant, who is sometimes seen at night, patrolling the empty tracks, as if trying to guard against another tragedy.

The barn is still there where the survivors suffered and died. Some people, passing on foot, have been shaken to hear faint cries and hopeless sobbing from the building's dark interior.

And Steve told me, too, about repeated sightings of a ghostly child in old-fashioned clothing. This diminutive phantom is occasionally seen at dusk, hovering a few inches above the water, as if standing on a sheet of ice that had long ago melted.

Those who have seen him think he's the ghost of a young boy who watched his father burn to death in the crash. Though the child escaped then, he returns now—again and again—reenacting a rescue attempt that will never be successful.

GOOSE RIVER'S GRACIOUS GHOST

WHY GHOSTS SHOULD CHOOSE to haunt structures as uncomfortable as bridges is a mystery all its own. But Emily and the railroad ghosts are not New England's only bridge-dwelling phantoms.

If we continue east, passing New Hampshire and crossing into Maine, we're likely to find ourselves on another haunted bridge. However, the spirit here seems quite calm and well-adjusted. Perhaps that's because he's been in the haunting business longer than the Vermont ghosts. Or maybe he was more mature when he switched planes. Whatever the reason, this unusual apparition is often described as downright hospitable.

A typical confrontation occurred in the mid-1960s. Two couples were at their romantic work, parked in a lover's lane area near a bridge in Rockport, Maine.

Needless to say, they were not paying much attention to what was going on around them. It would have been easy for an intruder to sneak up to the car. It was far easier for a ghost to materialize right beside it—and that's apparently what happened.

One of the young men rolled down his window, perhaps to admit a little air into the car's steamy interior. What he saw outside, looking him directly in the face, lowered his temperature almost instantly. It was a man dressed in old-fashioned clothing, and he had something in his hand. He was holding it out as if offering it to the car's trembling occupants.

Later, when the teenagers compared notes on the strange incident, they all agreed on one thing: whoever or whatever had disturbed them seemed to intend them no harm. He was, after all, offering them what for all the world looked like a pitcher of beer.

Although reports of Rockport's hospitable haunt date back at least to the 1920s, researchers trying to identity him believe his story begins far earlier. It is likely that he is the ghost of a local hero, a fisherman named William Richardson.

During the Revolutionary War, the town—then called Goose River—was repeatedly under siege by the British. Since there were no resident colonial troops to protect the area, the citizens had to defend themselves as best they could. But it was impossible to guard against sneak attacks. Using these covert tactics, the British often destroyed their crops, slaughtered their livestock, or burned their houses.

In 1779, a private vessel captained by Samuel Tucker was being pursued by a British warship. William Richardson came to the rescue. He used his small fishing boat to meet the privateer and guide it to safety. With Richardson's help the ship eluded the British, allowing it to continue unmolested to Portland, then on to Salem, Massachusetts.

This retaliatory maneuver was tremendously satisfying to the citizens of Goose River, who'd been much abused by the Royal Navy. But they enjoyed far greater pleasure in 1783 when the Treaty of Paris was signed, finally putting an end to the Revolutionary War and recognizing America as a nation.

Richardson threw a huge party to celebrate. There was much laughter, music, dancing, and feasting; according to all accounts, he did it up right. Needless to say, the ale flowed nonstop.

Wanting to share the celebration with everyone in town, Will Richardson went wandering off. He carried a pitcher of beer from house to house, peeking in windows and rousting his neighbors.

Just as he was walking across a wooden bridge over the Goose River, he confronted three horsemen. Smiling and singing, he raised the pitcher, offering the travelers a drink.

The men, however, were Tories, and in no mood to celebrate. To them, this lone, drunken townsman was easy prey. One of the riders smashed Will over the head with his rifle-butt and left him beside the road for dead.

When Will woke up in the timeless void of the spirit world, he might have been confused. After all, the familiar wooden bridge has been replaced and just didn't look the same. Even the name of his hometown was different; now everyone was calling it Rockport.

But Will still has his pitcher with him, and—even today—he freely offers to pour a glass for anyone he meets on the bridge.

For example, the young couple walking on the bridge one summer night in 1953 had anything but spirits on their minds. But as they approached the bridge, something was approaching them. It was a man, strangely dressed, staggering slightly. He stepped out of the darkness, holding something in front of him. Unable to see the object clearly, the young man stepped protectively forward.

Before an altercation occurred, the young man and his frightened girlfriend watched as the stranger vanished before their disbelieving eyes. After all, believing in ghosts is one thing, but spirits carrying spirits is almost too much to swallow.

Ghost-Hunting

Sometimes people ask me where to go looking for ghosts.

As you might conclude from the previous chapter, ghosts are none too choosy about where they hang out. In Europe, castles have long provided permanent lodging for spirits. But here in New England, castles are in short supply.

There is one, however. A huge stone place with a three-story tower, it was built in 1871 by publisher Sylvester Beckett. Its address: 1 Singles Road, Cape Elizabeth, Maine.

Although Beckett died in 1882, he has neglected to leave. Maybe that's why the old place is still called Beckett's Castle. Mr. Beckett sometimes shows himself in the form of a transparent blue-colored cloud. Apparently, he continues to enjoy the view from on high, because the door from his bedroom to the tower always remains open—even after people have tried nailing it shut.

Maine seems to be hospitable to ghosts; it provides plenty of diversion so they won't die of boredom. For example, there is a haunted movie theater in Skowhegan. The mean-spirited spirit who lives there likes things just the way they are. He recently demonstrated his objection to building modifications by spilling paint, throwing tools, and zapping workers with electrical shocks—even when the power was turned off.

For ghosts with more elevated cultural demands, Maine also offers a haunted opera house in Boothbay. Mostly, the ghost confines his activities to a single upstairs room. There, since 1949, certain human beings have sensed they were not alone.

The spirit will subtly announce his presence by playing the piano. Some people believe the ghostly musician is Earl Cliff, a pianist featured there around the turn of the century.

And what can be the motive of the invisible squatters who have taken up residence in Bellingham, Rhode Island's Center Library? I don't think they are there to study. They repeatedly ignore the library's "silence rule" as they thump around, moving chairs, and mumbling in empty rooms. Staff members gave up shushing them long ago. "It's been going on for years," one librarian said. "I don't pay any attention to it anymore . . ."

But Maine and Rhode Island are not the only New England states that appeal to ghosts with education, taste, and breeding. Take Lenox, Massachusetts: what most people think of as the summer home of the Boston Pops, others recognize as the abode of a music-loving spirit.

On the grounds of the Tanglewood Music Festival, there is a three-story Victorian house called Highwood Manor, built during the first half of the nineteenth century. Its invisible occupant became reanimated in 1986 when workmen disturbed a memorial marker on the grounds.

Suddenly, water faucets turned themselves off and on, doors opened and closed, and something unseen tossed the hair of house manager Marcia Duncan. Perhaps it was the same entity that materialized in front of Leonard Bernstein, causing his fearful leap from a window seat.

Subsequently, John Williams joined a group of ghost-hunters, but their target remained invisible. Some people theorize it might be the spirit of Oreb Andrews, who died on the grounds in 1822. Others believe it might be some spirited musician, living or dead, who enjoys performing his very own fantasia.

While Maine has its haunted opera house and Massachusetts has its Tanglewood, we might expect something entirely different from Connecticut. And that's just what we get.

Many of us have heard about the "stage-door-Johnnys" who haunt strip joints. But in New Haven, there's a strip joint called "Stage Door Johnny's"—and it's actually haunted! Could performers like Bethany Bustin and Selena Steele have an admirer from the spirit world? Or are his inexplicable antics puritanical protests from the great beyond?

Whatever its motive, the mysterious, invisible presence has employees on edge.

According to owner John Kraft, a former railroad man, weird events began immediately after he bought the club in 1990. Equipment broke down. Objects moved around on their own. People heard bells ringing, footsteps in empty rooms, and low, indistinct voices when no living soul was near.

Kraft ignored the occurrences at first, but one night when he and his wife were sitting at a table talking, all the house lights came on.

An Australian stripper, who is also a witch, conducted an after-hours Halloween seance. Kraft ended the seance abruptly when a cordless microphone rocketed across the room.

So far, no one has been injured, though everyone's fears are thoroughly aroused. My curiosity is aroused, also. What type of entertainer, I wonder, is responsible for these strange things that go bump and grind in the night?

I wonder, too, if ghosts keep up their odd antics forever? Or do they eventually give up? If so, where do they go when they retire?

Perhaps to Northampton, Massachusetts, where there's a retirement home called Rockridge. There, residents are likely to hear soft, pleasant chords from an electric organ at all hours of the night. No melody, no individual notes, just a harmonious progression of chords. The instrument was donated by resident Lee Thornsten. Before she passed away in 1986, she used to get up early, sit in the dayroom, and play the organ. But, because of her severe arthritis, all she could play was chords.

ISLES OF FRIGHT

FOR SOME REASON GHOSTS seem to like water. In fact, there are contemporary theories that suggest water may play a part in creating ghosts, either by somehow recording fragments of their earthly existence, or by providing a medium that allows departed souls to swim or sail back into our reality.

We recall classical stories about Charon ferrying souls of the dead across the river Styx—perhaps some souls stowaway for the return trip.

Anyone living along the New England seacoast probably can recall a good story about a phantom ship's captain, an eternally patient seaman's widow, or a pirate's ghost.

If water is a factor in creating ghosts, then islands should be especially haunted. Surrounded by water, they're like little countries all their own. Invariably, these countries have a minority population of specters.

There are many examples, of course. Whole books have been written about the hauntings on this or that island.

In Massachusetts, Nantucket island boasts over forty stories about haunts, chronicled in at least two books.

Among the spirit-plagued islanders is Joanne Shaw. Like an extraordinary number of her neighbors, Ms. Shaw had a resident ghost in her nineteenth-century farmhouse in the middle of the island. She reported that it came downstairs one day "right in front of me." Apparently, it's the ghost of a 10-year-old child, with a cloak covering her face. Ms. Shaw said, "I watched her for a minute, and then when I started getting scared, she disappeared." The ghost, christened Emily by Shaw's family, seemed to operate out of a third-floor bedroom. She'd occasionally appear there; if not, she'd at least make the floorboards creak.

According to many people, including *Jaws* author Peter Benchley, the old William Coffin house on Nantucket is also haunted.

Back in 1795, wig-maker Coffin was accused of robbing a local bank and making off with $21,000. Then in 1816, another man confessed to the crime. After 21 years of public scorn, Coffin had been pretty thoroughly humiliated. Because he was never able to forgive the townspeople for the false accusation, Coffin ultimately took his anger to the grave.

But that wasn't the end of it. Being a true Yankee, he was still able to keep a good firm grip on a grudge. Coffin continues to make his discontent known from time to time, and has been doing so for over two centuries.

During the 1960s, Peter Benchley summered at the Coffin house. He claims he woke from an afternoon nap to see an old man in eighteenth-century dress, sitting in a rocking chair in front of a roaring fire. Then, in a heartbeat, the old man and the fire vanished. Eventually, the rocking chair came to a stop.

At Nantucket's old Sankaty Lighthouse, U.S. Coast Guard officers claim their nearby dormitory is occasionally disrupted by, among other things, flying pots and pans. Interestingly, the ghost, quite possibly an ex-military man himself, will always cease immediately when ordered to do so.

Although ghosts who follow orders might be unusual, haunted lighthouses are fairly routine. In fact, I have come to suspect every lighthouse on the New England coast has its resident specter.

The Penfield Reef Light in Fairfield, Connecticut, for example, was the scene of a Christmas tragedy—and is the birthplace of a Christmas spirit.

In 1916, lighthouse-keeper Fred Jordan wanted to go to the mainland to spend some holiday time with his family. With judgment perhaps slightly impaired by loneliness, he set out alone in a rowboat, just as a storm was brewing.

It was a one-mile trip, and Jordan was an experienced seaman, but it must have been a wicked night. Ten-foot waves swatted at the tiny boat, quickly capsizing her.

A few days later, Fred Jordan's body was found and buried.

Shortly thereafter, the two men who replaced Jordan watched a ghostly figure coming down the lighthouse stairs, making toward the room where records and other lighthouse data were kept.

When they summoned enough courage, they entered the room. Though it was absolutely empty, they found the log book opened to the page that recorded the lighthouse-keeper's death. There, in ink that was barely dry, they read fresh notations about wind and weather. Fred Jordan's ghost still walks the reef, and hovers protectively in the now automated lighthouse.

A slightly more assertive ghost is said to walk the New London Ledge Lighthouse at the mouth of the Thames River in Connecticut. Even without a resident haunt, it would be a pretty amazing place. It is a big, square, three-floor Georgian mansion that seems to float upon the tide. There is no traditional tower; instead, the light is housed in a sort of cupola positioned at the center of the rectangular roof.

Built from 1909 to 1913, its $94,000 price tag included a handmade crystal lens crafted by Henry LePaute in Paris in 1890, and a system of intricate weights and gears that had to be wound three or four times a day.

In 1987, this imposing structure was the last lighthouse on Long Island Sound to become fully automated.

Why last?

Well, some people say it is because the Coast Guard feared the resident ghost would sabotage the place if left unsupervised.

During the many years the New London Ledge Lighthouse was staffed, no one ever actually saw the ghost, but he aggressively made himself known. He opened windows, moved radios around, turned TVs off while people were watching them, and raised a ruckus stomping around overhead when everyone was accounted for on the lower levels. Perhaps not wanting to be left alone, he'd sometimes cut boats adrift, even when they were securely tied fore and aft.

He seemed to enjoy plaguing Coast Guard crews by setting off the foghorn on bright, cloudless days. Specially trained technicians were unable to determine why the lights flashed on and off or what overrode the atmospheric sensor, triggering the foghorn mechanism at inappropriate times.

No one is sure who the haunting spirit really is, but for some reason, people took to calling him Ernie. According to tradition, Ernie was a distraught lighthouse-keeper who, back in 1939, jumped off the building and drowned. His suicidal mood overcame him when his wife ran off with a ferryboat captain from Block Island.

When machines replaced men, Fireman William Grace was among the last Coast Guard personnel to leave the island. His final entry in the lighthouse log was, "Take care Ernie, this will always be your lighthouse."

And with that, the Coast Guard was replaced by a ghost guard who'll never be put out of work by automation.

SHEFFIELD ISLAND

THERE'S ANOTHER HAUNTED ISLE where the unnatural seems perfectly commonplace.

Accessible only by boat, Sheffield is one of several Connecticut islands that make up the Stewart McKinney Wildlife Preserve. Though it is the most distant of the islands, some people might prefer to describe it as the "farthest out." That's because strange things happen there. For years, the island has had the reputation for being haunted.

An archaeologist named Karen Orawsky, working on historic site preservation, experienced the strangeness for herself in 1991. On a clear fall day, she heard music as her boat approached the island. She described it as hypnotic and mystical. This Siren song was definitely mysterious, for Ms. Orawsky could not determine where it was coming from.

Sheffield's haunting air was continually accompanied by other uncanny sounds. For example, occasionally Ms. Orawsky heard the blare of a foghorn—but not a wisp of fog or mist would be visible anywhere. And perhaps more unsettling, there were the distinct cries for help. She'd hear these at night, when no one was in trouble.

But Ms. Orawsky's strange experiences while researching Sheffield Island were not all aural. During a sunny, 80-degree summer day, she suddenly felt cold, as if a draft were enveloping her. She looked at the trees to see if wind was moving the leaves. She shuddered again when she saw the branches perfectly still.

As an archaeologist, perhaps Ms. Orawsky pays more attention to rocks than other people might. How surprising it must have been when she returned to the island several times over a three-day period to find that certain rocks had changed places, apparently all by themselves.

Between trips, they'd reassemble into distinctly different formations—circles and partial walls—that Ms. Orawsky insists "weren't there before."

Perhaps an examination of the island's history can provide explanations for some of these ghostly phenomena.

Robert Sheffield, Sr., was part of the island's original family of settlers. He died there in 1807. During his lifetime, he had enjoyed music and played an obsolete instrument called a "Long Spell." It was similar to an oversized violin, but the strings were played with porcupine quills. Could that explain the haunting Lorelei lullaby that greeted Ms. Orawsky upon her first arrival?

And what about the cries for help? Could they have been a supernatural echo reverberating in the island air since 1832? That's when the 27-year-old Nelson Smith drowned while loading stones on his boat. And perhaps it's Nelson, or all that is left of him, who keeps repositioning stones . . .

But the sound of a foghorn on clear days? That remains a mystery.

There is a lighthouse on the island. Its stark stone walls have stood for more than a century and a quarter. Though the sounds don't originate from there now, perhaps they did a long time ago. Could people today be hearing the warning blasts that failed to save long-dead sailors from their watery doom?

Pat O'Shaughnessy, a lighthouse-keeper on Sheffield, said he had never seen any of the island ghosts. "But," he added, "if there was ever a place that could be haunted, this is it."

For Karen Orawsky, there were enough contemporary oddities blended with island history to inspire a book. Her *Sheffield—From Legend to Lighthouse* speculates about ghostly sounds and moving rocks in a place where the air, like the sea, is full of mysteries.

All of which brings us to this next fascinating tale of a highly unusual haunting. It is from the files of artist and international ghost-hunter James Reynolds and takes place around the turn of this century on an island in Maine. The scene is the appropriately named Dark Harbor, a village on Islesboro, in Penobscot Bay . . .

A DEADLY IMPULSE

SALATHIEL STONER had made a big mistake, though it was difficult to say exactly when he first realized it.

Looking back, he knew it had been an impulsive thing; his friends never had a chance to warn him. But now it was done, twenty years done, and it seemed way too late to set things right.

If he had it to do over again, he would have married a local girl, just as his brother Asa had done. Anyone in town would have told him importing a woman was a bad idea, especially a Southerner. When Salathiel came home with that Virginia woman, it was as if he had invited the Devil right into his house.

He'd met her during that long trip to Church Falls, Virginia, the time he'd gone down to settle his uncle's estate. She was 29 years old—as was he—and pretty enough, too. He especially loved the musical softness of her speech.

So Salathiel Stoner had married Amanda Carter, just like that.

Oh, she'd been friendly enough at first, all sweetness, smiles, and Southern hospitality. Maybe she'd thought he was some rich Yankee land baron with a mansion on the sea. Or maybe she'd figured Maine was a far more romantic and temperate place. But from the moment she set foot in Dark Harbor—where the Stoners had lived for generations—the sweetness ended, the smiles faded, and the Southern hospitality vanished forever.

By 1900, Sal's wife had the reputation for being the most ornery woman in town—a shrew. She scared his friends away with her sharp tongue, discouraged visitors with her better-than-thou airs, and rarely left the remote spit of land where their white house was forever lashed with wind and rain.

Sal's brother Asa, and all the Stoner boys' fisherman friends, remembered Sal as a good-natured lad. He'd enjoyed spinning yarns down at the dock, or joking around the fire at the general store. But they had watched him erode, worn down by his wife's relentless tongue. Now he was a grim, sullen shadow, who spent hours alone and who remained uncommonly quiet in the presence of his longtime friends.

No one could imagine what went on behind the walls of that white house on the knoll overlooking Dark Harbor. They just knew the hard life of a fisherman could be made a hell on earth by the wrong companion. And there were no two ways about it: Amanda Carter Stoner would not be fit company for anyone but the Devil himself.

Vicious arguments ended in sullen silences that would last for days. Months passed without a kind word being shared. Years slipped away, blurred in misery and pain. And tensions grew.

At first, Sal had tried to see things from Amanda's point of view. Sure, Maine was a very different place from Church Falls, Virginia. Hard storms could cripple the community any time of year. The island air was never free of dampness. The winters were long and difficult.

And the sea never offered riches, only sustenance—and sometimes not even that.

It was a bleak life if one chose to see it as bleak. Amanda made no effort to see it any other way.

Sal couldn't remember the last time they'd had company. His mother and sisters refused to come around. Even brother Asa wouldn't set foot in the house. If he wanted to talk, he'd summon Sal by yelling from the dooryard.

Must be the woman likes being miserable, Sal thought. Seemed like there was never a shortage of things to nag him about. Lately, she'd been on him again about a carpet for the parlor.

Well, why not, Salathiel thought. She had a birthday coming up and Sal was about due for a trip to Bangor. A nice gift might shut her up for a while.

Then, maybe just for a moment, Sal's thoughts for his wife softened. He knew she'd probably married him just to spite that Southern boy who'd jilted her more than thirty years ago. And she'd come to Maine to escape the whispers and the gossip. But when she'd settled in Dark Harbor . . .

Well, being a fisherman's wife was not easy, even for those who were used to it. And Salathiel knew he had never been the best husband in the world. Maybe, he thought, maybe it's time for a small kindness.

Two days later, Sal and Asa returned by boat from Bangor, sailing down the Penobscot River. It was dark when they crossed the bay, but the moon was full as Sal climbed the knoll to his house. Over his shoulder, he carried a sizable piece of rolled carpet.

Though tired after his trip, he was determined to get the carpet down before bedtime. He'd even bought just the right kind of nails to do the job.

He shifted his burden from shoulder to shoulder, noting that Amanda wasn't at the door to greet him. But maybe she'd be glad to see him when he showed her the birthday present, especially one she'd been hankering after for years.

He walked in the front door, entered the dimly lit parlor, and began to unroll the carpet. It sure was a fine piece of merchandise, an Axminster. It had come all the way from England. In fact, the salesman told him it was the nicest one in the store. Deep red colored, pile soft as a mossy riverbank, covered with clusters of tiny roses and green leaves.

"Amanda," he said, "come in here and see what I brought you."

Amanda didn't say anything. She walked to the table, lighted a small lamp, and carried it to where she could get a better look at her birthday present.

"Ain't that handsome, though," Sal said. "Now if you get me my hammer and give me a hand with this furniture, we'll have her down 'fore bedtime."

Amanda almost smiled as she went to fetch Sal's hammer. But by the time she handed it to him, the cold dead look had returned to her eyes.

"You make me wait twenty years for this and now you expect me to be grateful? You expect me to celebrate my birthday after you've used me up like an old plow horse? Well, I hate your carpet. I wouldn't wrap fish in the damn thing. And I hate you too, Salathiel Stoner. I might as well say it right out in the open: I hate you, and I always have."

It was then that Salathiel Stoner's years of silent seething, his decades of pent-up anger built into a mindless rage . . .

And exploded.

Before Amanda could tell Sal exactly how much she had always hated him, Sal lifted the hammer.

Something in him snapped, releasing a hammer blow against the back of his wife's skull. Amanda slumped like a bag of grain, her blood gushing onto the floral bouquets of her new red carpet.

He hit her again and again and again. Until she was still. Finally, finally still.

And quiet.

Sal sat down on the ottoman and, for the first time in thirty years, enjoyed a pleasant silence in his home.

Well, he thought, job's only half done. Guess probably I oughta bury her.

His first thought was to roll her up in her new carpet, make it a burial shroud. Then he got a better idea.

Sal pulled the shades over the windows, and he set to work. First, he began moving things. He moved chairs and tables, pushed the ottoman out of the way. Then he repositioned his wife's body.

By midnight, he had driven the last of the tacks. When he stood up to admire his work, he knew he'd done an excellent job. The carpet was stretched tight and was lined up perfectly with the corners of the room. Okay, so maybe there was kind of a hump in the middle of it, but hell, he could get used to that. If he could get used to Amanda, he could get used to anything.

Yup, this new carpet would keep her quiet, just the way he'd hoped it would. Sal walked over and poked the hump with the toe of his boot.

In the days to come, no one bothered Salathiel. Folks were no longer in the habit of dropping by, so it was easy to keep to himself.

But whenever he ventured into town, he'd stay just a little longer than usual. In fact, he could stay just as long as he wanted and not catch hell when he got home. Little by little, Sal started smiling again.

Tod Potter couldn't see a damn thing. The fog was so thick that all the lights on land were invisible. There was no way to get himself oriented.

Figuring he was somewhere around the spit, he called out, hoping Sal Stoner would hear him and give him some bearings. But no. Just the eerie sound of the waves on the beach.

So Tod continued rowing.

Pretty quick, his boat ran up on the sand. Tod recognized the spot. He dashed up the path to Stoners' place. He was sure they'd let him wait inside for the fog to clear. Even the old lady wouldn't turn him away on a night like this.

The little house appeared dark and quiet. Tod tapped on the door, thinking the Stoners might be sleeping. When no one answered, he knocked harder.

Still no answer.

He tried the door and found it locked. That was odd. Nobody around town locked their doors. No reason to. Probably had something to do with that odd wife of Sal's.

Tod walked around the house. Funny. All the shades were drawn. When he tried the other door, he found it locked, too. Maybe they've gone away, he thought.

Then motion startled him.

Something yanked the shade away from the window. Something hairy was moving around in there.

It was a cat. Wild-eyed. Panicky. Clawing at the glass.

Now Tod Potter was sure the Stoners had left home, abandoning the poor cat. Wonder how long it's been left alone? Poor thing's probably starving to death.

He cupped his hands and peered in through the window.

There was something funny in there. Something that just wasn't right. Even in the half light of the foggy evening, Tod could make out odd dark blotches on the red carpet. And there was something else. Something damned peculiar about that carpet . . .

About seven o'clock, Tod Potter ran into the Dark Harbor general store. Panting and pale, he looked as if he'd seen every ghost in town, all at once.

"There's somebody dead," he cried, "out at Stoner's place. You gotta come. Quick. Think I found a body!"

Then Tod noticed that Sal Stoner was sitting with the other men. Their eyes met.

"Yup," Sal said, his voice full of quiet resignation. "I guess you probably did."

When the men arrived at Stoner's house, none could believe what they found. A new-looking carpet had been put down in the parlor. But a dark stain eclipsed its rosy decoration.

Blood? And that bulge in the middle, was that Amanda Stoner's body? Could Sal have tacked her down under the rug?

As the men peeled the carpet away, things got even more gruesome. Although the woman's head had been damaged to the point she was no longer recognizable, the repeated hammer blows apparently had not killed her. Under the tightly nailed carpet, Amanda Stoner must have regained something resembling consciousness. She'd evidently come around enough to get some idea of her plight.

The poor woman must have thought she'd been buried alive.

Her bloody face was full of splinters from the floor. She'd bitten her tongue and lips. Her fingers had been reduced to raw stumps as she'd clawed at the unyielding floor beneath her.

And her new carpet? Well, it was an Axminster, known for its stiff backing and for the tightness of its weave.

Had she died from hammer blows, starvation, or suffocation? No one could say for sure. All they knew was that Amanda Stoner had lived a little too long.

Salathiel was committed to an insane asylum in Portland, where he died a few years later. In order to contribute to Sal's upkeep, the house was sold. But peace was never to return to its haunted rooms.

A man from Seal Harbor bought the place and moved in with his wife and their four children. They soon discovered that things were not right in their new home.

Furniture would not stay put. Every morning when they came downstairs, chairs and tables in the parlor had rearranged themselves.

Prowlers?

Perhaps. But nothing was stolen. Nothing was damaged.

Locking the doors and windows failed to put a stop to the weird intrusion.

On the fifth night, the man decided to stay up and see what was happening. He armed himself and sat in the parlor, waiting.

He didn't see anything.

But if he dozed off, or went to the kitchen for a drink, he'd come back to find things were not exactly as they had been. Something—a chair, a vase, a picture— had moved just a bit.

One afternoon, the family came home to find all the furniture in the parlor had been knocked down and strewn around. Yet the doors and windows were securely locked, just as they'd left them.

Another time, they returned to discover a hump in the center of the parlor rug. It seemed to be twitching, as if something were caught under there. Soft muffled moans seemed to emanate from the hump.

The man whisked the rug off the floor but found nothing underneath.

A few days later, the woman thought someone had hurt himself in the parlor. Otherwise, where did all that blood on the rug come from?

She checked with each member of the family. Everyone was fine. No injuries. And no explanation for the blood.

When she tried to get rid of the stain, no matter how hard or long she scrubbed, a few days later it would be back.

The family didn't stay long. Enough was enough.

And in the years to come, so the story goes, several families were plagued by similar events. No matter how many times the carpet is replaced in the parlor, a lump will take shape at the center. Then bloodstains appear.

A move off the premises is never long to follow.

Things Unseen?

JUST WHEN I THINK I HAVE A USEFUL THEORY ABOUT THE NATURE OF GHOSTS, some story comes along that confuses me. Okay, I can buy the notion that most, if not all, human beings have a "soul" that passes over into "Summerland" at the moment of death. And I can buy the idea that on occasion, for whatever reason, the Summerlanders return to their old three-dimensional stomping grounds to put in an appearance.

But if revenants are the paranormal remnants of human beings, how are we to explain such phenomena as ghostly animals? Should we believe animals have souls, too? Even weirder are the apparent ghosts of things that never were alive. For example, why are most ghosts seen wearing clothing? Do suits have souls? Are there bargain outlets in Summerland? Does Land's End have a division called Life's End?

TRAIN OF THOUGHT

AND THINGS CAN GET WEIRDER STILL. I'm talking about the occasional appearance of objects huge enough to suggest that Summerland has topography and technology very similar to our own.

Take that afternoon in 1958 when a man by the name of John Quirk from Pittsfield, Massachusetts, reported that he, along with several witnesses in the Bridge Lunch Diner, saw a phantom train.

A phantom train?

He described it vividly, saying it was made up of a baggage car and five or six coaches. He also said he could actually see the coal in the tender.

A month later, another ghost train passed the same spot at 6:30 in the morning, highballing at full steam toward Boston.

Wondering who was using their tracks without permission, railway officials looked into the matter. They quickly determined that no steam engine had run on that line for years. What's more, after the spirit express was spotted again, the same officials were able to verify that no train of any kind had passed along the tracks at that specific time.

GONE TO BLAZES

TRAINS ARE NOT THE ONLY MEANS of spirit conveyance. There is, apparently, a whole fleet of ghostly vessels, members of which are spotted from time to time all along the eastern seacoast. In fact, one of them is the most famous "ghost ship" in all of the United States, the *Palatine.*

For more than 200 years, people have been seeing America's flying Dutchman as it cruises along the North Atlantic coast, usually off Block Island.

It's easily recognized because it's eternally ablaze.

In life, the *Palatine* was a Dutch ship that sailed for Philadelphia in 1752. It was crowded with immigrants eager for a new life—but life wasn't in the cards for these unfortunate travelers.

As food ran low, living conditions grew bleaker by the nautical mile.

During Christmas week, somewhere between the mainland, Long Island's Montauk Point, and Block Island, the *Palatine* was threatened by a wicked storm. Stressed to the breaking point, the crew went berserk. They murdered the captain, plundered the ship, robbed the passengers, then took off in the lifeboats at the first sight of land. Deserted to fend for themselves, the immigrants—by now little more than walking skeletons—had no idea how to navigate the ship.

With no one to sail her, the *Palatine* tossed helplessly at the mercy of wind and wave. Finally, she ran aground on Block Island.

The Block Islanders, I'm sure, have their own version of the story. But in most tellings, they are portrayed as looters who boarded the distressed vessel. When they found the crew had left nothing of value, they got angry, torched the ship, and let the tide take it back out to sea. An especially gothic touch included in some versions holds that they left a madwoman aboard because she refused to come ashore.

A gentler version says the Block Islanders helped the seventeen ill-fated survivors, conveying them to Simon Ray's farm on the southwest side of the island. There, some were nursed back to health. Most, however, were unable to overcome the horrible ordeal and perished. Their graves are on Ray's land, marked by boulders.

The hulk of the ship, leaking but still afloat, was sure to become a navigational hazard, so the islanders torched it. A freak wind brought the flaming ship and its one mad stowaway back out to sea. In time, it vanished from sight—but only briefly.

The ship is still occasionally spotted, generally on the anniversary of the fire. It is seen as a burning hulk, a fire on the sea.

As newsman Edwin C. Hill reported in 1934, "There are people living on Block Island who will tell you, with their hand on the Book, that they have gazed seaward in the blackness of the night, startled by a bright radiance at sea, and have watched, with straining eyes, while the *Palatine*, blazing from trunk to keelson, swept along the horizon."

GHOST HOUSE

NOT LONG AGO, while driving north along coastal Route 1 in Maine, a vacationing family passed through Rockland and Camden, heading toward Belfast. It was an overcast day, not warm enough for the beach, so a seaside drive seemed like just the perfect thing.

The kids, however, were getting restless in the backseat. Before tempers erupted, the man and woman decided to stop and let everyone stretch their legs.

The family found themselves in the little town of Northport. Right away, they could sense something charming and timeless about the place. The surrounding forest seemed uncommonly dense, and houses, partially hidden among tall, old trees, were like architectural ghosts from two centuries passed.

After leaving the children in the town park to play, the couple grabbed their camera and started walking uphill along one of the old estate roads.

An eerie sight soon met their eyes. At the center of grounds that had obviously once been cleared and cared for, they spotted the ruins of a mansion. Clearly, there had been a fire some time back. Amid the cluttered remains, a perfect stone chimney rose like a phoenix from decades-old ashes.

This gothic tower, stark against the cloudy sky, would surely make an artful photograph. The couple took turns snapping pictures of it. Then they photographed the surrounding area.

When they got back to town, the couple asked about the fascinating ruins. Everyone knew the story.

It was the Cosgrove Mansion. Generations ago, its owners had become rich in the real estate business, then surrounded themselves, and their descendants, with luxury. The last Cosgroves to occupy the place had been a well-liked young couple with three fine sons.

On December 16, 1954, Mr. and Mrs. Edward Cosgrove left their Northport mansion, heading to Boston to do some Christmas shopping. Full of effervescent Christmas cheer, they didn't hesitate to leave the boys with Mr. and Mrs. Walden, two trusted employees who loved the children and treated them like family.

The boys—ages 5, 7, and 9—were caught up in the excitement of the season. On this special night, they were permitted to stay up later than usual, playing, singing, and putting the final touches on the Christmas decorations. The ever-watchful Mrs. Walden baked cookies and made hot chocolate.

Later, Mrs. Walden read to the children until they got sleepy. Then the couple put the boys to bed before retiring themselves.

At that moment, silently, invisibly, and unexpectedly, seven lives began to change.

By the time the fire department got there it was already too late. Flames licked at the black sky, menacing trees and neighboring houses. The inferno burned so intensely that the firemen, try as they might, couldn't get close enough for their hoses to do much good.

Neighbors joined the firefighters, and everyone did what they could, working to exhaustion. Through their combined efforts they were able to save the house next door, but the Cosgrove mansion was reduced to a pile of blackened rubble, twisted pipes, and smoldering squalor.

The next day, Mr. and Mrs. Cosgrove returned home. All that remained recognizable were their metal appliances and tall stone chimney, blackened by the flames.

Later, when it was safe enough to explore, five charred corpses were recovered from the ruins—two adults and three children.

The cause of the fire was never determined. Perhaps it was the result of a faulty oven or overworked furnace. Perhaps the electrical system was taxed too greatly by the Christmas decorations. Perhaps a million other things.

None of it mattered.

The only important thing was the good life enjoyed by the Cosgrove family was over forever.

Or was it?

Understandably, Edward Cosgrove and his wife moved away from Northport. The property changed hands several times, but no new house was built where the chimney stands.

In time, the pain of the catastrophe faded in the community; that horrible December night in 1954 became an uncomfortable memory.

And life—as we shall see—went on.

One evening, a local farmer named Brent Severson was walking along the road near the Cosgrove ruins. Suddenly, he heard the shrill cacophony of screams.

He froze. Listened.

No doubt about it, children were crying out as if someone were torturing them.

The only thing nearby by was a trailer with a light in the window. But clearly the screaming wasn't coming from there.

It was unlikely, Mr. Severson knew, but the cries seemed to be coming from the direction of that old chimney. With his heart pounding like a fist, Mr. Severson began to approach the source of the screaming. As he did so, the cries died out as suddenly as they had begun.

His pulse still racing, Brent Severson hurried on home.

A local minister, Calvin Owens, was walking in the same area with his two daughters. Suddenly, the still morning air was rent by the plaintive cries of tormented children. Rev. Owens knew what they were hearing. Immediately, he offered help in the most appropriate way he knew; Rev. Owens and his daughters knelt at the roadside and prayed.

The family of tourists soon learned that ghostly stories of this type are plentiful in the area around the Cosgrove estate. Though they personally had experienced nothing supernatural while photographing the ruins, at least they'd have a great story to tell about their Maine vacation. And they would have the photographs to go along with it.

But in a week or so, when they got their pictures back from the lab, the shots of the old chimney simply didn't come out. Oh, the chimney appeared in the photographs all right. But it appeared as part of a huge white mansion, perfectly intact, just as it had been in 1954.

The idea that ghosts of human beings can linger at the location of an earthly tragedy may thoroughly tax our imaginations and belief systems. Yet certain people find it easy to accept that something once alive might be living still.

A house, a ship, a train, these are another matter entirely. Can such things leave their ghosts behind?

Or can a human being, especially one with psychic abilities, occasionally look back across the years and see a person, place, or thing that is no longer with us? Only the most hard-headed individuals would completely disallow such a possibility.

But a ghost house being recorded by a "psychic" camera . . . ?

Just exactly what are we to make of that?

In any case, this was not an isolated incident, according to the citizens of Northport, Maine. Since about 1985, the vanished house has reappeared in a fair number of photographs. According to Carol Olivieri Schulte's account, one such photograph is even on public display on the wall of a Northport diner.

Now that's certainly food for thought.

Communication

WAY BACK AT THE BEGINNING OF THE BOOK, I TALKED ABOUT THE GOLDEN AGE of American Spiritualism and how human beings made various attempts to communicate with those who had "passed over."

It was a fascinating era.

Sir Arthur Conan Doyle endorsed Spiritualism "as the greatest event that ever occurred upon American soil." Eventually, phenomena associated with this "great event" were actually embraced by the scientific community in one form or another.

A SOUL IN THE BALANCE

IN 1906, DOCTOR DUNCAN MACDOUGALL of Boston's Massachusetts General Hospital did some unusual research; he tried to determine whether the human soul is corporeal, or completely intangible. If found to have substance, then of course it could be said to exist.

His technique was to build a light framework on a delicately balanced scales. The frame held a bed on which a dying patient would spend his or her last few hours.

From among the volunteers, Dr. MacDougall chose only people whose death would follow profound exhaustion. That way there would be no last-minute agitation of the scales.

Tuberculosis deaths were perfect for the experiment.

The weight of substances escaping from the person's body, including the air in the lungs, were factored in. The scales were sensitive to within one-tenth of an ounce.

Surprisingly, Dr. MacDougall found that in every case there would be a minor loss of weight at the moment of death, measurable in ounces. Of one such volunteer, Dr. MacDougall wrote, "At the end of three hours and forty minutes he expired, and suddenly, coincident with death, the beam end dropped with an audible stroke, hitting against the lower limiting bar and remaining there with no rebound."

In some cases, Dr. MacDougall discovered there would be a second sudden loss of weight.

Many spiritualists and psychic scientists saw this as proof that some part of us leaves the body at the time of death and survives. And by extension, if something survives death, we should be able to communicate with it.

As early as 1892, Elijah J. Bond had invented the modern Ouija Board, sort of a "spirit telegraph" system for communicating with the great beyond. Then, as now, it didn't stand up to the rigors of objective scientific scrutiny.

Later, and a bit more scientifically, Thomas Edison tried to manufacture a kind of telephone machine with which he could talk to the spirits. He died before it was complete, perhaps preferring personal visits to phone calls.

DEADLINE

BUT OF COURSE, long before people began making "scientific" attempts to communicate with the spirit world, spirits were trying to communicate with us.

Sometimes they'd appear to us directly with messages they had no time to deliver in life. Sometimes they even tried more exotic means.

One such tale never fails to make my skin crawl. It isn't that the events are especially gory or even sinister, but for some reason this certain alchemy of ingredients leaves me trembling.

I learned about the story in Curt Norris's book *Ghosts I Have Known*, published in 1994, and I spoke with him about it in 1996. It has to do with Curt's father, Lowell Ames Norris.

The Norris family had had ties in Pembroke, Massachusetts, for decades, but it wasn't until 1940 that Curt's parents purchased a house there. It was a century-old New England cottage on Brick Kiln Lane that came with three acres, a barn, and a garage.

Back then, Pembroke was an isolated farming community. It offered only the bare essentials of modern conveniences, including a very few street lights.

There was no electricity in the Norris's new house and no bathroom, either. The family quickly updated both these situations, but preserved certain elegant mementos, among them a handsome old copper hand pump in the kitchen and an antique telephone with crank and bells.

Curt's father was a writer, so he renovated part of the barn to use as an office.

One night, while the elder Norris was working at his desk, racing against a quickly approaching deadline, he was suddenly overwhelmed by a sensation of discomfort. It was irrational: he could determine no reason why he should be feeling ill at ease.

Mr. Norris looked around suspiciously. Nothing. With an effort of will, he returned to the story he was working on, refusing to be further distracted.

A short time later, the uneasy feeling began to intrude again. Mr. Norris jumped when he heard a ringing sound. Concentration totally broken, he looked this way and that, trying to spot an alarm clock, or door bell, or anything that could be responsible for the shrill, persistent ringing.

It seemed to be coming from that old crank telephone hanging on the barn wall. The antique instrument had been there when his family bought the property and Mr. Norris had left it in place as a decoration. He hadn't realized it was still working.

He rose from his desk and walked over to the phone, then—with mounting suspense—he lifted the receiver to his ear.

"Hello?"

He didn't recognize the woman's voice. She sounded elderly and well spoken, but her words came fast, with a definite urgency. "I've taken a fall," she said, "and I can't seem to get up again. And I can smell smoke. Could you come down here and help me, please? And please do hurry. It seems that there's a fire here."

Mr. Norris didn't know what to say. Of course he'd be willing to help, but he had no idea who was speaking. How would anyone know to call him here at such an hour? In her near panic, had the woman misdialed and reached him by mistake?

"Who's calling, please?" he asked, trying to keep his voice from betraying his confusion.

As if slightly surprised at not being recognized, the woman said, "Why, this is Abby Magoun. At the end of the street."

Mr. Norris couldn't place her. He knew the Turners lived at one end of Brick Kiln Lane; Andy and Mary Washburn lived at the other.

Mr. Norris was about to ask for more specific instructions when the line went dead. It is difficult to imagine what he must have been feeling as he left the barn and got into the family car.

The night was absolutely dark, so if there was a fire anywhere in the neighborhood, he should be able to spot it easily. He drove slowly down toward the North River end of Brick Kiln Lane, looking both ways, keeping his window down and sniffing the night air for smoke.

He passed one house and then another. All were dark; there was no sign of any activity along the way.

Finally, he stopped in front of the Macy place, trying to decide what to do next. How could he help an old lady in trouble if he didn't know who she was or where she was calling from? Perhaps, he thought, he should go home and telephone the police.

In the light of the dashboard, he checked his watch: almost two o'clock in the morning.

Then, from the corner of his eye, he caught a flash of light. It was within the dark Macy house. Soon, he saw the interior illuminated by what he recognized as the glow from a kerosene lamp. In moments, a dark form emerged, carrying a flashlight.

"What do you want?" Mr. Macy demanded from a good, safe distance. When he recognized Mr. Norris, he approached the vehicle.

As Mr. Norris explained his dilemma, he watched Macy's expression grow more and more disbelieving.

Macy thought for a minute, then said, "Used to be a Mrs. Magoun, lived up there by the river." Mr. Macy pointed to an overgrown driveway barely visible in the headlights of Mr. Norris's car. "House burned down, though, some twenty-odd years back. Woman died in that fire. Nobody got there till too late."

Mr. Norris sat frozen in profound silence, a professional writer at a loss for words. As he drove home, a total sense of unreality spread through him. He walked back to his study, hoping he could summon the concentration to finish his article.

Before he sat down at the keyboard, he walked over to the telephone. He picked up the receiver. Yes, the line was still dead.

Then, for the first time, he took a careful look at the old telephone. It was hanging from the wall by a nail. There were no batteries to power it. Severed wires dangled from its back.

The old instrument wasn't even hooked up.

CALL RETURN

MY ONLY CONCLUSION is that Massachusetts must have some pretty odd phone systems. Since the days of the crank telephone, even updating the technology hasn't eliminated these unique crank calls.

Consider the equally baffling case of James R. Middleworth of Malden, Massachusetts. On a Friday evening in June 1981, Mr. Middleworth and his wife were returning from dinner at a local restaurant. On the spur of the moment, they decided to stop to visit their friends, John and Lisa.

This unplanned stop turned out to be something of a family gathering, for Jim's brother and sister also were there.

After about 20 minutes of refreshments, TV, and softball-related conversation, the telephone rang.

Jim's sister was beside the phone so she picked it up. She listened briefly, then said, "Whom do you want? Lisa? Hold on, please."

Lisa took the phone. It was her house, so surely the call was for her. But no. After listening quietly for a moment, she realized it wasn't for her at all.

"It's for you, Jimmy."

James Middleworth took the phone from his puzzled-looking friend.

"Hello?" he said.

The line was strangely quiet, as if no one were there.

"Hello?" he persisted.

The soft voice on the other end said, "Jimmy, this is Mama and us over here."

Mr. Middleworth recalls that everyone in the living room saw him turn white. His legs weakened, and a feeling of lightheadedness came over him.

"Who *is* this?" he demanded, with all the severity he could muster.

The voice replied, "Jimmy, this is Mama and us over here."

James Middleworth stood there utterly paralyzed. His friends looked on, saying things like:

"Who is it, Jim?"

"What's the matter?"

"What's going on?"

Finally, when no more words came from the mysterious caller, Jim hung up. Slowly, he moved back to his chair and sat down. Deep in thought, he tried to decide if he should tell the others what the caller had said.

Without a doubt, it had been his mother's voice.

Further—and there was no question about this—his mother had been dead for five full years.

And if that weren't puzzling enough, James R. Middleworth also knew that his stop at John and Lisa's house had been unplanned; nobody knew he was going to be there. So how would anyone know to call?

Of course, that was in 1981, long before the days of high-tech telephone services. If he'd been able to dial *69 for the "Call Return" option, I can't help wondering where his return call would have been directed.

Terrible Tricksters

ONE OF THE STRANGEST STORIES OF THE SUPERNATURAL THAT HAS EVER CROSSED my desk came by way of the *New Haven Register.* Columnist Neil Hogan managed to resurrect a newspaper article published in the *New Haven Union* during late December of 1875.

This was a period during which the phenomenon of Spiritualism had pretty well taken root in New England soil. It was the year Colonel Olcott investigated the Eddy Brothers in Vermont, and it was the era when seances were routinely conducted in parlors all across America.

Though there were many believers in spirit phenomena, there was an equal, if not greater, number of skeptics.

MR. X'S FILE

THE 1875 ARTICLE, involving a terrifying confrontation with the unknown, was concerned with the skeptical and anonymous "Mr. X" who, on the evening of December 14, received an unsigned message.

It suggested that if he wanted to see the work of a convincing spirit medium, he should visit a certain address, only about a mile from the center of the city of New Haven, Connecticut. Determined to satisfy his curiosity about the validity of spirit communication, Mr. X and a friend visited the address that very evening.

The medium, they discovered, was "a scared-looking" man in a room that contained only a stove and a large pine box. This box—the so-called "spirit cabinet"—was standard seance-room equipment during that era.

As was the custom of many mediums, the frightened-faced fellow offered to let the visitors tie him up to prevent trickery. Mr. X and his friend accepted the invitation. At almost the instant they tightened the last knot, the newspaper reported, "a tempest of knocks began in all parts of the room as caused Mr. X and his friend to look at each other in amazement."

The investigators responded by checking the cabinet, suspecting the trickster might be hiding inside. However, the box was completely empty. But when they closed its door, it flung back open again. This time the cabinet was occupied. Where a moment ago they had seen only empty space, now they stood gaping at "the dried-up face and figure of a little old man, dressed in the fashion of a hundred years ago."

The wizened figure then floated out of the cabinet and somehow remained suspended in the middle of the near-empty room. He began to move his arms in the hypnotic gestures associated with mesmerism. Immediately, the two men "felt an indescribable influence begin to creep over them."

Feeling panicky and paralyzed at the same time, Mr. X realized the scared-looking medium would not be able to come to their aid—he was either in a deep trance, or had passed out entirely.

It was then that the spirit began to speak. He commenced an oration about the nature of life and the cosmos. This promised to be exactly the sort of revelation all Spiritualists hoped to gain from the enlightened denizens of the world beyond. But before he imparted any truly useful wisdom, he paused. "Before I speak further upon first principles," he said, "let me materialize my daughter for you."

With that, the spirit vanished, leaving the two investigators in a baffled silence. Within moments, a new commotion began within the spirit cabinet. In the midst of the disturbance, what sounded like a woman's voice protested, "I do not want to be materialized."

The noise increased; the cabinet shook, teetered, and eventually toppled. The terrified visitors ran to the window, hoping for escape, but, "They were seized by invisible hands and immediately lost consciousness."

When he regained consciousness, Mr. X found that he was in his own home. Bewildered and fatigued, he made his way upstairs to his bedroom. But the rest he sought wasn't to occur, for there, waiting for him, was the "dried-up little spirit" who greeted Mr. X with a harsh laugh. "I have come to pay you a visit . . . and I brought my daughter with me. You see her?"

Mr. X glanced toward the corner of the room where he saw a female form kneeling in front of his safe. The old man informed Mr. X that his daughter was "spiritualizing the safe to get at the contents, which she will also spiritualize and carry away with her."

Then, on a more sinister note, the old man continued, "Your friend has also been spiritualized and is now in the spirit world, but he will be returned to you in a few days."

At that, Mr. X lunged for the revolver he kept at his bedside. He was able to fire one round at the apparition before he collapsed a second time into preternatural unconsciousness.

Next morning when he awoke, he found himself stretched out on his bed. His safe was still exactly where it should be, but when he checked, he found its contents—some $700—to have vanished completely.

Understandably reluctant to have the whole episode become known, Mr. X hired a pair of private detectives to conduct a secret investigation. They were unable to shed any light on the dark business.

Later, Mr. X's vanished companion showed up again in New Haven. He could not account for his whereabouts, saying that he had remained "spiritualized" until he heard someone call his name. Thus summoned, he returned to normal, waking up in his own room.

Eventually, news of the events leaked out. Although the *New Haven Union* published the story, they scoffed at it, using terms like "preposterous" and "unmitigated nonsense."

One suspects that either Mr. X, the newspaper, or the reader was victim of a hoax. If we delete the supernatural elements from the equation, what we have left looks remarkably like an elaborate con game. Was Mr. X victimized? Was his trusted companion actually in league with the medium and "phantom" family?

Any slightly skilled stage magician, trained in hypnotism, could have pulled off most of what occurred. And certainly a rogue magician would have much more need of $700 than any disembodied spirit.

Of course, there is always that other possibility. Maybe events transpired exactly as described. Maybe this was an example of malevolent spirits messing in human affairs. If so, then clearly they didn't need any cash. They just wanted to deprive Mr. X of his.

The conclusion here is the same as in almost every story in this book: the ambiguity remains.

There is only one thing we can say for sure. In the words of Mr. X's companion, it was "a passing strange experience."

No matter how we read the story of Mr. X, we see evil at work: either evil hoaxers or evil spirits. But of the total population of ghosts, how many can be up to no good? It may be a point worth considering . . .

Around 1991, when I began collecting strange stories for my radio series, my perception was that ghosts were rare and haunted houses rarer still.

I was wrong.

Ghosts, I find, are surprisingly plentiful, especially in New England. And haunted houses . . . ? Well, take a city the size of Burlington, Vermont, where I live. If we were to round up all the haunted houses in town and cluster them together, we'd have a good-sized neighborhood. As in any neighborhood, of course, the diversity of behavior patterns among residents can be pretty vast and somewhat vexing.

For the most part, the routines of a conservative, middle-class ghost are predictably mundane, even boring, the metaphysical equivalent of mowing the lawn or washing the car. Human beings can cohabit for years with a spirit who confines his activities to turning lights on and off, producing bodiless footsteps, and moving tiny objects around.

But occasionally, a more radical ghostly presence will slip into a neighborhood and take up residence on a nice quiet street. Soon, it will begin to act out in ways that truly twist our concepts of common sense, consensus reality, and natural law.

In fact, such ghosts can become so demonstrative and destructive that we grope for new names to call them—names like poltergeist or even demon.

THE DEVIL IN CONNECTICUT

NOW, WHEN IT COMES TO DEMON-INFESTED STATES, Connecticut gets the prize. I'm not sure if I can explain why, exactly. Maybe it all dates back to the Puritans, who saw devils everywhere (which also might explain their habit of avoiding mirrors).

Or perhaps folks in the Nutmeg State are just less secretive about the manner of skeleton they keep in their closets.

However, Connecticut's demon-consciousness is evidenced in the number of locations that bear the Devil's name. Some of these places may just look like hell, but others, certain legends assert, are spots where Old Nick himself spent some time. At least two dozen—and as many as thirty-four—such areas appear all over the map, flaunting names like "Devil's Den," "Devil's Meditation," and "Satan's Ridge."

The proof of satanic presence is forever stamped upon the landscape. Ol' Nick leapt from Montville across Long Island Sound (aka "Devil's Belt") to Montauk, and left a footprint on each side to prove it. He left the imprint of a similar cloven hoof on a stone in Devil's Den in Weston. Apparently, there was a third track in Branford, but it was blasted back to perdition during road building.

And it was Connecticut, you'll recall, that first offered "demon possession" as a defense in a murder case.

Surprisingly, this didn't occur during colonial times.

In 1981, Arne Johnson of Brookfield went on trial in Danbury for murdering his employer, Alan Bono. Attorney Martin Minnella planned a "devil-made-me-do-it" argument but Judge Robert Callahan refused to permit a demonic possession defense in his courtroom.

Another diabolical incident took place in 1986, when Carman and Allen Snedeker rented a house on Meridan Avenue in Southington. Turns out, the place was already occupied. The residing family of demons then tried to occupy the Snedeker's 15-year-old son, Phillip. Family members were pinched, slapped, and sexually molested by malignant unseen forces. They discovered their new "home" was actually a converted funeral parlor, and eventually had to flee for their lives, if not their very souls.

Of all the instances of demons in Connecticut, the Southington case is the only one where I have had any direct involvement. After a business associate suggested I do a book about the events, I spent a few days in the area.

Following many interviews and much soul-searching, I ultimately decided against the book. There were many reasons, but here are the main two: if it *was* a hoax, I didn't want to help perpetrate it. And if there really were demons in the Snedeker home, I didn't want to mess with them. Still, it gave me an opportunity to hear about the events firsthand and to spend time with some of the principal players.

Admittedly, stories about demons interfering with humankind are a little tough to accept. Believers argue that reflexive disbelief and easy dismissal are all part of demonic design. I must admit I've noticed one factor to support that notion: more often than not, there is some element that's so profoundly absurd that it imposes a kind of grim, dismissive humor on an otherwise terrifying situation.

For example, back in 1974, an East Hartford man named Anthony Rossi was heard to shout, "You're nothing but a toy!"

Why?

Because he was being attacked by an oversized Raggedy Ann doll that was supposedly possessed by the satanic spirit of a dead girl. The demonic doll, Annabelle, was up and walking around the apartment, just like some animated, special-effects puppet from a horror movie.

Now really, what villain could be more absurd than an ambulatory Raggedy Ann doll? Yet, somehow it attacked Rossi, burning his chest and leaving seven bleeding claw marks slashed across his skin. This wound was observed by two nurses, Margarite Tata and Annalee Goetz, who shared the apartment with Rossi.

GOOD IN EVIL

MY FAVORITE CASE of New England deviltry includes one highly absurd and ridiculously comic element. It involves a sinister entity that moved into a quiet working-class neighborhood in the city of Bridgeport. Today, the house at Lindley Street still has a sinister atmosphere about it. Many people discuss it in whispers, if they dare discuss it at all.

Clearly, there is nothing strange about the house's appearance. This unassuming one-story bungalow, containing just four rooms, was built around 1915 by a local manufacturer. It changed hands a number of times. Then, in 1960, a Roman Catholic couple, Gerald (in some accounts Gerard) and Laura Goodin, moved in.

The couple's first few years were not pleasant. The son they conceived there died tragically in 1967. In their forties at the time, the grieving couple decided to adopt a 3-year-old girl, a Native American from Canada named Marcia.

Not much is known about the years from 1960 until 1972, when all hell broke loose on Lindley Street. Early in '72, the family began hearing noises. Something unseen pounded on the walls of their home. Typically, the disturbance could commence at any hour of the day or night. It might begin as a series of tiny taps, then escalate to a baleful banging that rattled the whole building. One troubling detail is that the concussions were not random; instead, they were executed with a certain rhythmic precision that suggested some sort of intelligence was behind them. At first, of course, mortal pranksters were suspected.

Mr. Goodin informally reported his suspicions to a neighbor, a Bridgeport police officer named John Holsworth. Working together, the men were able to tape-record the sounds, but both remained mystified as to the source.

When the disturbance persisted on and off for several months, the Goodins finally asked city officials for help. Perhaps it was something in the sewers or waterlines. Or maybe some irregularity of electrical service was causing the discord.

City engineers, policemen, and representatives of the fire department showed up at different times to conduct investigations. However, the reason for the noises remained elusive: walls, pipes, and the foundation all passed rigorous examination. Everyone agreed the cause must be natural, but none of the experts could determine exactly which natural law accounted for the problem.

And the sounds continued.

Then things escalated. Over the next few months, a series of odd and unsettling occurrences contributed to the family's growing unease. A disembodied hand appeared and vanished in a front window. Other windows broke, smashed from the inside while family members were elsewhere and all together. Once, three loud raps sounded from the front door. When Mrs. Goodin opened it, no one was there. All she saw were wet footprints on an otherwise dry sidewalk.

And that's the way it continued over the next two years. Who can guess what tension and terror the Goodins endured as the situation gradually worsened? Who can know how isolated they must have felt during those strange months?

Then, on Sunday, November 24, 1974, forty-eight nonstop hours of absolute pandemonium began. Finally, just in time for Thanksgiving, the Goodins' private terror went on public exposition.

At 10:11 that morning, Bridgeport Police Officers Joe Tomek and Carl Leonzi responded to a distress call from Lindley Street.

"The lady [Laura Goodin] came to the door," Leonzi recalls, "and I asked, 'What's the problem?' She was crying . . ."

Mrs. Goodin pointed, directing the officers to a living room that looked as if a bomb had detonated there. Objects were scattered everywhere.

"Were you burglarized?" Officer Leonzi asked.

"No," Mrs. Goodin said. "This is always going on."

In his initial report to Capt. Charles Baker, Patrolman Joseph Tomek wrote that he and Officer Leonzi "observed the inside of the house in disarray: furniture, pictures, religious articles, personal belongings etc., were thrown about in all rooms except one."

Dishes and silverware littered the floor. Papers were strewn helter-skelter. A big television set lay on its side.

The Goodins then briefed the officers about events that preceded their arrival. Loud pounding had moved from wall to wall and from room to room. A table turned over all on its own. Chairs moved about the kitchen as if they were living things. The big television set seemed to rise into the air before it crashed to the floor. Perhaps odder still, the set wasn't damaged at all.

"Things were flying around in the front room," Gerald Goodin said. "Whatever it was, was acting like a demented person and I felt I had to get my family out of the house."

But whatever-it-was was completely invisible.

Officer Tomek reported, "While conducting the initial investigation [we] observed one or more of the following happen: the refrigerator rose approximately 6 inches off the floor; a 21-inch portable TV set in the living room rise off a table and turn around; furniture move away from the wall and fall over; object[s] on shelves and hanging from the walls start vibrating . . ."

More policemen—some ten in all—arrived at the building, as did a group of firemen. Fire Chief John Gleason's men saw "dinner plates rattling, pictures jumping off the wall . . . and a heavy leather chair jumping at least six inches off the floor."

A fireman summoned Father Edward Doyle from St. Patrick's Church. He blessed the house and occupants, then left to make some phone calls.

Shortly afterward, witnesses saw a plastic crucifix "explode" from the wall, shattering into pieces.

Someone in the neighborhood telephoned Ed and Lorraine Warren, well-known ghost-chasers from nearby Monroe. They in turn called Father William Charbonneau, a young Catholic priest from St. John of the Cross Church in Middlebury, and Paul F. Eno, a 21-year-old seminary student living in East Hartford.

Somewhere along, reporters got ahold of the story and soon journalists, TV crews, and radio commentators were flocking to Lindley Street from all around the country. Predictably, such media activity attracted droves of curiosity seekers. Crowds grew rapidly.

In less than 24 hours, authorities estimated a gathering of 10,000 people. News leapt around the world and suddenly Bridgeport, Connecticut, was known for a horror to rival its drugs, crimes, and murders.

There was plenty to keep newsmongers busy: two of Mrs. Goodin's toes were broken when a television set seemed to pounce on her. Inexplicable cold spots manifested in the various rooms. A gray-white cloud formed and began to grow in the kitchen. The stench of sulfur and ozone permeated the house—source unknown. Something dark and malignant followed Eno to a neighbor's house and bashed on the door there.

CAT TALES

AND ALL THE WHILE, there was the grimly comic behavior of Sam, the family's pet cat.

Of all the instances of bizarre activity in the Goodin home, Sam's antics seemed to be most interesting to media representatives.

It was Marcia's habit to cuddle Sam, holding him tightly against her body. She'd lean her head close to Sam's and talk to him in a low voice.

Somewhere along the way, the Goodins and certain of their neighbors became convinced that occasionally they could hear Sam answering back. In fact, Mr. Goodin said that sometimes it was as if Sam had "swallowed a myna bird."

But Marcia didn't always have to be present when it happened. Sam would come upstairs from the cellar and bang on the door to be admitted to the house. If rapping didn't work fast enough, the impatient feline would try calling out in a grotesque voice, using colorful language befouled with inappropriate epithets. One of the milder was, "Open this door, you dirty Frenchman!"

Other people told of standing in an empty room with Sam on the floor nearby. Someone would speak, but no one would be there but Sam—the only possible source of the voice.

Once, Marcia's tutor was visiting the house when she heard cursing and swearing coming from the next room. She opened the door to confront the offender, but . . . After a thorough check, she determined no one but Sam was around. And with this incident, Marcia's home-tutoring came to an abrupt end.

Sam's soliloquies may be entirely folklore. Then again, on rare occasions, poltergeists have been known to speak. And demons, according to Ed Warren, will sometimes try to rattle their victims by making animals appear to use human language.

Though it is unlikely Sam ever said anything more than "meow," investigator Eno enjoys recalling the sight of several TV and radio reporters clustered around a house cat, shoving microphones in his face, and begging him to speak.

WHAT WAS IT?

POLTERGEIST IS A GERMAN WORD meaning "noisy ghost." Rather than haunting places, the poltergeist generally attaches itself to a specific person, usually an adolescent. It manifests with motion, sound, and the creation of general disorder. Modern thinking is that the poltergeist is not a spirit but rather a telekinetic force generated within the troubled mind of its "host."

I'm not sure when the term "poltergeist" was first applied to Goodin's situation. And who knows when someone upped the ante from poltergeist to "demon"?

All we can say is that tremendous excitement generated by word-of-mouth and media—all in the wake of 1973's blockbuster film *The Exorcist*—quickly convinced scores of people that Evil had indeed visited the Goodin home. Surely, no one doubted the bewildered family had spent time in hell.

If chaos is an indication of the Devil's reign, then quite possibly Satan really did come to Connecticut in 1974. Crowds grew; confusion spread. Things were quickly getting out of hand.

While well-intentioned clerics wrestled to regain control inside the house, Police Superintendent Joseph Walsh faced an equal problem outside. The potential for trouble grew with the size of the crowd. Soon, both ends of Lindley Street had to be cordoned off to help manage a mob so immense and unruly that arrests had to be made.

It may have been a chance remark by Edward Warren that gave the superintendent inspiration for the solution to his division of the pandemonium.

At some point, Warren speculated that because Marcia was an unhappy and troubled child, her inner turmoil was released in the form of telekinesis, producing poltergeist phenomena. If Marcia's unbridled psychic energy was responsible for the extraordinary activity on Lindley Street, then by extension, the whole thing was Marcia's fault.

So, perhaps more interested in social order than truth, and wanting to end the unexpected ruckus that plunged his city into turmoil, Superintendent Walsh announced on November 26 that the whole thing was a hoax perpetrated by Marcia Goodin. He said she confessed. And that's what he maintains to this day.

But others present on the scene remember things differently. In spite of Superintendent Walsh's ruling, and Marcia's alleged "confession," several police officers later told the *Bridgeport Sunday Post* that they'd definitely witnessed events at the house that could be psychic phenomena.

Remember, the Goodin house was tiny—just four rooms. In such a confined area, wouldn't it be next to impossible for 10-year-old Marcia to fool repeatedly numerous adult investigators simply by pushing furniture around and hurling objects when no one was looking?

And what about the initial police report quoted above? Can we discount the on-the-scene statement of two of Bridgeport's finest?

Then, there's WNAD radio reporter Tim Quinn, assigned to cover the story firsthand. He personally witnessed a big leather chair move all by itself.

Father Charbonneau recalls sitting in the house with Marcia when she screamed and pointed behind him. He turned around to see a bureau slide from one side of the room to another—with no one having touched it.

In full view of several witnesses, Lorraine Warren suffered a spontaneous burn on her left hand. She was simply sitting in a chair when it happened, nowhere near a heat source.

In a recent account of the events, then seminary student Paul Eno has come to discount the idea of demons. Today, he believes that Marcia "literally and unconsciously created a poltergeist." He goes on to say, "Her personality was textbook: a lonely, introverted, frustrated but intelligent child overshadowed by domineering parents and about to enter puberty."

She was, after all, a Roman Catholic child being raised by Catholic parents and assisted by Catholic rescuers who perceived the telekinetic phenomena as demonic. Is it any wonder the events took on an evil cast?

Today, it is difficult to get satisfying closure on the bizarre events at Bridgeport. What are we to believe? Was it hoax or horror? Demons or deceit?

Those who know for sure—the Goodin family themselves—are not available for comment.

Mrs. Goodin died in an auto accident in 1994.

Marcia seems to have successfully disappeared.

And Mr. Goodin—who I understand still resides in the Lindley Street house—has an unlisted telephone number and, perhaps understandably, has never replied to my letter of inquiry.

Maybe it's just as well. I'm not really sure I want to know.

PART IX

The
Last Word

" Nobody has any conscience about adding to the improbabilities of a marvelous tale. "

— NATHANIEL HAWTHORNE
The Marble Faun

FINAL THOUGHTS

BEFORE CONNECTICUT RESIDENTS suspect I'm accusing them of providing aid and comfort for the Devil, let me hasten to add that other New England states have reported demonic activity, too.

We all remember that Stephen Vincent Benet classic, "The Devil and Daniel Webster." Well, those events transpired in New Hampshire.

And there's no need to time-travel way back to the Salem witch trials to find the devil in Massachusetts. In 1981, a Roman Catholic family in Lee was repeatedly attacked by a "demonic spirit." It decapitated religious statues, threw crucifixes around, and jabbed a butcher knife into a nondenominational kitchen table. An 11-year-old boy seemed to be the target of this hostile activity. Frequently, he would go into convulsions as various poltergeist-type phenomena occurred around him.

The family tried to fight the malignant force using the power of religion. Unfortunately, that approach seemed only to anger the dark presence. In retaliation, it yanked a golden religious medallion from around the boy's neck and hurled it into the air. When a Capuchin friar was administering holy water, a stone from nowhere knocked the vessel out of his hand and smashed it to pieces. Later, four priests arrived and began reading prayers and invocations. This caused a virtual bombardment of stones to rain down on the boy.

Some years later, another Massachusetts case found its way into the news. This one involved evil spirits not only entering a house, but also entering a human being.

According to reports in the *Springfield Morning Union* and the *Boston Herald*, Maurice "Frenchy" Theriault, a tomato farmer from Brimfield Road in Warren, spent six weeks in hell during the first months of 1985. He suffered indignities that ran the gamut from bleeding eyes to a "doppelganger," or exact double, that did foul things for which the farmer was blamed. Family members claim to have seen both Frenchys at the same time.

Although he had only a fourth-grade education, Frenchy was able to speak Latin while under the control of his internal visitors. And in spite of his slight stature, only 5 feet 4 inches, he was observed picking up the front of a farm tractor, presumably assisted by his "possessing" spirits.

The dark intruders were finally subdued by a renegade Catholic priest and Connecticut demon-hunters Ed and Lorraine Warren.

And there are a thousand more such stories—enough to fill several more books this size. They're all fantastic, all fascinating. Each calls to mind that deceptively simple question posed so long ago in Machiasport, Maine, by Abner Blaisdel. Remember when he asked the specter of Nellie Butler why, of all possible places, did she pick his house to haunt? It's a good question. And, to conclude our little safari into the strange, I think it deserves a bit of speculation simply because it applies to almost everyone discussed in these pages.

Why did Bill Bartlett see the Dover Demon while Andy Brodie, riding in the same car, missed it altogether?

Why did puddles appear in Dr. Waterman's house while his neighbors' homes remained properly dry?

Why did John Fuller and David Buckley see a big hairy monster in their Connecticut barn while Sgt. Fred Bird saw nothing but two frightened farmhands?

And why did the Devil come to Lindley Street, Bridgeport, Connecticut?

Were the events completely random? Or were they part of some mysterious, unfathomable design?

In Blaisdel's case, it may be simply that he, or one of the members of his household, possessed a fair amount of undiscovered mediumistic ability. Perhaps, of all the people in the Machiasport area, Blaisdel was the only individual with whom Nelly could communicate. If so, she arrived at Blaisdel's house by necessity.

The same, presumably, would be later true of the Fox sisters. If one or more of them had not been mediums, the entity called Mr. Splitfoot—whatever it was—could not have communicated at all.

It is beyond the scope of this book to explore the nature of mediumship or to speculate if it is indicative of elevated spirituality, supernatural ability, inborn talent like perfect pitch, or whether it might even be some form of mental illness, sort of a controllable schizophrenia. All we can say is whatever mediumship may be, it has been around in one form or another for thousands of years. Before the term "medium" became fashionable in the nineteenth century, such individuals were known as, among other things, oracles, soothsayers, prophets, mystics, and most recently, channelers.

It might just be that Mr. Blaisdel and many of his neighbors in this book are yesterday's and today's "shamans," isolated individuals among the population as a whole who are predisposed to having, or facilitating, paranormal experiences. Perhaps it is through such people that all "monsters" are kept alive.

Or maybe the "monsters" survive because of the storytellers, the Nathaniel Hawthornes, H.P. Lovecrafts, and Stephen Kings. Perhaps the writer and reader, the yarn-spinner and the listener, are partners in world-building. Together they weave complex wonders from the fabric of imagination. And it is this very act—the creation of the marvelous—that dignifies our species, that contributes to personal fulfillment and heightens the enjoyment of life.

To dismiss the stories, to call them subjective or hyperimaginative is to do them a great disservice, for it is to suggest they are fraudulent and without value.

In my mind, stories like those presented here should be celebrated. Perhaps each New England state should embrace one, bestow dignity upon it, and call it its own. After all, we each proudly display our state bird, state tree, and state flower.

So Massachusetts has its witches.

Rhode Island its vampires.

Vermont has the Lake Champlain Monster.

And Connecticut is most welcome to the Devil.

This leaves just two without official state monsters.

I'd like to nominate Bigfoot as a likely candidate for Maine, home of the giant Quoddy Moccasin.

And now we have one left: New Hampshire. Considering the odd aerial goings-on in Exeter, the puzzle in McCarthy's pond, and in recognition of that grand dame of interplanetary abductions—Betty Hill—maybe we should call New Hampshire "The Alien State."

Though as we have seen, it is no more strange than any of its neighbors.

NOTES, ACKNOWLEDGMENTS, AND SOURCES

BEFORE I'M OFF AGAIN on my eternal quest for more New England mysteries, I must remember my manners and acknowledge the people who helped me with this project.

First and especially, many thanks to Fred Hill and the staff of the Fletcher Free Library here in Burlington, Vermont. Amazing what ghosts Mr. Hill can conjure through the Interlibrary Loan system.

Another very special thank you goes to Gary Mangiacopra of Milford, Connecticut, who willingly answered my occasionally stupid questions and then supplied me with hundreds of pages from his files. Photocopying alone must have been tremendously labor-intensive. Such generosity of time and spirit is very much appreciated.

And thanks to Faye Ringel, Ed Rhodes, Paul Eno, Bob DiGiulio, Greg Guma, Judy Ranney, Arlene Tarantino, Tom Fagan, Steve Marshall, Curt Norris, Nick Bellantoni, James Guyette, Howard Coffin, Robert Cahill, Chris Cate, Tina Ferris, Steve Bissette, Brian and Allison Citro, Alan and Melody Clark, John Coon, Ed Desany, Barry Estabrook, Michael Johnson, Derek Muirden, Ken Horseman, Betty Smith, Sam Sanders, Linda Davies, Stanley Wiater, Will Lang, Marie Tedford, Floyd Ramsey, Sandra J. Taylor, Susan McClellan, David Diaz, Alice Lawrence, Kerry Lawrence, Emily Stetson, and all those who, by request or oversight, must remain anonymous.

A final tip of the hat to those intrepid Bigfoot baggers and bashers, including Bill Green, Joseph DeAndrade, and George Earley.

My sincerest apologies to anyone I've forgotten.

I tried to mention as many sources as possible within the text, if doing so was not a distraction. But there are several that I either didn't mention or that I'd like to give special recognition.

First, there are the works of Robert Ellis Cahill of Salem, Massachusetts, whose New England series includes some twenty small books that thoroughly cover the region's lore and legend. In fact, just about everywhere I went looking for ghosts and goblins, I always seemed to find myself following Mr. Cahill's footprints.

Two books from Connecticut writers are more than worthy of special mention: *Legendary Connecticut* by David E. Philips seems to be the definitive work on the Nutmeg State, and Faye Ringel's *New England's Gothic Heritage* is an amazingly comprehensive and readable work that illustrates the merging of folk and literary traditions of the region.

Curt Norris's interesting and entertaining titles include *Ghosts I Have Known*, *The Boston Boogeyman*, and a terrific series of columns called "New England Mysteries," written for the Quincy, Massachusetts, *Patriot Ledger*.

Paul F. Eno's pamphlet *Faces at the Window* provides an insightful look at some of New England's strange events from the point of view of a firsthand investigator.

Other fun and useful books include most anything by Robert Pike, the ghost-story collections of James Reynolds, Alton H. Blackington's *Yankee Yarns*, and Edward Rowe Snow's collections.

A partial list of other reference books includes:

Jean Anderson, *The Haunting of America*; Paul Barber, *Vampires, Burial, and Death*; Raymond Bayless, *Voices from Beyond*; Raymond Bayless, *The Other Side of Death*; Raymond Bayless, *The Enigma of the Poltergeist*; Horace Beck, *Folklore of Maine*; Henry Beckwith, *Lovecraft's Providence*; Paul Begg, *Into Thin Air*; Katherine Blaisdell, *Over the River and Through the Years*; Fessenden S. Blanchard, *Ghost Towns of New England*; Janet and Colin Bord, *Mysteries of the 20th Century*; B.A. Botkin, *Treasury of New England Folklore*; Ruth Brandon, *The Spiritualists*; Ann Braude, *Radical Spirits*; Katherine Briggs, *An Encyclopedia of Fairies*; Slater Brown, *The Heyday of Spiritualism*; Carrington and Fodor, *Haunted People*; Milbourne Christopher, *ESP, Seers & Psychics*; Allen Churchill, *They Never Came Back*; Jerome Clark, *Unexplained!*; J. Clark and L. Coleman, *Creatures of the Outer Edge*; Daniel Cohen, *Encyclopedia of Monsters*; Sylvia Cranston, *H.P.B.*; Marion M. Daley, *History of Lemington, Vermont*; Richard M. Dorson, *Jonathan Draws the Long Bow*; Arthur Conan Doyle, *History of Spiritualism*; Arthur Conan Doyle, *The Edge of the Unknown*; Samuel Adams Drake, *New England Legends and Folk Lore*; Eastman and Bolte, *Haunted New England*; Frank Edwards, *Stranger than Science*; Frank Edwards, *Strange World*; Frank Edwards, *Strangest of All*; Nandor Fodor, *Between Two Worlds*; Charles Fort, *The Books of Charles Fort*; J.R. Greene, *Strange Tales from Old Quabbin*; Rosemary Guiley, *Encyclopedia of Mystical and Paranormal Experience*; R.J. Hagermas, *Covered Bridges of Lamoile County*; Judson Hale, *Inside New England*; Gerry Hunt, *Bizarre America*; John A. Keel, *Our Haunted Planet*; John A. Keel, *Operation Trojan Horse*; John A. Keel, *Complete Guide to Mysterious Beings*; Major Donald Keyhoe, *Aliens From Space*; Gerald McFarland, *The Counterfeit Man*; R. DeWitt Miller, *Forgotten Mysteries*; Edwin V. Mitchell, *Yankee Folk*; Edwin V. Mitchell, *It's an Old New England Custom*; John Mulholland, *Beware Familiar Spirits*; Arthur Myers, *The Ghostly Gazetteer*; Arthur Myers, *The Ghostly Register*; Henry Steel Olcott, *People from the Other World*; Lynn Picknett, *Flights of Fancy*; Harry Price, *Poltergeist Over England*; Jenny Randles, *Mind Monsters*; Ethel Colt Ritchie, *Block Island Lore and Legends*; D. Scott Rogo, *An Experience of Phantoms*; Carol Olivieri Schulte, *Ghosts on the Coast of Maine*; Robert Somerlott, *Here, Mr. Splitfoot*; Lewis Spence, *The Encyclopedia of the Occult*; Allen

Spraggett, *The Unexplained*; Herbert Thurston, *Ghosts and Poltergeists*; Lee Vincent, *Ten Years on the Rock Pile*; Lee Vincent, *Instant Legends from the Rock Pile*; Colin Wilson, *Encyclopedia of Unsolved Mysteries*; Colin Wilson, *Poltergeist*; Herbert Wisbey, *Pioneer Prophetess*; David Yeadon, *Hidden Corners of New England*.

And a number of editor-assembled books such as *Vermont Life* magazine's *Mischief in the Mountains*, edited by Walter R. Hart, Jr., and Janet C. Greene; Sharon Jarvis's *Dead Zones*; Austin Stevens's *Mysterious New England*; John Lovell's *Those Eccentric Yankees*; Eva A. Speare's *New Hampshire Folk Tales*; Kerr and Crow's *The Occult in America*.

And the list goes on . . .

I am indebted to several individuals who were kind enough to share their unpublished papers, among them: Dr. Robert DiGiulio's work on Dudleytown; Greg Guma's work on the Eddy Brothers; a manuscript called "Monsters of the Northwoods" by Robert and Paul Bartholomew, William Brann, and Bruce Hallenbeck; and a history of the Vermont State Police by Michael J. Carpenter.

Journals, periodicals, and newspapers consulted are too numerous to list completely. However, I am especially in debt to Neil Hogan's column "Our Connecticut," in the *New Haven Register*.

Other newspapers include, but are not limited to: the *New York Times*, *New York Herald*, and *Washington Post*.

VERMONT: *Rutland Herald, Burlington Free Press, Bennington Banner, Newport Daily Express, Times Argus, Vermont Journal, Brattleboro Reformer*, and *Vermont Vanguard*.

CONNECTICUT: *Connecticut Post, New Haven Register, Hartford Courant, Bridgeport Sunday Post, Bridgeport Post-Telegram, Connecticut Sunday Herald, Litchfield County Times, The Advocate, Milford Citizen*, and *Southern News*.

NEW HAMPSHIRE: *Claremont Daily Eagle, Concord Monitor, Keene Sentinel.*

MASSACHUSETTS: *Springfield Morning Union, Patriot Ledger, Boston Globe, Boston Sunday Herald*, and *The* (Framingham) *Middlesex News*.

MAINE: *Kennebec Journal, Portland Press Herald*, and *Maine Sunday Telegram.*

A few magazines were consulted. Chief among them were *Vermont Life, Yankee, Fate, Strange, Fortean Times*, and *Window of Vermont*.

THE WHOLE POINT IS, I COULD NEVER HAVE DONE THIS ALONE.

GEOGRAPHIC INDEX